Minneapolis Madams

Minneapolis Madams

The Lost History of
Prostitution on the Riverfront

PENNY A. PETERSEN

University of Minnesota Press

Minneapolis

London

Maps drawn by Ted Tucker

Published by the University of Minnesota Press
111 Third Avenue South, Suite 290
Minneapolis, MN 55401-2520
http://www.upress.umn.edu

Library of Congress Cataloging-in-Publication Data

Petersen, Penny A.
    Minneapolis madams : the lost history of prostitution on the riverfront / Penny A. Petersen.
    Includes bibliographical references and index.
    ISBN 978-0-8166-6523-5 (hc : alk. paper)
    ISBN 978-0-8166-6524-2 (pb : alk. paper)
    1. Prostitution—Minnesota—Minneapolis. 2. Brothels—Minnesota—Minneapolis. I. Title.
    HQ146.M5P48 2013
    306.7409776'579—dc23

                                                    2013010354

Printed in the United States of America on acid-free paper

The University of Minnesota is an equal-opportunity educator and employer.

20 19 18 17 16 15 14 13   10 9 8 7 6 5 4 3 2 1

To Ted Tucker and Erin Vasseur

CONTENTS

LOCATION   212-14 11th Ave. S.

LOT   6   **BLOCK** .113 ADD.   Town of Minneapolis

6612 1389 0105 1347

PERMIT NO.	CONSTRUCTION	DATE	CONTRACTOR	COST	O. K.
A 2214	42x80 Br. & Sto.Flats	12-16-90	L. Anderson	12000.	
D 5784	Plbg. Flat	3-14-91	C.A.Brooks	1000.	6-18-91
A 3267	Alt.	10-31-92	E.O.Tronered	30.	
A 5650	Alt.	10-28-97	John Erickson	75.	
F 3401	Elec. Sporting Hse.	5-13-99	Minn. Elec. Co.	30.	
F 3425	Elec. Hse. of Ill Fame	5-17-99	Minn Elec. Co.	20 .	
D 20108	Plbg. Dwlg.	2-13-03	G.A.Kelly	225.	3-11-03
F 9744	Elec.Dwlg.	6-25-04	Mpls. Gen.Elec.Co.	20.	
F 9839	Elec. Dwlg.	7-11-04	O.F.Chidester	50.	
F 15652	Elec. Dwlg.	1-9-06	Minn Elec. Co.	10.	
D 35528	Plbg. Dwlg.	7-30-07	Bjorkman Bros.	110.	8-19-07
F 22132	Elec. Dwlg.	8-14-07	Hortig & Hellier	200.	
F 22139	Elec. Hotel	8-14-07	Pike Elec. Co.	225.	
F 22270	Elec Dwlg.	8-28-07	John Trevor	310.	
G 883	Steam Htg. Plt.	9-14-07	Bjorkman Bros.	1600.	
A 14865	Alt.	2-21-20	Bert Thompson	700.	
F 235957	Elec. Rm. Hse.	11-19-29	I.C.Jensen	150.	12-18-29
A 18680	Alt. Br Flat to Fac.	11-22-29	Ruhen Blumberg	300.	
F 245938	Elec. Cafe	2-24-31	A. Ingebredtson	25.	2-26-31
A 20957	Alt. Cafe	9-17-32	E.Bamble	200.	

The building permit index card for 212 Eleventh Avenue South. The fifth line notes a "Sporting House" and the sixth line a "House of Ill Fame," evincing the degree of prostitution's visibility with city officials. Similar permit cards used terms such as "pleasure resort" or "boarding house–saloon," all common euphemisms for brothels. Photograph courtesy of the Minneapolis Collection, Hennepin County Central Library.

PREFACE

This book began as a bike ride. One morning, instead of staying on the usual course along West River Parkway, which parallels the Mississippi River in Minneapolis, I veered off to nearby Eleventh Avenue South. There I noticed a handsome, three-story, Richardsonian Romanesque building. It appeared to be the residence of a wealthy family or an elegant apartment house dating from the 1890s, but its proximity to the west bank flour milling district was disconcerting, as the Minneapolis elite had long abandoned the central riverfront as a residential neighborhood when this building was erected. It was in the wrong place, to my way of thinking. I decided to visit the Minneapolis inspections department and check the building records for the address.

The simple phrases for the address's building permit index card read: "Elec. Sporting Hse." and "Elec. Hse. of Ill Fame," meaning two permits for electrical work had been knowingly issued by the municipal authorities to a brothel.[1] I looked at permits for adjacent buildings and found others in the same vein. In time I began searching for municipal and district court records but learned that these had mostly disappeared. Fortunately an index of criminal cases at the district level had survived, and as I reviewed it I wrote down the date and name of everyone who had been charged with "keeping a house of ill fame," almost all of whom were women. I started reading period newspapers and over time discovered that madams and prostitutes regularly entered guilty pleas to the charge of prostitution, paid fines to the municipal court, and then returned to their usual business. Occasionally a madam would be charged at the district court level and face the possibility of higher fines or even a prison sentence.

This new knowledge was bewildering, as I thought I was very familiar with Minneapolis history. For the past twenty-some years, I had studied and written about the downtown riverfront. I was certainly aware that prostitution existed in nineteenth-century Minneapolis, as it did (and does) in every urban center across America. I had read the annual reports of the Sisterhood of Bethany, a women's group devoted to rescuing "fallen women." Yet I had never heard of the names I was running across in the newspapers and property records: Nettie Conley, Ida Dorsey, Jennie Jones, Edna Hamilton, and Mary E. Allen, to name a few. None of these names appears in the Sisterhood of Bethany reports, where I might expect these women to be listed as bad examples, if nothing else.

Each tiny fact I discovered whetted my curiosity to know more. Further searches into building and property records suggested a vanished urban landscape. The building on Eleventh Avenue was not a lone aberration but one of many bordellos that existed along the central riverfront. City directories revealed that madams often operated out of the same location for years. Everyone knew their names and where to find them. Some madams built up extensive real estate holdings, both inside and outside the established sex districts. The madams and the sex trade were deeply entrenched in the city.

During my decade-plus search, I assembled a narrative of the city's history of prostitution from land records, court documents, probate files, and newspaper accounts scattered over six decades. The revelations led me to reassess my understanding of Minneapolis history. Illuminating the lives of these entrepreneurial women added new dimensions to accounts of local reform movements and politics. The riverfront madams were an important component of the complex sexual ecology of nineteenth-century Minneapolis. Usually written off as deviants, the madams were actually crucial components of a larger system of social control and regulation. One seemingly small detail would often open up an entirely different venue of investigation. For example, at the close of 1880, several newspapers vaguely alluded to a petition being circulated in regard to the madams. A little more digging led me to a box at the municipal archives that contained a petition, signed by the city's leading citizens, urging the release of three madams from the state penitentiary. Interestingly, some of those same signers had been instrumental in putting the madams into their prison cells. Slowly, it became clear that city officials both tolerated and suppressed this subculture, depending on the direction of the political winds at any given time.

This study does not pretend to be a complete account of the commercial sex trade in Minneapolis from its beginnings to the present, or even a study of all the madams and prostitutes who worked in the city from the nineteenth century to the early years of the twentieth century. *Minneapolis Madams* primarily follows the fortunes of several successful madams whose life stories I was able to reconstruct, despite their multiple identities, the general secrecy concerning their business operations, and large gaps in the public records. The madams and other sex workers made only a few public statements, and evidently none of them left firsthand accounts of their lives. In time, other writers may be inclined and more able to continue to develop this history.

ACKNOWLEDGMENTS

This book owes its existence to many people. Erin Vasseur first pointed out that my research was more than just an interesting collection of arcane facts to be shared with my friends. Dave Stevens provided early support and encouragement for this project. Bill Huntzicker pointed out the close connections among the local newspaper reporters for whom the madams and red-light districts were a source of stories. Gauti Sigthorsson enlightened me that the sex workers, their clients, the politicians, reformers, and respectable citizens were all part of the greater sexual ecology of Minneapolis. Barbara Bezat of the Northwest Architectural Archives patiently answered my questions and tracked down information on the various architects who designed the river-front bordellos. Edna Brazaitis introduced me to the wonders of the state law library and showed the way to supposedly lost transcripts from the Doc Ames trial. Richard Reed provided help with the gene-alogy of several madams. Victor Thortenson, with his knowledge of rare books and photographs, helped me obtain some of the illustra-tions for this project, and Ted Tucker drew the maps. The very helpful staff at Special Collections of the Hennepin County Library referred me to several resources that I would never have found on my own, as did the marvelous reference librarians at the Minnesota Historical Society. The Hennepin History Museum was the source of a photo-graph with a very rare view of Main Street and a Sanborn Insurance map. Pieter Martin at the University of Minnesota Press encouraged the completion of the manuscript and gave good feedback along the way, and many reviewers worked diligently as the reader's friend to make the manuscript readable and offered fine suggestions of sources on nineteenth-century prostitution.

Finally, a group of loyal friends talked me through my many doubts, read seemingly endless versions of the manuscript, and offered good advice, and I thank JoEllen Haugo, Eric Boyer, Erica Webb, Sarah Tittle, Ross Edwards, Jen Edwards, Cindy Johnson, and Jan Richardson.

The Public Women of Minneapolis

> This city is known abroad as a moral, upright city, and
> its citizens are noted for their honesty, integrity and
> enterprise; and many a person has referred with pride
> to the fact that no house of "ill-fame" could flourish here.
>
> —"THE 'SOCIAL EVIL,'"
> *MINNEAPOLIS CHRONICLE*, APRIL 30, 1867

In 1867 a *Minneapolis Chronicle* article sounded the alarm on the "Social Evil," as prostitution was often called: "It is the duty of a public journal to look after the morals of the community, and warn the people when the approach of an evil threatens to destroy or mar their happiness." The newspaper's concern was prompted by a rumor that "notorious prostitute" Mary Robinson, a successful St. Paul madam, was planning to open a bordello in Minneapolis. While the historical record proves otherwise, the reporter seemed to believe Robinson's plans would be the first documented instance of the commercial sex trade in the town. He noted, "Our city has been so free from prostitution and the standard of morals so high, that there has been no need of reference to this evil," asserting that not even one brothel could thrive in the city. However, if this prostitute was allowed to establish her business here, "the damning effect, which this monster will have upon our hitherto uncontaminated people is too dreadful to contemplate." Once the contagion of prostitution touched the city, the reporter believed, its ruination would be complete. Even virtuous women, the writer opined, would fall victim to the commercial sex trade. The parade of well-dressed prostitutes through the streets would be a constant advertisement to respectably employed women that crime paid very well. According to the writer, even women uncorrupted by these sights would still be at risk, as every woman would be seen as a potential prostitute: "for, however high-minded and pure the lady may be if prostitution is in our midst she will be watched with evil eyes and talked about by licentious tongues."[1]

This "notorious prostitute" exerted a powerful influence on the imagination of the reporter. The article warned, "It is well known that this crime is destroying the native American population of our country, and that the 'old puritan stock' will soon become extinct as a fit punishment for this same social evil. If this great evil once gets a foothold in our city there is no knowing at what stage it will stop." By way of contrast, the writer observed that Minneapolis's neighbor St. Paul "licenses it as a legitimate business," allowing any sex worker to "openly engage in her nefarious traffic in the character and standing of young men, if she will only pay into the city treasury the sum of $20," and he added, "nothing breeds more vice and crime than that same licensed 'social evil.'"[2]

Despite the claims of a crime-free past by the *Chronicle,* there were certainly lawbreakers in the town prior to 1867. St. Anthony had a city ordinance concerning houses of prostitution by 1855, stating that the keepers of such establishments could be fined one hundred dollars. Perhaps the *Chronicle* reporter was unaware of an 1857 incident in which a mob of citizens forcibly closed a bordello. In 1858 the *Minnesota Republican* noted that lumbermen had jailed the prostitute known as "the Norwegian" because of some unnamed bad behavior. A short time later, the same newspaper reporting on an attempted jailbreak by three prisoners noted, "The general feeling seems to be that the authorities have been trodden on long enough, by rowdies, and thieves, and ruffians, and that it is high time that law-abiding people come to the rescue. In the first place, all the rummeries and harlot-hells ought to be destroyed and torn to pieces by an indignant community. Then the *root* of the evil would be torn up." What the reporter and others seemed to miss was that the true root of all these ills was human nature itself—saloons and brothels existed in the town because there was a demand for them.[3]

This otherwise obscure *Chronicle* article identified almost all the players and issues that would define the city's forty-odd-year struggle with the commercial sex industry, as practiced from the late 1860s to 1910, when the city closed the last openly operated red-light district:

the madams and prostitutes who ran the industry, the eager consumers of prostitution, the reformers in the shape of "benevolent ladies" who hoped to open an "asylum for abandoned women," and the municipal authorities who alternately strove to suppress the sex trade and worked to accommodate it. While Mary Robinson never actually moved her brothel to Minneapolis, plenty of other "public women" were attracted to the city's growing wealth and the opportunities it offered.[4]

The *Chronicle* article also combined two strands of Minneapolis history: the first, a well-known narrative of a sober, moral, entrepreneurial population engaged in building an industrial and commercial powerhouse at the Falls of St. Anthony. Versions of this story can be found in many accounts of the city, ranging from Isaac Atwater's *History of Minneapolis* to Lucile Kane's *The Waterfall That Built Minneapolis*. The other thread is an account of the city's fight against vice as well as its strange dependence on the very foibles that would tempt and distract the virtuous citizenry. It is the second, and lesser-known, version that will be explored in this book.

Minneapolis began as two towns nestled on either side of St. Anthony Falls. On the east side, the town of St. Anthony was laid out in 1849. Meanwhile across the river, Minneapolis sprang up in the early 1850s with a collection of squatters occupying land that was still part of the Fort Snelling Military Reservation. The first waves of white settlers were lured to the area by the possibilities of waterpower provided by the falls and the seemingly inexhaustible white pine forests to the north. In 1855, Minneapolis was platted into a town with streets and blocks laid out. By 1872 the two towns would merge under the name of Minneapolis.[5]

Within a couple of decades of its founding, Minneapolis had three significant sources of wealth: sawmilling, flour milling, and warehousing. All three operated on or near the city's riverfront. From the beginning, Minneapolis not only manufactured lumber for its own needs but supplied out-of-state demand as well. During the period 1890–1905, the Minneapolis lumber industry reached its zenith; by 1897 the city had "finally attained the position of the leading lumber market of the world."[6] Flour milling at St. Anthony Falls grew from very humble beginnings during the 1850s, when, in the words of historian Lucile Kane, "residents of the community tried hard to be proud of the flour" produced in an early mill, despite its obvious inferiority. In time, local millers mastered the art of producing high-quality flour from the hard spring wheat that could be grown in northern climates. The city became the flour milling capital of the world in 1880 and held that title for another fifty years.[7]

The milling industry not only shaped the city's commerce, it also played a determining role in the physical appearance of the riverfront. The concentration of mills that would later be known as the West Side Milling District was well established by the early 1860s. In time this industrial area would line the riverbank from Third to Tenth Avenues South. Although largely composed of flour and sawmills, the area hosted numerous other industries as well: ironworks, barrel factories, woolen mills, paper mills, and railroad facilities. Some of these buildings, such as the Washburn "A" Mill, the Crown Roller Mill, Engine House No. 1, and the Hall and Dann barrel factory, survive to the present day, although their appearance and functions have changed. Across the river the story was much the same, with the Pillsbury "A" Mill complex dominating Main Street Southeast.

Just as the lumber industry had funneled the resources of the northern white pine forest to St. Anthony Falls, the flour millers drew raw materials, in the form of wheat, from the vast prairies to the west and north. Minneapolis's ever-growing web of railway connections allowed raw materials such as wheat or logs to flow smoothly into the city and sped the higher-value, finished products on to eager customers. The whole process deposited a layer of wealth in the city, and those riches, in turn, attracted more people and industries to Minneapolis.

The wholesaling industry in Minneapolis got its start during the Panic of 1857, a time of tight money, especially in the Midwest as eastern capitalists were reluctant to extend credit to those in remote areas. Minneapolis jobbers, who had the capital and merchandise, stepped into the breach, extending credit to country storekeepers and in the process building long-lasting relationships. One account noted that "this first wholesaling was more of an accommodation than anything else, but the idea took ready hold."[8]

The wholesale trade began with a concentration of small warehouses along North First Street, soon required massive warehouses and rail lines to serve them, and would fan out up to six blocks back from the river and ten blocks upstream to present-day Plymouth Avenue North. One writer traced the growth of warehousing in the city to the 1880s: "At this time the Northern Pacific Railroad was rapidly opening up the Dakotas for settlement, and agricultural implements were in great demand. Realizing that Minneapolis offered the best rail connections to the new western farm land, national manufacturers of farm machinery began seeking warehouse space in the city." By 1908 one historian asserted that Minneapolis was the largest distributor of agricultural implements in the world.[9]

As sawmilling, flour milling, and warehousing were established at the falls, another industry, prostitution, gained a foothold at the riverfront. It was along the streets that lined both sides of the river that the first two red-light districts coalesced. Along the riverfront, madams would begin their careers in low-down saloons, catering to rough lumberjacks and itinerant laborers, and some would go on to accumulate large bankrolls and build elegant bordellos. On the east bank, sex workers settled on or around Main Street between the present-day Hennepin Avenue Bridge and the Stone Arch Bridge. Across the river, Bridge Square, where the Hennepin Avenue Bridge connected to Hennepin Avenue proper, served as the commercial focal point of the town. By 1873 the first city hall would be located on the triangle of land where Hennepin and Nicollet Avenues met. Not surprisingly, the early madams chose to locate their establishments within easy walking distance of Bridge Square along River Street (no longer extant), High Street (the present-day Robert Fisher Drive, which runs along the back of the main post office), and First Street on either side of Hennepin. In time, the bordellos would be largely concentrated into recognized red-light districts.

Although operated and controlled by the scorned class of madams and ordinary prostitutes, the sex industry exerted a surprising influence on the civic life of Minneapolis. In 1868 the necessity of a commercial sex trade forced extremely reluctant city leaders into a partnership with vice. Bowing to pragmatism, the city began a system of regular fines for prostitution that enriched the municipal treasury. Madams and prostitutes appeared in court on designated days each month, entered guilty pleas, and paid a fine. Then they were free to conduct their business until the next month. Among the first to be charged under the ordinance was a "'fair but frail creature.'" At first, the unnamed woman denied the charge, but she finally pleaded guilty and chose a ten-dollar fine over thirty days in jail.[10]

Within a short time, newspapers would not only name women charged with prostitution but announce the location of their bordellos as well, showing customers where prostitution could be found, as well as warning others away. One newspaper noted a typical case: "Maggie Morse introduced her High Street ballet troupe by special request—four besides herself. The individual members of the company were encored by the court and paid $5 and costs each, after which they were told to go and sin some more, for thirty days."[11] Typically, a madam's fines were based on the number of prostitutes she employed each month. During the 1860s and 1870s, the most common fine for ordinary prostitutes was between five and ten dollars, plus court costs. The system operated smoothly, but occasionally a madam would receive a harsher sentence. In 1869 nineteen-year-old Nellie Sullivan, using her professional name of Nell Stack, became the first person in Hennepin County to be prosecuted in district court for operating a bordello. She was convicted and sentenced to six months in Stillwater State Prison. It is not clear from surviving accounts why Sullivan received a prison sentence instead of the usual fine.[12]

While Minneapolis leaders might fear for their city's reputation by allowing prostitution to exist at all, the system of monthly fines offered advantages to both sex workers and the city on a practical level. Regulated prostitution was confined to certain geographic areas, offering assurance that it would not spread to other neighborhoods. Once established, these segregated areas or "red-light districts" were stable and long lived: the Main Street district was in place by at least the early 1870s and continued until 1904, when the city closed it. On the other side of the river, the First Street and Eleventh Avenue districts operated openly for many decades. Under this system, the madams had an obligation to run orderly businesses, with the knowledge that they could call the police for help when trouble arose. Monthly fines for prostitution offered the city a way of controlling the sex industry and allowed scarce police resources to be allocated to other more serious crimes. The fines also provided revenue for the city, which, at the time, had relatively few sources of income. Still, there were disadvantages to the system of monthly fines as it made the city a partner in the sex trade by allowing it to openly exist. This inherent conflict of interest would be a recurring theme in Minneapolis politics for decades to come.[13]

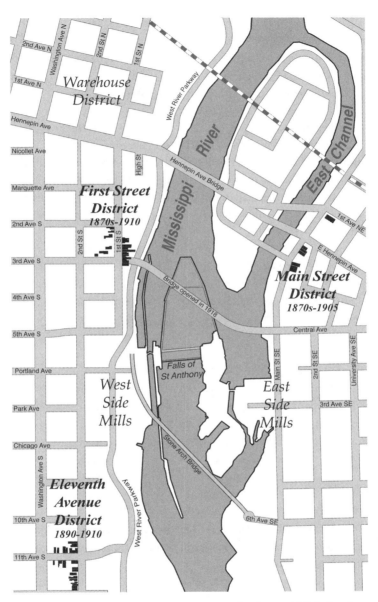

Minneapolis riverfront brothels, 1870s–1910. The three established red-light districts on Main Street, First Street, and Eleventh Avenue are placed on a map that shows the central riverfront of Minneapolis as it appears today. West River Parkway and the Third Avenue Bridge did not exist during the era of regulated prostitution, and previous versions of the Hennepin Avenue Bridge had no connection to First Avenue Northeast.

Despite their low status, the public women of Minneapolis would come to occupy a great deal of civic space, influencing the city's life in ways both direct and indirect. Many respectable citizens, such as grocers, dressmakers, carriage drivers, architects, contractors, and merchants, provided goods and services to those within the red-light districts. Over the decades the madams took on the privileges usually limited to males, running their businesses, regularly appearing in court, often as criminals, sometimes as the objects of civil lawsuits, sometimes as the originators of those suits. They bought and sold real estate, and hired prominent architects to design their buildings. During the 1890s the madams redeveloped at least one neighborhood to suit their needs. Their accumulated wealth also hints at a substantial underground economy, although this activity did not show up in the standard reports of goods and services sold. The riverfront madams not only appeared in newspaper stories but also played a significant, if unacknowledged, role in the city's economy and politics.

Prostitution provided synergy to Minneapolis, and vice versa. Migrant workers, whose labor supplied the riverfront mills with the essential raw materials, expected to find basic amenities in the city, including opportunities for female companionship. The sex industry also served as a tourist attraction for the city and contributed to its economic security. It was hardly a secret that bordellos would develop a reputation beyond the city limits. A Minneapolis newspaper reporter detailed a conversation he overheard in a hotel: "'Oh, be hanged!' said one of the speakers, 'if we are going to have a city, let us have a city, and everybody knows that we cannot have a city without such places [brothels]. If our country visitors cannot see and enjoy city sights here, they will go to Chicago or New York where they can, and buy their goods there, too.'"[14]

As the reporter's complaint implies, the increasing visibility of prostitution was a contentious issue throughout this period, and led to an equally visible movement to shut the brothels down. The seeds of reform were planted as early as the area was settled. The founding elite of Minneapolis had a noble vision of what the city should be as it was forming in the late 1840s. The first waves of white settlers in St. Anthony and Minneapolis were mainly from northeastern states such as Maine, New Hampshire, Massachusetts, Vermont, and New

York. They carried with them a strong Yankee culture that placed a high value on literacy, hard work, and the expectation of high moral values.[15]

That culture would long survive and dominate local affairs, even as the actual number of New Englanders dwindled. From the beginning, many settlers from the East seemed to envision St. Anthony and Minneapolis as a special place where the fight between good and evil, virtue and vice would be played out. In 1850 lawyer John North observed, "Indeed I never knew so young a village, where there was so little vice. It is said there is no man here who does not earn his own living, and I believe it is true. We already have two schools, a public library, and regular preaching by Presbyterian, Methodist, and Baptist denominations." North hoped to attract settlers to the city who shared his beliefs.[16]

North was also contrasting his town with its rival, St. Paul, nine miles downstream. One writer noted, "His [North's] acknowledged purpose was to build Saint Anthony—the future Minneapolis—with citizens of such sterling worth that the community would become a political makeweight to what he believed was the dissolute, ignorant, drunken, Democratic, pro-slavery capital city down the river [St. Paul]. He wanted as few wandering fur traders, lumberjacks, military men, Indian agents, immigrant Irish, and western roughs as possible."[17]

Not surprisingly, St. Paul had its own opinion of its upstream neighbor. When reporting on a public brawl, one newspaper observed, "It must have shocked the nerves of St. Anthony, for the *[St. Anthony] Express* has always represented their town as a perfect Pecksniff in religion and morals." The reporter continued that all too "often has Saint Anthony said, 'See how much better, more industrious, more temperate and more moral I am, than that rowdy, Saint Paul.'" The writer opined that "a few fights and rows at the Falls, will cure our perfectionist neighbor of rolling up her eyes at the sight of a dog-fight or a gin cocktail, 'like a dying duck in a thunderstorm.'"[18]

In 1857 the founders of Minneapolis and St. Anthony began the tradition of New England Society dinners, with the date of the party coinciding with the anniversary of the Pilgrims landing at Plymouth in 1620. Two hundred people sat down to dinner at the Cataract Hotel, in a hall hung with banners proclaiming, "The Sons and the Daughters of New England." After dinner was finished, the room was opened up to allow several hundred more participants to listen to speeches.

Cyrus Aldrich, the president of the society, opened his talk by recounting that their forefathers came to the New World on a mission: "to bear arms against the world, the flesh and the Devil." In his view, "Their religion was an armor that might well put to flight the powers of darkness. It was not so much a love of God as a resistance of evil." The idea that the world could be cleanly divided into good or evil would guide many of the decisions of Minneapolis leaders as they confronted problems that were, and still are, common to cities. In some instances, the application of this principle backfired spectacularly and led to unexpected consequences.[19]

Over time, reformers such as the Sisterhood of Bethany, ministers of various denominations, nativists, and progressives would occupy themselves with prostitution. Some would speak or write against it, while others led public crusades to eradicate it. The Sisterhood of Bethany actively offered aid to erring but repentant women of all types ranging from sex workers to unwed mothers.

As we will see in subsequent chapters, sex workers would exert a powerful influence over the city far beyond what their apparent low status would suggest. Efforts by the elite to recruit industrious workers resulted in a flood of ambitious newcomers who held very different ideas about vice than their patrons. Actions aimed at tamping down prostitution only caused it to spread to new neighborhoods. One member of the Pillsbury family would champion a crusade against prostitution, while another Pillsbury would have an intimate and quasi-public relationship with a well-known madam. A civic culture that promoted the ideal of free public education for all sought to ban "children of vice" from attending public schools. Attempts to prosecute "Doc" Ames, a notoriously corrupt mayor, would backfire and heap even more shame upon the city. A contradiction was built into the cultural foundations of Minneapolis. On the one hand, there was a strong faith that its moral convictions could withstand any force. But at the same time there was pervasive fear that outsiders, harboring strange ideas and customs, could easily overwhelm the city.

Minneapolis's response to the rise of the commercial sex industry was both typical of nineteenth-century American cities and in some respects unusual. Minneapolis was hardly the first or only city to impose a system of regular fines on madams and prostitutes that, in effect, licensed the sex trade. St. Paul had a system of fines in place by 1863. Nor was Minneapolis alone in the creation of recognized red-light districts. The historian Mara Keire called vice districting "a distinctly American phenomenon [that] arose out of the United States' creole cultural heritage and the new science of city planning," and she noted that Shreveport, Houston, and El Paso passed vice district ordinances. Keire observed that reformers not only segregated prostitution in many cities but also limited other vices such as alcohol and gambling to specific areas in downtowns. The establishment of the notorious Storyville red-light district in New Orleans in 1897 was not the city's first attempt at controlling the commercial sex trade. In 1857 the Common Council of New Orleans enacted an ordinance requiring a license to engage in prostitution. However, the licensing requirement was declared unconstitutional by an appellate court, unlike the establishment of the Storyville district, which was held to be legal by the U.S. Supreme Court; the court found that while municipalities could not legalize prostitution, they did have the authority to isolate vice.[20]

The largely female-operated bordello system began to decline owing to a number of broad social changes. Courtship rituals and sexual mores were rapidly evolving and the new telephone technology facilitated "call girls," who were not tied to a specific location and the supervision and protection of a madam. The eroding system made it easier for reformers and municipalities to wage successful campaigns to close down red-light districts. Keire observed that during the seven years prior to the United States' entry into World War I, Progressives had "a programmatic agenda: closing down the segregated red-light districts found in most cities across the country," often waging this battle on a "city-by-city" basis. After several attempts, Minneapolis finally managed to shutter the Main Street district in 1904, making the city a kind of national leader in this campaign. The other two wide-open red-light districts were officially closed by 1910, although clandestine prostitution was still practiced in those areas afterward. By contrast, St. Paul did not shut down its red-light district until 1913. The city of New Orleans finally closed the Storyville district at the insistence of the War Department in the autumn of 1917 to prevent soldiers from patronizing prostitutes.[21]

The underlying urban culture may offer an explanation of why Minneapolis, unlike some other cities, often denied the presence of prostitution despite plenty of contrary evidence. There seemed to be an underlying belief that if Minneapolis's citizens gave in to vice, be it alcohol consumption or patronizing brothels, the entire city would follow suit and turn away from both its ideals and the building of a commercial and industrial powerhouse. The mere acknowledgment of vice seemed dangerous. When faced with the practicalities of administering an expanding commercial and industrial city, Minneapolis leaders would agonize over their choices, then come to a realistic compromise and, in time, often forget the whole process. The deep-seated rivalry with St. Paul played a significant role as Minneapolis defined itself in contrast to its downstream neighbor. If St. Paul had a somewhat more relaxed attitude toward vice, then Minneapolis would be compelled to take a hard line on the same issue.

The madams who regularly appeared in the local newspapers during the nineteenth century never made it into the history books. Unlike other cities, Minneapolis's history has not recognized the women who directed its nineteenth-century sex industry. Chicago, New Orleans, Denver, and St. Paul all own up to bordello keepers in their colorful urban pasts. Chicago had the storied Everleigh Club run by sisters Minna and Aida Everly. New Orleans not only acknowledges the Storyville district and madams such as Kate Townsend and Lulu White but also uses them as selling points to tourists who want to explore the city's naughty past and musical heritage. Denver's Lower Downtown Historic District includes the "House of Mirrors," complete with a plaque that identifies it as a former bordello built by madam Jennie Rogers in 1889. St. Paul freely accepts Nina Clifford as its most famous madam. When Clifford died, one St. Paul newspaper published her obituary on the front page; decades after her death, St. Paul newspapers still ran stories about her. Modern-day tour guides relate the probably apocryphal tale of how Clifford's bordello was connected to the Minnesota Club at 317 Washington Street via tunnel, allowing respectable businessmen the opportunity to secretly patronize her place; tour guides also note that a portrait hanging in the bar of the Minnesota Club supposedly depicts Clifford.[22]

Minneapolis's tidy version of its past is not only inaccurate, it also denies a much richer history. Studying the lives of nontraditional women and other groups who were left out of the official version yields a larger and more complex view of a city's heritage. Acknowledging the madams sheds light on the lives of ordinary workingwomen and why some of them ended up in the commercial sex trade instead of respectable work. Recognizing the madams yields a more complete understanding of the sexual ecology of nineteenth-century Minneapolis and the political passions that drove the reformers. As the Minneapolis riverfront is being rediscovered, it is time to bring to light a group of enterprising women who lived on that riverfront, who both acknowledged and challenged traditional notions of gender in the nineteenth century and our own.

ONE

Women's Work of All Kinds
Paid Labor, Sex Work, and the Reform Movement

> Time was when the servant occupied a subordinate
> position in the household, when it was considered that
> obedience and not command was her function. In those
> days, they are long past now, and live only in history or
> tradition, the servant looked up to the lady of the house
> as authority. . . . Minneapolis has suffered with the rest
> of the world, and even more, perhaps, judging from
> the trouble our housewives report in obtaining efficient
> help. It is not an infrequent thing to hear of housewives
> changing girls two or three times in a single week.
>
> —"THE SERVANT GIRL PROBLEM,"
> *MINNEAPOLIS TRIBUNE*, OCTOBER 14, 1879

In 1874 a nineteen-year-old woman named Mary Rasette came to Minneapolis and found work as a domestic. But according to a *Minneapolis Tribune* article, she soon "willfully entered a life of shame" when she joined a bordello run by madam Mollie Ellsworth. Once Mary's father learned of her situation, he removed her from the brothel despite her objections. She later escaped from his custody, and a reporter concluded that it was "probable she has left the city." While one can only speculate, Rasette may have been avoiding an abusive family situation or looking for adventure, new opportunities, or better wages.[1]

The newspaper article provides only the briefest sketch of Rasette's life, but it highlights the fluid and changing relationships among women's growing mobility, opportunities for paid labor, and sex work in nineteenth-century America. The massive migration from rural to urban areas brought many single women into the labor force, including the sex trade. Joseph Kett, a historian of American adolescence, observed that by the mid-nineteenth century young men were leaving their parental homes in great numbers. Kett argued that "girls probably left agricultural communities at earlier ages than boys, for girls were less valuable on farms. According to the 1830 census, girls aged fifteen to nineteen generally formed a smaller portion of the population of New England villages under 1,500 people than did males of comparable ages, but a larger proportion in cities."[2] Another scholar, Faye Dudden, noted a high degree of mobility for workers in the nineteenth century, especially those who were young, unmarried, and without property. In part, for female workers, domestic "service itself helped to stir the streams of geographic mobility because its entry requirements were virtually nil, the ability to do housework being practically a secondary sex characteristic. Girls and women who needed work knew that they could go to a city, any city, and find work as servants."[3]

Increased mobility provided more opportunities for both men and women to seek their fortune away from parental control. Once in the city, young women became acquainted with a variety of employment opportunities, including prostitution. They also discovered that many of the old rules governing social interactions were different in the city. These young women might try out a number of jobs, encounter all manner of men, and perhaps move on to another city that seemed to offer better opportunities.

This chapter explores women's work in the nineteenth century, ranging from "respectable" work in factories and private homes to volunteer work meant to provide charity for the less fortunate and promote social change, to the disreputable labor of prostitution. It will provide a picture of the wages offered for different classes of female employment, as well as a rough estimate of what those wages would buy. The chapter also examines careers in prostitution and shows some of the reasons and routes that led women into and sometimes out of the commercial sex trade, as well as outlining the working life of one Minneapolis madam who flourished in the 1870s. Finally this chapter will introduce a group of female reformers, the Sisterhood of Bethany, who hoped to offer a chance at redemption to women who had violated, in one way or another, the bounds of sexual purity.

WOMEN'S LABOR IN MINNEAPOLIS

During the second half of the nineteenth century, women in Minneapolis engaged in a variety of paid and unpaid occupations, ranging from housekeeping and child care to working in factories or retail stores, teaching school, and occasionally operating small businesses. Housekeeping, which covered a broad range of tasks, such as washing, ironing, cooking, cleaning, and sewing, was the most common female occupation, whether performed for a woman's own family or as paid work for others. Without the now commonplace devices such as vacuum cleaners, dishwashers, prepared foods, microwaves, washers, and dryers, housekeeping was a full-time and endless job. For the most part, females occupied the lower end of the pay scale, and their choices were usually constrained by gender roles. Generally women did not perform "men's work," nor did men do "women's work." Usually this division of labor favored men in terms of pay and status; however, there were exceptions.

Two studies examined the subject of paid labor in Minnesota in the late 1880s. The Bureau of Labor Statistics of Minnesota conducted one formal study, looking at wages and conditions for both men and women. Its first report painted a mostly dismal picture of female wage earners. Generally, women who lived with their families were better able to live on their wages, as they often did not have to pay market rates for food and shelter. Employers preferred hiring this class of women, as they could be paid less. By contrast, women who had to rely only on their earnings often faced difficulties paying for rent, food, clothing, transportation, and medical expenses. The report offered a series of tables listing hours worked, weekly wages, and the number of women in each occupation sampled. Laundresses worked between nine and ten hours daily with an average weekly wage of $5.53. Women who made paper boxes worked a similar number of hours, and their wages averaged $3.63 per week. Some jobs were better than others. Women who did "copying" (i.e., writing out documents by hand; photocopiers had yet to be invented) worked eight-hour days and made an average of $9.27 weekly. Bookkeepers in the study were paid $13.07 for the same number of hours.[4]

The investigators went searching for cheap but comfortable boardinghouses and interviewed the female workers who lived there.

Women engaged in factory work in Minneapolis at the turn of the century. These workers label boxes at the International Stock Food Company, which moved into the Exposition Building in 1903. Photograph courtesy of the Minnesota Historical Society.

One woman told her tale: "I boarded [fed] myself at the cost of $1 per week for about six months and was taken ill at the end of that time. The doctor said the cause of my illness was insufficient food. So now I have to spend about $1.50 per week." Another one explained: "Two of us board ourselves and have good food at a cost of $5 per week for both, but it's hard to cook your own meals after working all day." Some tried pooling their resources: "Four of us hired a large room. We cooked, sewed, washed and ironed for ourselves and managed to live. Our wages were $3 per week apiece, but our clothes were always shabby [so] that we did not go to parties or to church on Sunday. We were so tired after doing our own work that we had no time to read or do anything but sleep."[5]

Devising ways to improve the lot of workingwomen, or any laboring class for that matter, presented a conundrum for the investigators. The report continued: "Here we come in contact with one of the most elevating and yet, in many cases, one of the most demoralizing forces in modern society. Familiarity with comfort, convenience, and elegance has a refining tendency; it awakens aspirations and desires for higher modes of life, and, no doubt, generally stimulates commendable effort; but on the other hand, it often breeds contempt for plain and honest surroundings, and where the foundations of character are not strong leads to extravagance, dishonesty, and often to ruin."[6] In other words, a woman who became more financially secure might spend her free time visiting libraries, attending lectures, or going to church. Or she might become dissatisfied with her lot in life and turn to other means to obtain an even better material life.

A later Bureau of Labor report described the dangers faced by children in the workplace. Sometimes the risk was to their character; sometimes it was bodily harm. "The chief occupation in which children in Minnesota are engaged where the occupation tends to endanger their morals is that by which many lads as messengers are sent daily into saloons, gambling hells, and the vilest dens of prostitution. There they are brought face to face with evil in its most seductive and destructive forms." For that writer, physical injuries were of less importance compared to endangering a child's soul. "For one child in Minnesota during the past year who has had his or her hands crushed in stamping machines or ironing mangles, there must be another who, led by the business mentioned, has had the moral fibre of his budding manhood ruined."[7]

The 1893 report also provided a county-by-county list of injuries investigators had uncovered in workplaces. Their clipped notes enumerated them: "Girl had her hand caught between feed rolls of ironing mangle. The flesh on her hand was badly burned." Or, "Girl had hand caught in rolls of ironing mangle and was badly burned and bruised"; "Girl, about 12, had her hand caught between rolls of ironing mangle. She was badly injured"; "One girl had two fingers mashed on a stay machine, necessitating the amputation of the ends. Another girl had three fingers on each hand pinched on a pressing machine."[8]

The Bureau of Labor report may have inspired a St. Paul newspaper to hire Eva McDonald, writing under the name of Eva Gay, to conduct her own investigations. During the spring and summer of 1888, the *St. Paul Globe* ran a series of articles on various jobs commonly held by women in the Twin Cities. Gay went undercover, posing as a job seeker in Minneapolis factories, retail stores, laundries, and employment agencies. Her findings echoed those of the Bureau of Labor Statistics investigators. In the basement of the North Star Woolen Mills, where the blankets were washed, women worked in a humid, ninety-eight-degree room and were paid ninety cents a day. The windows, which might have provided some ventilation, were kept shut so that dirt and dust would not soil the drying blankets. Gay asked one girl, "Do you think it's worthwhile to ruin your health by working in this place for such wages?" "I don't know as it is," was the weary reply, "but when a girl's got her living to earn she can't choose where she'll work."[9]

Gay talked to the female employees in each establishment to learn how much they were paid, their working conditions, and how they lived; the women painted a vivid picture of their employment. Gay learned that factory knitters earned two and a half to four dollars per week while working in dirty, poorly ventilated rooms.[10] Working as retail clerks, women had pleasant surroundings and their pay averaged about four dollars a week, but they were required to dress in fashionable clothes. Clothing, like room and board, was another expense that might not be covered by their earnings, which provided them with little more than carfare and pocket money.[11]

Female cigar makers made from six to nine dollars per week. Women workers in the shoe and boot factory considered themselves lucky to earn nine dollars per week, as the conditions and pay were far better than they had encountered in the East.[12] Female workers in some shirt factories had to furnish their own sewing machines and thread, worked in dim light for ten hours a day, and earned between three and nine dollars per week.[13] Women who worked for individual dressmakers were required to complete a three-month, unpaid apprenticeship. After their apprenticeship, they would earn about four dollars per week, which would barely allow them to live in a cheap boardinghouse.[14] The cheapest boardinghouse cost two to three dollars per week and did not include laundry.[15] Gay's investigation also turned up an account of an employer's organization. "The condition and wages of the girls in many laundries are nearly alike, wondering why it was thus I was told that a union exists among employers so that they may the more readily dictate wages. . . . Also a system of blacklisting exists."[16]

THE SERVANT PROBLEM

If factory, sewing, or retail jobs were not appealing, a woman could reliably find work as domestic help. Paid housework was often the job most readily available to uneducated women as well as immigrants who did not speak English. Servants were in demand regardless of geographic location. It was also the occupation that was most commonly held by those who later became prostitutes, although it is not clear whether something in the nature of housework led women into the sex trade or simply reflected the sheer number of women who worked as domestics during this period.[17]

Gay wrote, "Having sometimes met factory girls and others who could hardly manage to live on the wages received, I often asked why they didn't hire out as servants. It seemed to me that if a girl did housework she did not have to pay board nor many other incidental expenses." But Gay learned, "Among all classes of working girls I found a deep-rooted aversion to this sort of work. They persistently refused to see the advantages, which I urged. Some having tried house service claimed that hours were long, lasting all day and most of the night, or mistresses treated help in a harsh unreasonable manner."[18]

Gay's findings were similar to those of the Bureau of Labor Statistics. Female employees in other industries told interviewers that they refused to work as domestics for several reasons: "The hours are too long for the wages paid, and a girl is treated as an inferior." Or, "They treat their help very badly as a rule, and are not particular as to whom they hire; so that in houses where they employ several girls one must room and associate with strange girls, about whose characters and habits she knows nothing."[19]

Gay tried her hand at domestic labor. She began her investigations

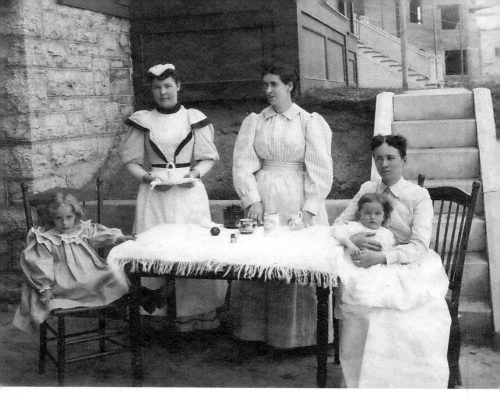

Three Minnesota women employed as domestic servants, with the two children in their care, 1895. Photograph courtesy of the Minnesota Historical Society.

at an "intelligence office," that is, a private employment office that connected employers with potential employees. Once there, Gay learned she would have to pay the office twenty-five cents for a referral and provide her own carfare to the interview, whether she was hired or not. One girl in the waiting room said she had been sent many places over the past two weeks, some of which did not even have any jobs available. Gay found other pitfalls faced by women going through an intelligence agency. Several young women there urged Gay to be very careful about accepting out-of-town assignments as these jobs were often in brothels. After Gay promised anonymity, several girls revealed that they had been sent to work in bordellos, although Gay did not elaborate whether these girls had been expected to work as domestics or as prostitutes at the bordellos, which often offered food to their customers and inmates, and had the same washing and cleaning needs as a boardinghouse or private family. After registering at another intelligence office, Gay finally got to interview a prospective employer. The woman told Gay that she would be expected to wash, cook, and iron for the family of five, work until 10 p.m. most days, and skip church services on Sundays because Gay would have to prepare the Sunday dinner while the family was at church. The woman explained, "If you're a smart girl you can get up at 4 o'clock in the morning on washing and ironing days, to get your extra work done early; then do the regular work the rest of the day." The woman offered two dollars or up to "two-fifty" per week to a "real good girl."[20]

The *Minneapolis Tribune* aired the opinions of employers, who complained their domestic workers did not work very hard and frequently left their positions whenever a better offer came along. The writer stated that servants should be denied night keys so they could not stay out late on their evenings off, that servants should be required to remain in their jobs until a replacement was found, and that employers should band together to set uniform wages. In this article, the domestics were portrayed as having most of the power in their relationship with employers. Apparently, these employers believed their only option was to institute a system akin to indentured servitude.[21]

PROSTITUTION

Neither Eva Gay nor the Bureau of Labor Statistics explored prostitution, and there were a number of good reasons for this omission. Prostitution was both illegal and shameful; its practitioners were unlikely to reveal exactly how much or little their services cost, since this was always subject to variations such as local supply and demand. The Bureau of Labor Statistics would have invited ridicule, at the very least, had it published the average pay and hours of Minnesota sex workers, even if such information were available. However, the commercial sex industry was always in the background of these reports, whether investigators were worrying about the morals of children who ran errands for bordello operators or women who struggled to survive on meager wages and might be tempted to turn to an illegal but more lucrative line of work.

Prostitution, as practiced in nineteenth-century America, took a variety of forms. At the top of the hierarchy were "kept women," who had one patron who paid their expenses in exchange for sexual favors. On the other end of the economic scale, streetwalkers trolled the by-ways or saloons for customers, taking their customers to their rented rooms or performing sex acts in out-of-the-way public areas. Since streetwalkers were more visible to the public, they usually suffered more police harassment, and by working alone were often more exposed to violence from their clients, although on occasion it was the customer who came out the worse. The *Tribune* reported on two "innocents" who had arrived in Minneapolis after working as harvesters and intended to seek work in the northern lumber camps "after seeing the elephant" (a euphemism for having sex). The two men walked along South Washington Avenue, where they connected with "two dusky damsels." The foursome "walked down Third Avenue until they chanced into an alley near the railroad and First Street." After a "short chat," the women hurried away and later the two men discovered they had been robbed of a total of $255. Although their wallets were kept inside their pockets, one woman was "so smooth that she returned the purse without the owner noticing the transformation."[22] Despite being the most visible of the public women, streetwalkers are the most difficult group to follow historically. Unlike the established madams, streetwalkers did not own the real estate, nor did they work in the same location for years. They rarely showed up in census lists or were not listed as prostitutes, as brothel inmates were.

Somewhere between kept women and streetwalkers were brothel prostitutes. In this arrangement, customers came to a particular location, often a dwelling, to buy sex from prostitutes who lived there. Women who lived in brothels were often called "inmates," a term that today suggests a prisoner confined to a jail. In this context, however, the term simply meant resident. Brothels could range from well-appointed mansions that offered its patrons several services such as live music and sumptuous food and drink, to low dives where clients were serviced as quickly as possible. Brothels were described with a variety of euphemisms such as house of ill repute, house of ill fame, parlor house, bagnio, low resort, sporting house, female boarding-house, or sometimes house of assignation.

Not all houses of assignation were brothels. Some of them were more like hotels where rooms could be rented for a few hours by illicit couples. The landlady would be willing to supply patrons with prostitutes if requested, but such a house did not necessarily have sex workers living in it. In 1889, Lena Leppala operated such a house at 829 Twentieth Avenue South. Leppala, according to several newspaper accounts, catered to the unhappily married of both sexes. During the raid that closed the operation, the police found six scantily clad individuals, posing for an "artist," and several prominent men in various stages of undress, including a naked man who jumped out a window.[23]

As Minneapolis grew rapidly, women poured into the city and experienced, firsthand, that in most cases their wages were far lower than those paid to men. The contrast between low pay for women's work and the relatively high "wages of sin" made the sex industry seem like a better alternative for some. The rising number of factories and commercial establishments in Minneapolis ensured a steady supply of homegrown talent for local bordellos, as some poorly paid female workers calculated that the sex industry offered the best opportunities.

It is difficult to determine how much or how little money Minneapolis prostitutes earned, as this information rarely was reported in newspapers or in other accounts. In 1879 one reporter gave an example, possibly hypothetical, of a brothel inmate who earned sixty dollars per month. Typically, a brothel prostitute would turn over half of her earnings in exchange for room and board and other overhead expenses, as well as paying a monthly fine to the municipal court ranging from $5 to $12.50. A woman earning sixty dollars per month would still have at least $17.50 for herself at the end of the month.[24]

Perhaps successful Minneapolis sex workers made even more money than the reporter imagined. Historian Timothy Gilfoyle cites examples of New York prostitutes who made four to five dollars per night and another who was paid five dollars for every sex act. A *Minneapolis Journal* article from 1886 stated that a customer would pay two dollars to meet a prostitute at a house of assignation. An assignation house prostitute would share some portion of the two-dollar fee with the keeper, but still, she stood a fair chance of making several dollars per day. In the higher-priced parlor houses, where the client paid for the privilege of making his choice from among several women, a sex worker could make even more money.[25]

A stereograph of a young woman on a bed in a richly furnished room with her street clothes tossed aside. This stereograph was produced by the "Swidish [Swedish] American View Company of Minneapolis"; the setting and the circumstances of its subject are unclear. Stereographs were a popular form of visual media in the late nineteenth century and often depicted travel scenes or famous sights. It is not known whether this image served as an advertisement for the city's sex trade. Author's collection.

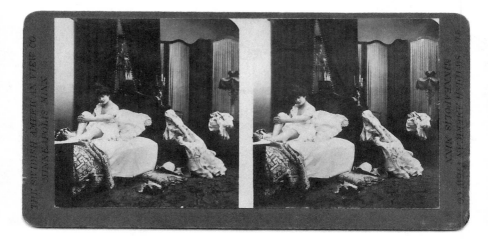

Like other workers, prostitutes faced workplace hazards, but instead of dangerous machinery or overheated factories, the biggest danger to sex workers came from their clients. The very nature of their work forced prostitutes into intimate contact with customers who might be unwashed, diseased, or drunken misogynists with violent streaks. For example, a customer who had repeatedly visited one particular woman at Lillie Goodrich's First Street brothel decided to shoot her, "proclaiming that he was Jack the Ripper." Fortunately the inebriated man's aim was poor and the bullets missed his intended target.[26]

Some prostitutes succumbed to despair and took their own lives. The story of Gracie Davis, whose life ended in suicide, suggested prostitution may have paid fairly well and offered mobility, but it did not necessarily bring its practitioners contentment. Although little was known about her previous life or identity, Davis may have first entered the sex trade in Chicago. From there Davis, described as a petite, vivacious, attractive blonde in her early twenties, moved to St. Paul and worked for madam Mary France; later she relocated to Minneapolis and a brothel run by Sallie Campbell. For a time, Davis went to live in the House of the Good Shepherd in St. Paul, where she hoped to reform her life. But for some reason, she returned to prostitution and went to work for other Minneapolis madams until she entered the bordello run by Kate Campbell. After spending a seemingly happy afternoon going about the city, Davis returned to the bordello, retired to her room, and overdosed on morphine. The reporter concluded that Davis committed suicide because "she wearied of a life of mocking shame and degradation."[27]

Although not specific to Minneapolis, William Sanger's 1858 study of the nineteenth-century sex trade, *History of Prostitution: Its Extent, Causes, and Effect Throughout the World,* directly addressed the longevity of sex workers. While Sanger's firsthand field research was impressive, some of his conclusions, or perhaps biases, appealed to popular attitudes regarding women, Europeans, and the general decline of public morals.

As resident physician of the Blackwell's Island penitentiary hospital, Sanger interviewed two thousand New York City prostitutes. He concluded that a woman who entered the sex trade died, on average, after four years in the business. As her charms quickly faded, a prostitute would always move from wealthy clients to miserable dives where

"none will be too low for her company." Well over half of Sanger's inter-
viewees were foreign born. Based on that number, he believed there was
a constitutive relationship between prostitutes' short lives and foreign
immigration. If one-quarter of New York's prostitutes died annually,
they would have to be replaced, often from the ranks of immigrants
pouring into the city. "Of every two hundred and fifty emigrants—
men, women, children, who land at our docks, at least one woman
eventually becomes known as a prostitute," Sanger asserted.

In Sanger's view the mere exposure to European culture could
weaken the morals of Americans. He decried the increasing number of
continentals who visited the United States and Americans who traveled to Europe. "We are rapidly introducing many of the absurd follies
and worst vices of Europe," Sanger railed. He noted that respectable
families now tolerate behavior that fifteen years earlier would have
caused the offender to be expelled "from the domestic circle." He complained that every day New York was becoming more like the "most
depraved capitals of continental Europe, and it remains for the good
innate sense of the bulk of the American people to say how much farther we shall proceed in this frivolous, intriguing and despicable manner of living." As for native-born prostitutes, Sanger concluded that
"fraud or force is used to entrap these females."[28]

Sanger's conclusions (such as the reason for sex workers' short lives
and the idea that women were forced into prostitution) would gain cre-
dence in Minneapolis and many other cities. In 1889, when Minneapolis prostitute Lou Williams died of tuberculosis at a rescue home,
her benefactors noted, "The four years that she lived the life of an
abandoned woman [prostitute] did their work quickly, and yesterday
morning she died at the [Bethany] Home." Ironically, fourteen years
earlier, the very same newspaper characterized Williams as "an old
habitué of Municipal Court," when she paid her monthly prostitution
fines. As chapter 4 will illustrate, Minneapolis reformers insisted that
the city's bordellos were filled with women who were "white slaves"
and had been entrapped into the sex trade, although evidence of this
practice was almost nonexistent.[29]

Starvation wages and dangerous working conditions often led
women to decide that prostitution was a better choice than respectable
work elsewhere. A poor home life, bad choices, desertion, divorce, or

even family tradition were also often determining factors. Seventeen-year-old May Anderson started working at a brothel at 220 First Street South after her parents turned her out of their house on Bohemian Flats. She later told a police matron that her parents had always treated her badly. After leaving home, Anderson found work as a domestic in the brothel, but soon realized she could make more money as a prostitute.[30]

In 1886 a woman calling herself "Marion Field" ran away from her home in Madison, Wisconsin, and soon found her way to a First Street bordello in Minneapolis. When her parents discovered Marion, her mother begged her to return home. When Marion declined, her father pulled out a revolver and announced, "You are going back home with me dead or alive." Marion remained adamant and just before her father pulled the trigger, the detective accompanying them intervened. As a prostitute Marion "had many admirers on account of her beauty and intelligence," and apparently sex work was preferable to her home life.[31]

Mrs. John Stewart ran away to Milwaukee with her lover, Hal White, a bartender, leaving her husband and three children behind in Minneapolis. Once White grew tired of Stewart, she wound up homeless on a winter night. Stewart appealed for help from an acquaintance who lived at what a reporter called "Wild Irish Rose's" bordello at 1019 Second Street South and soon began working there. Stewart explained she had no particular job skills or other sources of money. "It was night and so cold, and I was hungry. . . . What else could I do?"[32]

One St. Paul madam who relocated to Minneapolis exemplified the desertion-divorce-family-tradition route to prostitution. In 1851 teen-aged Mary J. France married Charles Butts. The couple was living in upstate New York but moved to Minnesota. While they were living in Mankato, Charles deserted Mary and their two daughters, Charlotte and Lola. France stated in her divorce petition that "since May 1, 1866, the plaintiff has been dependent on her own exertions for support and maintenance, and for the support and maintenance of her said children."[33] After her abandonment, France moved to St. Paul, first appearing in the 1867 city directory as an employee of Robert Street dressmaker Maria Denley. Within a few years, France was operating a brothel. It is difficult to determine whether France completely supported herself from sewing in 1867 or whether she was already engaged in prostitution. By that time, she had adopted the name France, which would serve as her professional identity as a madam and suggests that she was already working in the sex trade, although scholar Joel Best dates her St. Paul career from 1875 to 1883.[34]

France's two daughters followed their mother into the trade. The *St. Paul Pioneer Press* noted, "Mrs. France . . . has associated with her in the nefarious business two daughters, both of whom have grown up in St. Paul, and the younger, who can scarcely be eighteen years of age, is known to be gradually, but surely fading away to a consumptive's grave, probably the effect of the avocation to which she is forced."[35] Contrary to the newspaper's predictions, neither of the daughters died prematurely. Charlotte, the elder daughter, went on to manage France's Minneapolis brothel. She later inherited her mother's estate, married a veterinarian, and lived into her seventies.[36]

In his study of prostitution in New Orleans, Al Rose interviewed several survivors of the Storyville district. One woman whom he called "Violet" was born in 1904 to a prostitute. She grew up in a brothel and began performing sex acts at age ten with the approval of her mother. Violet stayed in the business for a few years, but apparently did not suffer any long-term ill effects. She later recalled, "I was always high priced. Not because, you know, I was so pretty or nothin', but because I was a novelty, and I didn't hang around long enough to get wore out." Violet concluded, "I know it'd be good if I could say how awful it was and like crime don't pay—but to me it seems just like anything else— like a kid who's [sic] father owns a grocery store. He helps him in the store. Well, my mother didn't sell groceries."[37] The examples provided by Charlotte France and Violet from the Storyville district suggest that at least some women were not permanently trapped in the sex trade, but could move in and out of it as they did with other jobs, if or when circumstances changed.

RECRUITMENT INTO PROSTITUTION

Some women were recruited to become sex workers. In 1889, the *St. Paul Daily Globe* ran several articles about Mrs. M. Hertogs, who operated a Minneapolis millinery and dressmaking establishment. At first she appeared to be a hardworking, respectable businesswoman. But there

These two photographs of St. Paul prostitutes were produced by the yellow journalist Howard Guilford in 1913. Guilford was a noted scandalmonger, but his images are among the very rare photographic depictions of early twentieth-century sex workers in the Twin Cities. The woman shown alone was a parlor-house prostitute who called herself "Birdie Foley," likely a professional pseudonym; according to Guilford, Foley came to St. Paul from Chicago. In the photograph of three prostitutes and a "john" posing in a St. Paul bordello, the large mirror in the background, patterned wallpaper, lace curtains, and polished furniture indicate a level of elegance. From Howard A. Guilford, *Holies of Holies of the White Slave Worshiper.* Author's collection.

were disturbing rumors that she supplied dresses to prostitutes living in the First Street sex district. Her respectable clientele began to drift away, supposedly because she was devoting too much time catering to the First Street trade. Hertogs closed her shop and "conceived the idea of bettering herself financially and building up her business at the same time by acting as a procuress." The recruits would need expensive dresses, which she would supply on the installment plan, "thus getting the girls in debt and placing them to a large extent in her power."[38]

Hertogs persuaded Nellie Turcotte, described as a black-haired and rosy-cheeked country girl, to join a First Street brothel after she lost her job as a waitress.[39] At Hertogs's libel trial, several people testified that she frequently visited brothels in Minneapolis and St. Paul where she was on good terms with the madams.[40] Apparently Hertogs recruited for local madams as well those out of state, hinting at the existence of a madams trade association that allowed them to communicate with one another, and move employees or themselves to other cities. Not surprisingly, these lines of communication followed either railroad lines or navigable rivers. Hertogs recruited four women for Kate Whitney, a madam in Butte, Montana, and had urged Nellie Kellar to go to Spokane, Washington, and work in a brothel there.[41] Both Butte and Spokane had established railroad connections to the Twin Cities by 1889. One newspaper account noted, "In fact, it had been shown the plaintiff [Hertogs] was a sort of 'clearing house' for these places of ill-repute and this had not been disputed."[42]

The account of Madame Hertogs underscores historian Faye Dudden's point that improvements in transportation allowed for greater mobility of laboring women of all sorts, whether they were domestic help or prostitutes. Nellie Turcotte may have come to Minneapolis to work as a waitress, but she apparently moved into brothel life without much difficulty. Even when Turcotte's mother managed to get her removed from the bordello, Nellie refused to return home, preferring instead to become the mistress of a bartender.[43]

On the surface, the Hertogs story tells of young women being lured into the sex trade. But it also suggests a pool of available women in Minneapolis who might end up working in any number of jobs ranging from "sewing girl" to sex worker. There was a connection between the needle trades and prostitution. A prostitute was expected to wear rich, showy clothes to attract customers, clothes that would be sewn by a dressmaker. Sumptuously dressed women who complemented the elegant brothel interiors would be part of the entertainment offered by a successful madam. Conversely, a struggling dressmaker might conclude through her contact with prostitutes that selling sex offered a better life than long hours spent stitching other people's clothing for little money.

BEING "RUINED," MALE PRIVILEGE, AND THE DOUBLE STANDARD

There were other ways women could be nudged or fall into prostitution. The contemporary social mores (namely, male privilege and a prevailing double standard of sexual purity) virtually guaranteed that a professional class of women would exist to provide sex to men outside the institution of marriage. If a woman had sex outside marriage, the resulting loss of reputation could lead her into the sex trade. A local domestic worker's story illustrates how the transformation from pure to tarnished might occur.

On February 16, 1877, Kate Noonan, age twenty-two, shot and killed Will H. Sidle as he walked along Nicollet Avenue.[44] Despite initial newspaper accounts that painted Noonan as a deranged woman who without provocation had coldly assassinated the sober and proper Sidle, a different picture emerged during her trial. The social chasm between Noonan and Sidle was vast. Twenty-four-year-old Sidle was the assistant cashier at First National Bank, which had been established by his father, Henry, and uncle Jacob Sidle. Noonan, the daughter of impoverished Irish immigrants, earned her living as a domestic servant. Noonan testified that she had been pursued by Sidle after meeting him at several "low" dances. He would leave his desk at the bank and follow her down the street. At first she resisted his attentions, but after a time Noonan agreed to accompany him to a restaurant, where, at some point, she lost consciousness. The next morning, she found herself in a hotel bed with Sidle. Deeply ashamed, Noonan began crying, but Sidle comforted her with the promise that he would always love her. When Noonan saw Sidle the following evening, he told her that he had previously kept another woman but had to send her away when his father became suspicious, so their affair would have to remain secret.

Their relationship continued until Noonan broke it off. Sidle eventually persuaded her to come back, promising to support her for the rest of her life although he said that he could never marry her, as his father would fire him from his bank position. Sometimes Noonan would meet Sidle for trysts at various locations, including Mollie Ellsworth's bordello. Sidle's parents began to pressure him to marry a girl of his own social class. At first Sidle told Noonan that he would never marry at the request of his parents, but in time he either acquiesced or grew tired of Noonan. Sidle promised her a sum of money so she could leave town and start over, but he later reneged. He began avoiding Noonan and she began plotting her revenge. On several occasions Noonan tried to confront Sidle at work, and at one point the bank's president, Jacob Sidle, asked Noonan to settle the dispute privately and to stay away from the bank's premises. After one confrontation, Noonan was arrested and spent the night in jail. Sometime after this incident, Noonan acquired a gun and later claimed that she planned to kill Sidle and then take her own life.[45]

Noonan was fortunate in that Charlotte Van Cleve, for whom she had worked as a servant, took up her cause. Van Cleve hired lawyers and assembled a group of reputable matrons to serve as character witnesses for Noonan. Van Cleve also provided Noonan with emotional support. In one instance a reporter noted, "The prisoner was in her accustomed seat, accompanied by Mrs. Van Cleve, who has been her constant companion in the court room since the trial commenced." Although some of Noonan's supporters were aware of her relationship with Sidle, they considered it an aberration, painting him as an aggressive seducer. Noonan's first trial ended in a hung jury. At her second trial her lawyers managed to locate two witnesses, one of whom testified that Sidle had wagered with friends that he would seduce Kate within a fortnight while the other said that he had seen Sidle drug Noonan's drink. This time, Noonan was found not guilty by reason of insanity.[46]

Afterward Van Cleve continued her help, enabling Noonan to learn the trade of dressmaking. More important, Van Cleve made sure that her respectable friends employed the "notorious" Noonan as a seamstress; and Noonan lived in the Van Cleve household until Charlotte's death in 1907. Without the aid of Van Cleve and salable skills, Noonan easily could have drifted into prostitution. Apparently she lacked even an eighth-grade education. In her testimony, Noonan stated that "she worked in a woolen factory as a little girl," then as a domestic for two families before coming to work for the Van Cleve family at age fifteen.[47]

By contrast, Will Sidle suffered no loss of reputation or status. Although his parents knew of his clandestine activities, they still wanted him to marry a respectable woman within their social milieu. Even after his cruel actions were revealed in court, Sidle had the sympathy of the community. He was fond of bragging about his amorous exploits, yet his victim was blamed for creating her own troubles.

During Noonan's first trial, an editorial in a St. Paul newspaper acknowledged that while Sidle may have been a seducer, ultimately it was the responsibility of the woman to guard her own virtue. Noonan's case "should warn girls of her class against accepting the attentions and familiarities of young men of higher social position, whom they must know seek their companionship for no honest purpose."[48] As an illustration of a victim of seduction, Kate Noonan's story differed from the usual only in that Sidle ultimately paid a very high price for his pleasure and his private actions became a public story.

If Noonan had been less determined to make Sidle acknowledge his debt to her, she might well have ended up in the sex trade, as other "ruined" women sometimes did. A formerly respectable woman, identified by the *Tribune* only as "Ethel," joined a First Street bordello after her lover, "a well known young man," abandoned her because she had become pregnant. Noonan and Ethel were identified as damaged goods, while the double standard shielded their male counterparts from any ostracism.[49]

RECONSTRUCTING THE LIFE OF A NINETEENTH-CENTURY MADAM

As Mary France's story illustrates, a small minority of women in nineteenth-century Minneapolis worked their way up to become madams. The Minneapolis madams examined in the subsequent chapters of this book operated high-end parlor houses, although one started out with a rough dive that served lumberjacks. None of the Minneapolis madams left written accounts of their lives, but some women from other cities did write about their experience in the nineteenth-century sex industry.

A woman using the name Josie Washburn recounted her life in prostitution and offered a general description of the sex trade. After entering an Omaha bordello in 1871 at age seventeen to work as a prostitute, Washburn became a madam during the 1890s. Her account compared prostitution to a sewer that safely contained men's raging lust and carried it away from respectable women. She maintained that if the "Necessary Evil," as prostitution was often called, must exist, its practitioners should be treated with respect, not contempt.

Washburn devoted an entire chapter to madams and offered her thoughts on how madams were made. She painted a picture of a tough-minded individual who maintained control of her business through manipulation and force of will: "The woman becomes a madam just as a man becomes a manager, boss, or an owner, by progression or chance. To a great extent it depends upon her qualifications." Washburn opined that just as a "successful boss is the one who commands obedience without unnecessary display of authority," a successful madam is someone "who can make things come her way without domineering. She knows when to be indulgent, and when the firmness that amounts to harshness must be applied." Washburn continued, "The successful madam must not lose the confidence of those she is directing and managing; if so she loses prestige, and loses control of her house." Ideally, a madam would be able to control both her customers and employees without appearing to do so, but some did resort to force in dealing with their workers.[50]

Not all madams possessed the subtlety that Washburn recommended. In 1887 Minneapolis madam Nellie St. Clair, described as one who "weighs 180 pounds and has a muscular development that would do credit to a club swinger," beat and kicked the frail Mabel Smith, an inmate of her First Street bordello. St. Clair was subsequently arrested and charged with assault.[51]

Washburn elucidated how madams both exploited and protected their inmates when they became involved with predatory men. "As a rule the landlady [madam] is kind to the girls, and if she has been obliged to 'lock her in,' it is usually to the advantage of the girl," who is either heading out on a drunken spree or supporting a pimp.

Washburn did not glamorize the role of the madam, but at times she seemed to believe that the madam was truly "the best friend the girl has," stating, "there is a goodwill and love between them that nothing can change."

Washburn said that she had worked in bordellos across the country and had never been a prisoner in any of them. She said a successful madam would be more likely to manipulate her workers on an emotional level by appealing to a shared history, rather than by using the threat of force. Most madams started out as ordinary prostitutes and gained experience in the perils of the trade. But once a woman rose from sex worker to madam, she would then, much like a male pimp, exploit her inmates for money. A pimp would exert control over women by offering a combination of professed love and outright force, while a madam might achieve the same ends by providing what appeared to be friendship and the protection of a bordello. Some madams may have been genuinely fond of their inmates, but that would never change the fact that the madam held the upper hand in this power arrangement.[52]

Another woman, who called herself Madeleine Blair, wrote an account of the sex trade during the nineteenth century. While Blair's identity has never been established, some scholars believe her memoirs provide a fairly accurate account of brothel life during the late 1880s through the early years of the twentieth century. Blair worked in St. Louis, Kansas City, Chicago, and later in Canada. She even visited Minneapolis and claimed to know an inmate of a Main Street brothel.[53] Blair recalled that Lizzie Allen, who ran a very exclusive bordello on Dearborn Street in Chicago, was on duty from 8:30 p.m. to 4:00 a.m. every day.[54] But certain duties of a madam, such as court appearances, could only be performed during the day, regardless of how many hours she had worked the previous night. Depending on the size of her staff, a madam might delegate some tasks, but she was still responsible for the overall smooth running of the business, which often operated seven days a week.

A flourishing madam would be a good judge of character. She kept watch on customers and removed those who could prove dangerous to brothel inmates before trouble started. She also had to develop a sense of what a customer might seek. The better a madam was at assessing a customer's wants, the more successful she would be at turning him into a repeat customer. Madeleine Blair observed that competition in the sex industry was "keen and bitter," and, as in any other business, advertising played a large role. Although madams could not use the typical venues such as newspapers to promote their business, Blair noted, "the adage that the best advertisement is a pleased customer is doubly true in this business." A happy client would become a repeat customer and direct business to that particular madam. Conversely, an unhappy customer would not return and would warn his friends away. Blair reported that men typically held the madam responsible for the actions of her inmates. If a man was dissatisfied, "she should have trained her girls better."[55]

In addition to anticipating a customer's desires, a good madam would be skilled at recruiting the right kind of inmate to her establishment. Surprisingly, youth was not necessarily an advantage in a sex worker. Blair noted that because they had no experience in determining what men wanted, "young girls just entering the business [are not] of much value, commercially, either to themselves or to the house." Physical beauty was undoubtedly an advantage to a prostitute, but it was not the most important quality. The apparent willingness to please and entertain a customer, acquiesce to his demands, and keep him coming back for more were the traits of a good sex worker. In her memoir, Blair explained that "the ability of a girl to make money does not depend upon beauty, although that may be made an asset. It depends entirely upon her ability to flatter and please men, to be 'all things to all men.'" Superior acting skills and engaging conversation would always trump simple prettiness. As Blair noted, "In the same house there will often be a beautiful woman who does not make her expenses and a remarkably plain one who is 'coining money.'"[56]

A successful madam would be skillful at choosing inmates who could not only satisfy the customers but get along with other workers as well. A typical bordello might house five to eight inmates. While each woman had her own room, the inmates took meals together and generally shared each other's company when they were not entertaining customers. This enforced companionship could lead to rivalries that disrupted the entire operation if left unchecked and even to unwanted publicity. In once instance, the *Tribune* reported a fight between Alice Jackson and Pearl Clark, inmates of a First Street bordello, over the affections of musician Henry Clay Webster. As the argument grew more heated, one woman pulled out a gun, while the other "produced a razor." Alice received a black eye, "Pearl was bitten severely on the body," and others received lesser injuries. Apparently, everyone in the bordello was taken to jail as a result of the fight.[57]

Although inmates vied with each other for clients, they were also expected to assist each other while customers were present. For example, a large part of a brothel's profits came from selling liquor to customers, and clients expected prostitutes to drink with them. The inmates tried to avoid alcohol while on duty, however, as they needed to be alert and fully in control. Brothel inmates would often help each other deceive the customer into believing they were drinking, while disposing of the liquor elsewhere. Blair recounted an incident when she and another woman collaborated in repeatedly selling the same bottle of champagne to one man, pretending to get drunk with him. As the client's judgment was increasingly impaired by liquor, he spent more freely on them.[58]

Washburn compared the treatment of female employees by department store owners to that of madams, explaining that clerks, like prostitutes, had to dress nicely and always appear to be composed and pleasant toward customers regardless of how they were being treated. However, the store paid so little that clerks could not possibly live on their wages. "The department store drives the girl to the madam by paying her as little as possible, and the madam tries to keep the girl by the same means." Washburn reflected, "The majority of madams do not stop to consider the immorality of their business. If she stops to think about it at all, she decides that the world would soon give her the 'cold shoulder' if she did not have the money to pay her way. To her it is merely a business, a disagreeable disreputable business, which she hates. Her plans are to retire when she has money enough to live upon."[59]

Both Washburn's and Blair's accounts of the brothel business make it clear that a successful madam had to be an unsentimental individual who could solve problems both inside and outside the brothel. The madam was the chief storyteller, setting the tone and providing customers with the words they wished to hear. A good madam would try to develop camaraderie among her inmates, while working them for maximum profits. Blair claimed she never sold liquor to her girls because "I had no wish to make money from the girls; I was keenly aware of my obligation in making money through them."[60]

Successful madams would strive to acquire real estate, starting with their own brothels. Well-chosen property was a safe place to invest their earnings and diversify their holdings. Once they owned a place, madams would not be subjected to landlords who could either charge them higher rents than respectable tenants could pay or threaten them with arbitrary evictions if they suddenly decided to terminate their connections with the commercial sex trade. As property owners, the madams also gained a certain foothold and protection in society. Lawmakers were reluctant to regulate how private property could be used; if the authorities made arbitrary rules against one owner, then all property owners were threatened.

Historian Timothy Gilfoyle recounted that during the Brothel Riots of the 1830s, some New York prostitutes used the law to exact reimbursement from their attackers: "Rioters were thus compelled to repair the damage even when the judge knew about the illicit carnal activities of the plaintiff. . . . When prostitutes exercised their property rights, the municipality was compelled to defend prostitution and prosecute its more violent enemies."[61] From a madam's point of view, owning the real estate provided several advantages, beyond freeing them from a landlord. Once a madam owned property, she could build a brothel to suit the needs of her particular business instead of making do with an existing building. A diversified real estate portfolio could sustain a madam once she left the business, and a brothel could be turned into a hotel should the times demand. Several Main Street bordellos became residential hotels after the sex district was shut down.

A successful madam would also collect expensive jewelry as part of her holdings. Stunning jewels were part of a prosperous madam's business wardrobe as well as an advertisement of her success. They were portable and could be used as collateral for loans. Local newspapers delighted in running stories about Minneapolis madams and their diamonds. In 1893 Mattie St. Clair, having pledged her diamond solitaire earrings in exchange for a $600 loan, tried to snatch them back from the moneylender. In another instance, a madam had diamond earrings, valued at $1,200, torn from her ears, but noted the thieves were really hoping to steal the $15,000 worth of gems from her bedroom.[62]

THE SEX TRADE IN MINNEAPOLIS DURING THE 1870s

By the early 1870s Minneapolis had a thriving sex trade that offered expensive parlor houses, saloon–brothels, and ordinary streetwalkers. Mollie Ellsworth ran a high-toned establishment at 16 Second Avenue North on what is now a portion of the campus of the Ninth District Federal Reserve Bank. She opened her brothel in 1871 after taking over a fifteen-year lease on the property from Sarah A. Medberry.[63] Ellsworth operated at that location until her death five years later, at age thirty-nine. The outlaw Jesse James may have visited her establishment just before he led the raid on the Northfield bank on September 7, 1876. Or at least that is the story Ellsworth told a reporter. She claimed members of the James gang visited her bordello and that Jesse himself recognized her as "Kitty Traverse," who had worked in a St. Louis bordello several years earlier. Jesse James reportedly said to Ellsworth, "I am going out into the country [presumably Northfield] for a few days, and I will be back soon, then you and I will go to the centennial."[64]

Whether Ellsworth actually knew Jesse James is impossible to verify, but by telling this story to a reporter she garnered publicity for her business, associating herself with a notorious criminal who was then very much in the news. Ellsworth advertised through the reporter that men who visited her brothel just might rub shoulders with infamous and dangerous men, but in a controlled setting. It was a cunning bit of storytelling, suggesting that otherwise respectable men could indirectly interact with criminals and later tell their own tall tales. Ellsworth was providing her customers with more than one form of entertainment.

Perhaps as a clever storyteller, Ellsworth decided to mix some verifiable facts into her tale. She did use the name Catherine Travis on the lease for her real estate, and her probate documents are listed under the name Kate Travers. Ellsworth's obituary described her as a native of Buffalo, New York. According to this account, she had run away with an older man when she was sixteen, and he later deserted her in St. Louis. It was then that "she entered upon her life of shame, living there, in Omaha and other places, until she came here about seven years ago."[65] Ellsworth's estate passed to her father, Frank Travers, of Allegheny, New York, suggesting that she may have come from that area. Ellsworth's probate documents offer a rare, room-by-room glimpse of an 1870s Minneapolis parlor house, as well as hints about her business dealings.

Ellsworth operated a two-story, six-bedroom house. While many of the town's citizens lived in sparsely furnished, often shared, rooms in boardinghouses or simple houses that accommodated several generations, Ellsworth's inmates had their own bedrooms that were carpeted and furnished with bedsteads, marble-topped washstands, and chairs. Most had pictures on the walls, a freestanding bathtub, a bureau or wardrobe, and perhaps a writing desk. One parlor had a sofa, six stuffed chairs, pictures, a piano, a marble-topped table, and a chandelier. Multiple parlors or sitting rooms allowed patrons privacy and were the mark of a high-class establishment. The inventory of Ellsworth's estate included lists of silverware and fine jewelry, and an unusually detailed account of the food in her larder, but what is notably absent is any mention of alcohol. Brothels routinely sold drinks as much for profit as to lower the inhibitions that might limit consumer spending. Whatever liquor was on hand seems to have disappeared before the appraiser had a chance to take his inventory. Ellsworth's probate also contained several promissory notes carrying an annual interest of 12 percent from Kate Campbell, another Minneapolis madam. Campbell took over Ellsworth's brothel less than a month after her death.[66]

As Ellsworth's estate suggests, Minneapolis madams often lent money to one another, and real estate was routinely sold or rented from one madam to another. Not surprisingly, madams preferred to do business within their own group. Who better than another madam to assess whether a particular woman would or could repay her loans? And once a property was established as a brothel, both in function and reputation, the natural purchaser would be another woman in the business. These business arrangements buttress the idea of an informal trade association for madams that allowed the exchange of information as well as credit. While this organization never officially existed, there are many accounts of madams offering shelter to others who were under indictment and hoping to avoid process servers, or warning each other during periodic police raids on brothels.

An 1873 newspaper account revealed that the authorities were aware of this self-help organization: "It was evident that it would not do to 'go for' one house of ill-fame and return for the occupants of others, owing to the mysterious telegraphic system in vogue between them," even though there were guards stationed around each brothel.[67] The mutual aid association allowed madams to communicate with one another, and when Minneapolis reformers declared war on the sex trade in the late 1870s, it probably facilitated a well-organized backlash by the madams. It also likely served as a negotiating vehicle that allowed city authorities to work with the madams discreetly to allow the emergence of a completely new sex district in the 1890s, balancing the need for expansion of the sex trade against outward respect for the law.

THE SISTERHOOD OF BETHANY

The urban migration of single, working-class women and the conditions of their paid work played an important role in the expansion of prostitution in nineteenth-century Minneapolis. A different form of labor, on the opposite end of the class spectrum, was significant in efforts to suppress sex work. Across America during this period, upper- and middle-class women devoted their time and energy to charitable organizations promoting various types of social reform. Scholar Peggy Pascoe noted that by the mid-nineteenth century, white, Protestant, middle-class women in eastern locales had formed antislavery societies, while "others organized female moral reform societies dedicated to eliminating prostitution. Members of one such group, the New York Female Moral Reform Society, made themselves notorious by bursting into brothels to hold prayer meetings and by publishing the names of men known to have seduced young women." Pascoe observed that "not surprisingly for women raised in a culture that prized sexual restraint, they zeroed in on groups whose behavior seemed to them to raise the spectre of unrestrained sexuality." She noted that during the 1870s, female benevolent societies that sought to aid workingwomen, widows, orphans, and "fallen women" sprang up in many midwestern cities. These societies not only promoted piety and female purity, they also offered a certain amount of autonomy by allowing their members to operate in a sphere free of male supervision.[68]

In 1875 several Minneapolis women formed what would turn into a surprisingly effective organization, the Sisterhood of Bethany. It was dedicated to helping and reforming women who had violated prevailing sexual mores, as unwed mothers or prostitutes. Charlotte Van Cleve, Harriet Granger Walker, Abby Grant Mendenhall, and

Martha J. Talbert were the charter members of the Sisterhood. Like the examples cited by Pascoe, the Sisterhood was a Protestant-based organization, although not associated with a particular denomination; Van Cleve was a Presbyterian, Walker a Methodist, while Mendenhall and Talbert were Quakers. Van Cleve was married to Horatio Van Cleve, a military man who was promoted to general during the Civil War; Walker was the wife of Thomas B. Walker, a very wealthy and influential lumberman; Mendenhall was married to Richard J. Mendenhall, prominent banker and greenhouse owner; and Talbert's husband owned a drugstore. In an era when few women made it into the history books, Walker and Mendenhall rated individual biographies in Isaac Atwater's *History of Minneapolis*.[69] Van Cleve was a prolific writer who published a memoir of her early life, *Three Score Years and Ten: Life-Long Memories of Fort Snelling;* Walker would later be counted among the founders of Northwestern Hospital for Women and Children. During its first year, the Sisterhood of Bethany operated as an auxiliary to the Magdalene Society of St. Paul. At first, the Sisterhood's mission was "confined to visiting among the abandoned women of the city, talking, reading the Scriptures, and praying with them, and endeavoring to induce them to abandon their sinful lives." However, the Sisterhood soon split off from the Magdalene Society, undertaking a more ambitious program that offered direct aid to fallen women.[70]

The Sisterhood of Bethany's first clients were two Minneapolis madams. The *Minneapolis Tribune* reported, "Two women known as Em Reeve[s] and Georgie Graham, who entered a plea of guilty were each sentenced to six months imprisonment in the penitentiary at Stillwater. The women displayed considerable feeling when their sentence was pronounced. Georgie Graham recited a rather touching history in the court prior to being returned to the jail." Meanwhile, another madam, who was indicted at the same time, was granted a continuance of her case because she had superior legal representation.[71]

The Sisterhood, troubled by the court's sentence on the grounds of fairness and consistency, began their campaign with a public statement. In a letter to the editor signed by "Charity," but probably written by Van Cleve, they asked if the sentences truly fit the crime: "We find four or five keepers of houses of ill fame indicted, three actually arrested and brought before the court, while the remaining two are al-

A portrait of the directors of Bethany Home, 1880s. From left to right: Mrs. C. A. Overlook, Charlotte O. Van Cleve, Harriet Granger Walker, and Abby Grant Mendenhall. Van Cleve, Walker, and Mendenhall were charter members of the Sisterhood of Bethany. Photograph courtesy of the Minnesota Historical Society.

lowed to leave the city undisturbed, in the face of the alleged fact that there are not less than one hundred and fifty houses of this character remaining in the city at the present time."[72] Despite intervention by the Sisterhood, Reeves and Graham were sentenced to prison.

Whatever the other merits of her argument, Charity's assertion regarding the number of brothels in the city was not credible. If Minneapolis, with a population of 33,000, truly had 150 houses of prostitution, it would be the equivalent of one bordello for every 220 residents, or more than five times as many as New York City. Timothy Gilfoyle, citing police numbers, estimated the number of bordellos in New York at the end of the Civil War to be from 615 to 697, or less than one for every thousand persons. Perhaps the Sisterhood really believed the city was teeming with prostitutes, or, more likely, they were trying to grab the attention of the reader with a bit of hyperbole.[73]

Although the Sisterhood lost the battle to keep Graham and Reeves out of prison, they persisted in their campaign. One account described Graham as a formerly respectable widow who fell into poverty and turned to prostitution to support her two children. The article pleaded for clemency in Reeves's case because her elderly mother had come to Minneapolis and found her only child in jail, sentenced to six months at hard labor.

Van Cleve set about lobbying the sentencing judge, Austin H. Young, for the women's release. In turn, Judge Young persuaded Governor John S. Pillsbury to place Reeves and Graham into the custody of the Sisterhood. The governor pardoned the two women, who were less than halfway through their sentences, on June 1, 1876. The Sisterhood then confronted another set of problems.

Harriet Walker, vice president of the Sisterhood, recalled the dilemma of what to do with the two women. The Sisterhood could hardly release them, as they would return to prostitution. "Send them out to earn an honest living? Only a little more round-about way of doing the same thing—for who would employ them?" Van Cleve rented a small house, which in time became known as Bethany Home, and as Walker recalled, "hired an elderly Christian woman as matron and housekeeper, and bade these girls welcome to the best she could do for them. One accepted the invitation, and the other returned to her friends. Two other girls came voluntarily to the Home a few days after." The Sisterhood's agenda was simultaneously altruistic and self-serving: if they could point to concrete examples of "fallen" women they had transformed, then they might persuade a skeptical community that their organization was worthy of support and funding.[74]

The Sisterhood's first efforts at rescuing sex workers did not go smoothly. The *St. Paul Pioneer Press* offered its opinion in a headline: "How Some Good Women of Minneapolis Are Being Deceived—Reformatory Measures Which Have Failed Badly." The article described how the Sisterhood's efforts were being undermined by their charges, who were engaging in prostitution while living at Bethany Home. When confronted by the police, the women "coolly inform the officers that they cannot be justly arrested because 'they are under charge of Mrs. ——' [Charlotte Van Cleve], naming one of the most highly esteemed and charitable ladies in the city or state." The story continued, "in short, so bold yet hypocritical have been their acts, that the more honorable members of the guild have applied the name of 'Mrs. ——'s [Van Cleve's] bagnio to the quarters established upon a motive entitled to all honorable commendation." To be publicly named the equivalent of a madam must have been a stinging blow to the widely admired Van Cleve. To have this situation pointed out by a newspaper in the rival city only added to the humiliation.[75]

Van Cleve was quick to reply, arguing that a true friend would have privately informed the Sisterhood of these failings, not announced them in a newspaper. Over the years the Sisterhood would generally receive favorable notice in the press. But upon occasion some of their presumed friends would use public forums to discredit them, as a reminder to stay within the boundaries of acceptable female behavior. While the Sisterhood retained its respectable status, its leaders were gradually expanding the scope of what decent Minneapolis women might publicly comment upon. That the Sisterhood of Bethany acknowledged the existence of the sex trade in Minneapolis was an indication that they were willing to step beyond the safety of their individual situations and stand up for their beliefs.

Upon occasion, the Sisterhood even worked openly with the demi-monde. When Gracie Davis killed herself, madam Kate Campbell and the Sisterhood insisted that the inquest be conducted at the brothel so that Davis's body could be prepared for burial there. The coroner was told that if the "Bethany ladies" could enter the brothel without ruining their reputations, "doubtless his immaculate official robes need not fear of being smudged." The inmates supplied Davis's burial clothes, coffin, and funeral services while the Sisterhood provided a burial plot.[76]

Despite their initial difficulties, the Sisterhood persevered in their fund-raising and rescue efforts. Bethany Home quickly outgrew its first quarters, described as a brick house (razed) on Sixth Street Southeast and from there moved to a larger building (razed) near the present-day intersection of Cedar and Riverside Avenues.[77] In 1878 Bethany Home moved to Plymouth Avenue and Third Street North. The ever-larger quarters of Bethany Home were just one indication the Sisterhood had grown into an effective organization. The Sisterhood published regular annual reports with an accounting of funds received and how they were spent. At first, the founders envisioned Bethany Home would be supported by charitable donations and by taking in laundry and sewing. The home's inmates would learn to wash, iron, and sew, allowing them to acquire useful job skills while providing income for the home. This approach proved unworkable, however. The December 1877 monthly report listed thirteen inmates living in the home while the treasurer's report showed cash on hand and donations of $76.33, with earnings of fifty cents. Meanwhile, the Sisterhood had spent $90.86 for groceries, rent, medicine, and the matron's salary. The Sisterhood would have to find another source of income if the organization was to survive.[78]

Although Charlotte Van Cleve had condemned the city's scheme of monthly prostitution fines "as a mockery of sin and justice," the Sisterhood had become politically sophisticated enough to exploit the existing system for their own ends.[79] The Sisterhood petitioned the Minneapolis City Council to allocate a portion of the fines for the maintenance of Bethany Home. In response, the council held a special meeting to amend the city charter. One of the proposed changes would allow the prostitution fines to support "institutions for the care and reformation of fallen women."[80] At that time, any Minneapolis city charter amendment had to go through the state legislature; on March 7, 1878, legislators approved a bill allowing half of all prostitution fines to be directed to Bethany Home.

The following year, the city council voted to give two-thirds of the monthly prostitution fines to Bethany Home. In only a few years, the Sisterhood had gone from an obscure band of women who only had persuasion and prayer to offer sex workers to a well-organized group that could offer food, shelter, and counsel to women who were hoping to change their lives. The Sisterhood's success matched the model laid out by historian Peggy Pascoe: "Nineteenth-century Protestant women held neither final religious authority nor the political power of the vote, but by virtue of their identification with piety and purity, they enjoyed unprecedented influence."[81]

Once the Sisterhood began receiving a share of the prostitution fines, their financial woes lessened, but they paid a political price with a new conflict of interest. Their main source of income fluctuated with the amount of fines collected; if fines from prostitution decreased, then so would their income. The Sisterhood's expenses would not decrease, however, as they would still offer shelter to unwed mothers and other women who had transgressed sexual mores. While their goal was the elimination of prostitution, their funding relied on its continuation.

Some of their supporters deemed the Sisterhood hypocritical for accepting "blood money" from the very evil they were dedicated to eradicating. Judge Young, who had earlier helped the Sisterhood obtain pardons for Emma Reeves and Georgie Graham and who served on the Bethany Home advisory board, excoriated the Sisterhood for taking this money. Judge Young signaled his change of heart during a public rally at the Academy of Music in 1879. Speaking to a standing-room-only crowd of an estimated two thousand people, Young began his remarks by saying that he did not want to criticize anyone and hoped what he was about to say would be the best for all concerned. He then proceeded to savage the system of monthly fines for prostitution, saying that those "who wink at the violation of the law without sharing in its enforcement are guilty of its violation." True, the prostitution fines increased city revenue by about $350 per month, but the law called for a strict prohibition of the sex trade, not its regulation. If levying fines on prostitution is called "regulating" it, Young continued, warming to the subject, "You might as well try to regulate the devil to make a good Sunday school superintendent out of him." Young asked if the Sisterhood's conscience would allow them to accept this money; he, on the other hand, believed that "God would provide the means to support a charity such as the ladies were carrying on."[82]

Young did not apply these strict standards to the liquor business. He said he would prefer to eliminate liquor in the city, but this could not be done, because public opinion would not support its complete prohibition. One might ask why one vice, prostitution, had to be completely suppressed, while liquor could be licensed and tolerated.

Liquor licenses provided considerable income to the city, about $15,000 annually, according to Young. Liquor was also tolerated more than prostitution because the increasing numbers of German, Scandinavian, and Irish immigrants often held more tolerant views on liquor consumption than the earlier New Englander settlers in Minneapolis. Another rationale was that prostitution spread contamination in the form of sexually transmitted diseases and a breakdown of morals by exposing pure young men to a depraved class of women. Another speaker at this rally noted, "The Anglo-Saxon race in America is degenerating, and it is a rare thing to see a healthy girl or hearty boy. Pale cheeks and listless eyes take the place of blooming health and youthful beauty."[83]

A more complex explanation for this contradiction lay in the low status of women. Most saloon keepers were men, while most brothel keepers were women. An outright attack on liquor interests could backfire in terms of public opinion, and more specifically with voters, all of whom were men.[84] Condemning prostitutes, who had little political power and few open defenders, carried essentially no political risk. Prostitutes might be viewed as the "necessary evil" that protected decent women, but they were also seen as the instigators of lust. Worse yet, the female brothel keepers not only catered to men's desires but reaped huge profits from them as well.

Young felt free to attack both the commercial sex trade and the Sisterhood of Bethany because women were in charge of both entities. If the madams were openly violating the accepted norms for female behavior, the Sisterhood was doing so in a more subtle form. By speaking out on prostitution and unwed mothers, actively working to change the existing system, and garnering a measure of financial support for their enterprise, the Sisterhood was pushing beyond the confines of domesticity and into the wider world. They were also implicitly finding fault with male privilege. Judge Young's criticism was a warning to the Sisterhood to quit interfering with male politics and to return to their proper sphere. Praying for the reform of fallen women was acceptable, but using fines from city coffers for their redemption was not, because it meant that the Sisterhood had gained a measure of power.

The Sisterhood of Bethany made a spirited reply to Judge Young. In an interview with a reporter, Harriet Walker noted that the system of monthly fines was established in Minneapolis long before the Sisterhood was founded. She also pointed out that the Sisterhood had asked Judges Young and Charles E. Vanderburgh in the past if more laws were needed to end prostitution. At that time, both men replied that the laws were severe enough; what was needed was stricter enforcement. However, when the Sisterhood pressed other officials for stringent enforcement, they were turned away with the reply that greater enforcement would simply drive prostitution underground beyond police surveillance. At that point, the Sisterhood reluctantly concluded that the system of fines was flawed but that it did serve as a control upon the "social evil."[85]

The most direct and scathing reply to their critics came in the Sisterhood's annual report in which Walker articulated just how badly the judge had treated his former allies, noting that Young had been on the bench for many years and had never been bothered by the city's collecting fines, "until he saw a handful of women striving to turn some of the stream to the benefit of humanity and the class of society so wronged." Walker continued by stating that Young failed in his duty as an adviser when "he allowed us to adopt this policy without protest, and pursue it for months without note or comment, so that the first intimation of his disapproval came to us in the shape of a caustic and stinging reproof delivered in the face of a great multitude." By 1880 Judge Young was no longer listed on Bethany Home's advisory board.[86]

Critics may have tolerated these respectable women associating with the city's scarlet women, as long as they were dependent on erratic private donations. The Sisterhood went too far, however, once they became organized enough to secure public funds for their endeavors. Securing a regular income from public money suggested that the Sisterhood was no longer a group of women who were mainly devoted to domestic life; that they were spending only a small portion of their energies on charity work. Rather, it indicated that they were coalescing into a dynamic political group capable of swaying public opinion and running an independent rescue mission. If Judge Young and other critics viewed prostitutes and madams as threats to municipal order, they also saw the respectable women in the Sisterhood as another threat to the status quo. Young's criticism of the Sisterhood indicates a shift in his allegiances and signals his alignment with a rising group of reformers who, unlike the Sisterhood, sought to use the full force of the law to eradicate prostitution in Minneapolis.

TWO

The War on the Madams
Purity Crusades and Liquor Patrols

> Frank Gillette and John H. Knox are said to be "gay
> gamblers" and each aspires to win the smiles of one
> Nellie Connolly, who runs a bowling alley on Maine
> [Main] Street, East Side. They are not firm friends any
> more, Gillette and Knox are not, since yesterday at
> 1 a.m. when from jealousy, or some other cause, they
> "fought, and fought, and fit," in the aforesaid Nellie's
> rooms. Just how long the tussle lasted is not definitely
> known, but it was finally terminated by Gillette, who
> with a five-shooter in his clenched hand, gave Knox
> a couple of rattling knocks upon his knowledge box.
>
> —"EAST SIDE AMUSEMENTS,"
> ST. PAUL PIONEER PRESS, DECEMBER 24, 1872[1]

The brawl between Gillette and Knox may have been the first mention of Nettie Conley in the local press, but it would hardly be the last.
Men like Gillette and Knox would frequently abandon their reason, as
well as their cash, while in her company. Over her long career as a public woman, Conley openly operated brothels and neither purity crusades, fines, nor a prison sentence kept her down for long. Accounts
of men fighting over her favors only added to her reputation, as well
as providing her with free advertising. The raven-haired, gray-eyed
Conley would be featured in local newspapers for three decades; yet
today no one knows who she is.[2]

Nettie Conley, along with such madams as Jennie Jones, Edna
Hamilton, and Ida Dorsey, became increasingly prominent and powerful figures whose businesses drew the attention and the ire of

Minneapolis's authorities. As this chapter shows, their activities initiated a purity crusade aimed at suppressing the sex trade and imprisoning the madams. This crusade ultimately backfired, resulting in a number of unintended consequences and political complications. This war on the madams also led to the imposition of the Liquor Patrol Limits, which created a moral geography that would concentrate the sex districts and define a large section of the riverfront for decades to come.

CONLEY CREATES A PUBLIC PERSONA

Like the other prostitutes and madams, Conley worked under an alias. It is often assumed that women involved in the sex trade changed their names both to shield their activities from their family and to protect their relatives from any notoriety that might attach to them. Conley, however, maintained contact with her family throughout her career and did not hide her profession. A more likely reason for a madam to use an alias was to separate her private life from her professional existence. A madam created a public persona for herself, not unlike modern-day actors who change their names, appearances, and biographies to create an image for mass appeal. Through careful planning and study, the unknown Norma Jean Baker transformed herself into the persona of Marilyn Monroe. In a similar fashion, Naomi Angle made herself into Nettie Conley, well-known Minneapolis madam. She tried out a number of names before settling on Nettie Conley. In one exchange with a newspaper reporter, she was asked if Nettie Conley was her genuine identity, and "she blushingly acknowledged that her name was really Carrie Blume."[3] Conley's apparent embarrassment at revealing her "true name" was either an invention of the reporter, who wanted readers to believe she had shame for her situation, or more likely just one of many roles a successful madam might adopt according to circumstance. If men wanted to guess her "real name," Conley would genially go along with the game. The reporter might even have been a customer and Conley did not want to spoil his bit of fantasy of being in the know. By the close of 1873, she had used at least four different public identities: Nettie Conley, Nettie Angle, Carrie Blume, and Nettie Edmonds.

As a madam, Conley had to master the art of storytelling, coaching her workers on their stories, giving evasive answers to various authorities, and soothing customers who might have a complaint. Conley also had to create an overall story or "brand" that would set the tone for her establishment, reinforcing the story of the brothel with her choices of personnel and decor of the house. Conley was one of the few Minneapolis madams who managed to change her story as she segued from operating a rough saloon–brothel, where she started her career, to managing expensive parlor houses.

A few clues as to how far Conley traveled over her life can be found in the inventory of her estate. In addition to numerous pieces of furniture, such as many walnut and mahogany bedroom suites and oak sideboards, there is "one artificial knuckle [brass knuckles], one Billy [club], one slugger, one dagger and one .22 caliber pistol." Hardly the sort of items one would expect to find in the home of an elderly woman. This list also reflects Conley's transition to a wealthier clientele. Her considerable library included a set of law books, the works of George Eliot, and a nine-volume set of Alexandre Dumas. There was also a twenty-volume collection of *Courtiers and Favorites of Royalty,* which purported to be the secret memoirs of European royalty.[4] These were the kinds of books that suggest she was entertaining better-educated customers from the city's elite. The variety of Conley's jewels provides more testimony to her wealth and how she might have presented herself in a business setting. She could have decked herself out with four-carat diamond earrings, a four-and-a-half karat pin with three diamonds, or perhaps coral and pearl earrings, a diamond ring with nine stones, and another ring with eight diamonds.

CONLEY SETTLES IN MINNEAPOLIS

Conley did not leave a written account of her life, but in spite of her multiple identities there are a few verifiable facts about her. She was born December 16, 1849, as Naomi Angle in the town of Rose in upstate New York.[5] Conley's parents, Charles Henry and Harriet (Converse) Angle, owned a farm and had deep roots in the United States, dating back to the eighteenth century.[6]

In about 1865 Conley's family left New York, relocating to Sparta, Wisconsin, about 160 miles east of Minneapolis. In 1872 Conley made her appearance in the local press under a variation of her best-known professional name. While she did not yet own any real estate, she was the proprietor of the business.[7] By 1873 she appeared in the city directory in boldface type as "Miss Nellie Conley, saloon, Main Street near 1st Avenue, South E[astern]D[istrict] [present-day Central Avenue]." That same year Conley made her first appearance in the Hennepin County District Court, where she was charged with running a house of prostitution.[8] One month earlier Conley had been charged with the same crime in municipal court, along with George Ferrin, who apparently was her business partner at the time. Through counsel she argued that she had already been convicted of this crime and "suffered the punishment" in the form of a $25 fine. Although Conley fought the charge, she lost and was fined a total of $145.[9]

From the beginning local newspapers delighted in reporting the details of Conley's often-messy personal life. In 1873 she precipitously married Joe Edmonds after he testified on her behalf in district court (although his testimony did not save her from being found guilty). Within a few months of their marriage, Conley ordered Edmonds from their home, "and enforced her argument with chairs, old bottles, etc." Edmonds retaliated by getting drunk, returning to her saloon, and getting into a fight with another customer that landed both men in jail. A day later the newspaper noted, "Mrs. and Mr. Nettie Connelly have made up friends and peace reigns in their domicile." The marriage lasted about a year. Conley divorced Edmonds, stating that she had managed their household prudently, treated him with "kindness and forbearance," and conducted "herself with propriety." By contrast, Conley characterized Edmonds as a chronic drunkard who did not support her, endangered her safety, threatened to burn down their house, and "called her bad names." The court never heard Edmonds's side of the story because he had deserted Conley two months earlier. Conley evidently liked having a male partner in her life and business, but once a relationship soured, she retained control of the assets and the man moved on. Edmonds was apparently the only man Conley ever legally married during her career as a Minneapolis madam, although she would have several more boyfriends.[10]

In 1876 a St. Paul newspaper offered a description of Conley's first Main Street establishment and how she worked with the police. Her rowdy saloon–brothel catered to the army of lumberjacks that regularly flowed into the city after a winter of working in the forests to the north and was located in a designated red-light district where madams could freely operate brothels provided they observed the local rules.

The reporter related that a traveling salesman, who sold insurance policies during the day, spent his free time "observing the various sights at night." One evening he visited Conley's establishment, "and the disciple of insurance elaborately costumed in spotless apparel, white vest and immaculate plug [hat], entered and found himself in a mass meeting of well-browned, but not elegantly dressed 'boys just down from the woods.'" Whether the salesman was confused and had intended to visit a more refined establishment such as that of Mollie Ellsworth on the other side of the river or was just "slumming," he got more adventure than he expected. The reporter continued that although the insurance agent tried to be sociable, "the boys seemed to detect a weakness about the stranger, and displayed a peculiar aversion to silk hats. After a rather ominous silence, one of the timber colony sententiously remarked, 'any man that kin wear a plug hat kin afford to treat,'" and the man acquiesced. After the first round, the lumberjacks continued to drink at the expense of the increasingly anxious salesman.[11]

As the crowd grew more boisterous, the police were summoned but did not immediately intervene. Captain Hoy "viewed the performance for a time, and while enjoying its ludicrous features at last interfered," rescuing the traveler. The policemen concluded that the dandified man had no business in such a rough place and should have known better. A few days later, Conley made a rare retort to the newspaper, asserting that she did not run a brothel, merely a saloon; the insurance agent had not been abused; and her place was "about as orderly as any on the east side of the river." She conceded this was not a good business for a woman and offered to sell the place to anyone who wanted to buy it.[12] Since Conley had been paying fines for running a house of prostitution for at least three years, her denial of running a bordello rang hollow. Still, she was more than willing to tell a story that would garner publicity.

During the 1870s, Conley was the best-known madam on Main Street, but later there would be other candidates for the title. Before any of that happened, however, Minneapolis reformers would make a serious effort to eradicate all prostitution in the city. This campaign would have unforeseen consequences.

WAGING WAR ON THE MADAMS

Conley was one of several prominent madams targeted by a purity crusade. Ironically, the Minneapolis war against the madams had its start in St. Paul when the Reverend William McKibbin wrote a letter to a newspaper inquiring if St. Paul had legalized prostitution.[13] His letter claimed that the regular monthly fines levied against the madams violated the spirit, if not the letter, of the law prohibiting the sex trade. He soon gathered a group of citizens into an organization called the Society for the Suppression of Vice, and by 1879 the campaign led to the indictment of several St. Paul madams in district court.[14] Most likely, Minneapolis reformers were encouraged by the apparent success of the St. Paul campaign, as well as a desire not to be outdone by their civic rival.

Beginning with a large public rally in March 1879 and into the following year, Judge Austin Young and others attacked the system of "tolerated" prostitution. At another rally, the Reverend W. W. Satterlee declared that prostitution was absolutely prohibited by law, despite the system of monthly fines that constituted "a sort of license." Satterlee compared licensing, whether of the sex trade or liquor sellers, to "licensing" horse stealing.[15] Several newspapers printed accounts of how madams exploited their employees, attempting to create pity for ordinary prostitutes while demonizing the madams. One article noted that $4,400 was collected that year from prostitution fines "wrung from the keepers of five houses of ill-fame—for whom there is no sympathy—and the inmates—for whom there is much more sympathy, because the monthly fine means to the unfortunate girl so much more debauchery."[16] The reporter guessed that there were at least five brothels that contained from two to eight inmates. This estimate did not include "kept women," who the writer claimed far outnumbered the denizens of bordellos.

While the writer of the *Tribune* article was attacking the madams, the Sisterhood of Bethany offered a dismal portrait of the few brothel inmates who came to Bethany Home. These women "furnish striking illustrations not only of total depravity, but of the utter lack of personal responsibility which results from a continual life of vice." According to this account, sex workers developed a "peculiar mental condition, the result of years spent in a life where there is not the slightest attempt at self-control, [and] is manifest in their actions and their ignorance of all social habits." In this account, prostitutes supposedly had no regard for the property of others and knew "nothing of the value of money, while they have it, are improvident, and are entirely careless of social and sanitary laws."[17]

Taken at face value, the Sisterhood's depiction of prostitutes' abilities and lives was an ungracious attack on the very individuals they were supposed to be helping. If sex workers truly lacked the most basic skills and socialization, they could not perform their jobs, much less sustain businesses, accumulate wealth, and thrive in spite of police raids and reformers. In this portrayal, prostitutes were more akin to vulnerable adults in need of protection, not prosecution. However, this account was less about prostitutes and more a reflection of the Sisterhood's utter frustration with their own situation and their difficulties in attempting to change an entrenched system. Their former ally, Judge Young, had publicly betrayed them, their success at providing steady funding for Bethany Home was criticized as "accepting blood money," and turning prostitutes into domestic workers was proving much harder than members of the Sisterhood originally anticipated. Finally, the ongoing purity crusade was taking civic attention away from their efforts at reform and reeducation with the promise of eliminating vice forever in Minneapolis.

By February 1880 the Minneapolis reformers scored a victory when four of the city's best-known madams—Nettie Conley, Sallie Campbell, Kate Johnson, and Anna Carnahan—were indicted by a grand jury on charges of running houses of prostitution. Each pleaded not guilty, posted a five-hundred-dollar bond, and continued to run her business while awaiting trial.[18] Campbell had operated a bordello at 208 North First Street for at least two years. Johnson, also known as "Swede Kate," had been part of the Minneapolis sex trade since 1876, when she was mentioned as an inmate of a Washington Avenue brothel.[19] By 1878 Johnson was in charge of her own house at the corner of First Street and Seventh Avenue North, and the following year she moved into the increasingly important First Street South red-light district, operating a bordello at 116 First Avenue South.[20] Anna Carnahan, who was also known as Sarah Carnahan or sometimes Mrs. Dunn, was already well established on First Street South.[21]

A few weeks later the *Minneapolis Tribune* announced that Conley and Campbell were found guilty, noting that "the 'social evil' is receiving a most vigorous rebuff." A day later, Johnson was also convicted.[22] Judge Young, who was one of the leaders of the purity crusade, presided at the trials of all three women. Carnahan's case was postponed because of an unspecified illness. The three madams were sentenced to six months at hard labor at Stillwater state penitentiary, but their sentences were stayed while their lawyers filed appeals, arguing the madams were being punished twice for the same crime.[23]

The question of double jeopardy would go all the way to the state supreme court when two St. Paul madams, Annie Oleson and Pauline Bell, made the same argument, pointing out the conflict between Minnesota statutes and the municipal ordinances in a case known as *State v. Oleson*. During the appeal process, newspapers speculated on possible outcomes. If the high court sustained the district ruling allowing dual prosecution of the madams, then "a perfect reign of terror" could be visited upon the sex trade. "There may come a happy time in the history of both cities when lewd women will not be permitted to flaunt the banners of shame on the public streets day and night." The newspaper opined that if the purity crusade proved successful, there would be no need for Bethany Home in the future. Thus one court ruling might rid the city of two groups of troublesome women: the madams and the Sisterhood of Bethany.[24]

In October 1880 the state supreme court handed down its decision, siding with the lower court. The St. Paul madams changed their plea to guilty, paid fines of three hundred dollars, and returned to running their brothels.[25] By contrast, the three Minneapolis madams were packed off to prison. Several local newspapers reported the details of their departure. The sheriff took custody of the three, who "yielded gracefully, discharged their female boarders, finally shut up shop." The following morning the three women deposited "the wages of sin—their wealth—in six-month interest-bearing certificates of deposit." Then, they were put on a train and escorted to Stillwater prison.[26]

Meanwhile, back in Minneapolis, Police Chief Munger was quoted as saying that he did not think it was proper that three notorious women were serving a prison sentence while many more were still in business. He announced that all known brothels should be closed, and he did just that.[27]

The *Minneapolis Journal,* which had called for a "perfect reign of terror" to be visited on vice, abruptly changed its editorial position when reporting that the brothel closings had not eliminated the sex trade, but rather dispersed it all over the city. No longer was prostitution confined to known areas where customers could reliably locate it, while others could avoid it. The paper observed, "The evil exists today in a form more obnoxious and distasteful to good citizens than ever before. The vacant rooms in the upper stories of the business blocks are fast being occupied by the women—four of them this morning moved into a certain block within gunshot of police headquarters." The purity crusade had inadvertently made prostitution more flagrant than before. The paper complained that prostitutes now "ply their dreadful traffic on the public street instead of awaiting men at the public houses."[28]

By sending the three madams to prison, the authorities had broken an unwritten but well-established arrangement. As a result, the madams had no incentive to control any prostitutes who remained in the city, nor did the scattered prostitutes who had lived and worked in the brothels have any reason to play by the old rules either. They now felt free to practice their trade anywhere, without regard for secrecy or privacy. Clients in search of prostitutes might proposition any female, as the sex trade was no longer confined to specific areas.

It was in this atmosphere that Anna Carnahan's trial began. Whatever illness afflicted Carnahan, it had not prevented her from running her business while she was out on bail. In October she was fined thirty dollars for keeping a house of prostitution, and her nine boarders were fined ten dollars apiece for working there.[29] Carnahan's first trial ended with a hung jury, with a newspaper dryly noting, "The court was engaged upon the investigation of Anna's shortcomings all the forenoon and is still on it."[30] Judge Young, unfazed by the turn of events, subjected Carnahan to a second trial, and this time the jurors took less than two hours to return a verdict of not guilty. If the jurors did not think Carnahan was being unfairly persecuted, they may have concluded that sending madams to prison did nothing to stop prostitution and refused to convict.[31]

City officials were faced with the uncontrolled spread of prostitution and a storm of citizen complaints. To alleviate this crisis of their own making, the officials took an unusual action: they petitioned the governor to release the three madams. Mayor Alonzo Rand was the first to sign this petition. The names of the other signers included aldermen, judges, the clerk of court, the sheriff, the registrar of deeds, legislators, and the superintendent of the poor. The petition, dated December 14, 1880, read in part: "In view of the fact that a custom has grown up of imposing fines upon keepers of houses of ill-fame . . . with an implied understanding that such keepers should not be further molested. . . . [We] respectfully request your honor to grant a pardon to said Sallie Campbell, Nettie Connolly, and Kate Johnson." The petitioners were still gathering signatures in February 1881.[32]

AMENDING THE CITY CHARTER

In addition to petitioning for the madams' early release, Mayor Rand and other city officials tried to amend the city charter in a way that would remove prosecution of prostitution from the state and grant the city sole jurisdiction. The first bill proposed to modify the state law regarding prostitution, while the second was an amendment to the city charter that would regularize the system of monthly fines for prostitution. A special committee of the city council discussed the proposed amendments at just about the same time the petition to free the madams was circulated.[33] Introduced to the Minnesota senate on February 10, 1881, the legislation was described in a St. Paul newspaper as "a voluminous bill which amends the charter of Minneapolis," and went on to list mundane items such as extending the city boundaries and preserving the improvement fund for its original use. On January 28, a measure had been introduced in the House that proposed amending the state law in a similar manner.[34]

What the newspaper did not report was that a provision buried deep within the charter amendment would have barred further prosecution at the state level for the same offense, once a madam had paid her fine in municipal court. However, at least some members of the public were aware of this clause. W. W. Satterlee, in a speech to the

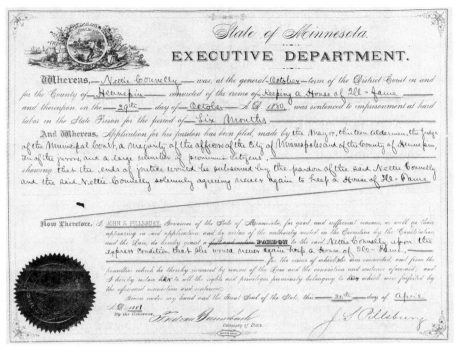

Nettie Conley's 1881 pardon signed by Governor
John S. Pillsbury and endorsed by "the mayor,
thirteen aldermen, the judge of Municipal Court, a
majority of the officers of the city of Minneapolis and
of the county of Hennepin, ten of the jurors, and a
large number of prominent citizens." Conley promised never to operate a house of prostitution again.
Courtesy of the Minnesota Historical Society.

Reform Club of Minneapolis, noted that the legislation would simply
reinstate the old system and asserted that city officials were complicit
in this arrangement. A writer identified only as T. A. N. countered
in a letter to the editor by saying Satterlee was mistaken; that in the
future, fines would be shared between the city hospital and Bethany
Home. Satterlee shot back that the effect of this legislation "will be
practically the old disgraceful farce of these criminals carrying into
court and laying the price of their shame, as fixed by the ordinance, at
the city's feet."[35]

The *Journal* offered an account of how the city was faring in the absence of the madams. The article commented that while Minneapolis was essentially a sober and moral city, unlike some other western towns, there were still pockets of corruption. The imprisonment of the three madams had not materially reduced vice in the city. At first, the writer seemed to provide an argument for returning to the old system of monthly fines: "The scarlet women have been driven from their recognized dens of infamy, they have scattered to various parts of the city, and it is an utter impossibility to intercept them in their crime." The writer was nostalgic for the previous system, under which the madams would arrive at municipal court "in a luxurious landau once a month, deposit the city's share of their sin-polluted earnings with the clerk of court, and return to their orgies and debaucheries." However, "deprived of the guidance of the chief harlots, the misguided and ruined girls scattered like foxes before the hounds." It did not take long for the prostitutes to find new hiding places "from which they emerged by night to parade the streets and lure to their lecherous arms, young men and boys, where they ruin their victims body and soul." The writer acknowledged prostitution was evil, but thought it was bound to exist in all large cities, suggesting that the proposed charter amendment was the best way to deal with the problem.[36] After all his statements about managing prostitution, the reporter wanted it both ways. Tucked in at the end of the article was his conclusion that the proposed legislation was a violation of both divine and civil law.[37]

The legislation passed both the house and senate with only a few modifications, but Governor Pillsbury vetoed it. Several newspapers ran stories similar to the article in the *Minneapolis Journal* that commended Pillsbury for his veto and chastised the legislature for passing the bill, concluding, "It is strange that law framed so palpably in the interest of immorality should get through the legislature."[38]

In April, two months after vetoing the charter amendment, Governor Pillsbury pardoned the three madams, freeing them nine days early. Without a doubt, the Republican governor was deeply conflicted by what the petition represented. Pillsbury had presided at the 1879 purity rally, siding with Judge Young on the need to eradicate prostitution. However, it was Mayor Rand and other fellow Republicans who had to face the day-to-day consequences of this policy.

Although the pardons stated that the three women promised to quit the prostitution business, even Governor Pillsbury understood that this was the last thing the petitioners wanted. They were counting on the three madams to return and impose order on the local sex industry.

The *St. Paul Pioneer Press* judged that Governor Pillsbury's pardon was correct and that no good had come from the prosecution of the madams. The writer concluded there were far more prostitutes now, and "the evil is more obnoxious and dangerous than then because it is scattered about the city, in apartments where they are to all intents and purposes practically beyond official control."[39]

In April Mayor Rand started his annual address by declaring, "One of the most embarrassing questions we have to deal with is the 'Social Evil.'" He enumerated the unintended results that had grown out of the failed campaign. In a rebuke to Judge Young and his supporters, Rand asserted, "Our city was exceptionally free from prostitutes. Those that were here were 'hived,' if you will permit the term, and kept under police surveillance. Our courts have broken up the evil in a concentrated form and most mischievously spread it over the city." Not only had the crusade missed its goals, it had also actively harmed other reform efforts. "The short-sighted actions of the reformers had changed the equilibrium" and "robbed Bethany Home of a means of sustenance."[40]

Mayor Rand's speech did not go unnoticed. One newspaper objected to his statement that the courts had spread prostitution over the city, and claimed the mayor was either misinformed or biased. The real problem, according to the writer, was that prostitution could not be ended with only one campaign; what was needed was a continuing policy of eradication.[41]

The failed war on the madams had both short- and long-term consequences. By mid-1881 the city reverted to the system of monthly fines, returning control of the sex trade to the madams, a tacit acknowledgment that the madams, acting in concert, could exert enormous power in the regulation of prostitution. Minneapolis citizens had been taught an object lesson that laws banning prostitution were unenforceable. As long as demand beckoned, the supply of prostitutes would rise to meet it. During the 1880s many, but not all, Minneapolis reformers would shift their energies from suppressing prostitution to eradicating, or at least limiting, the sale of liquor.

THE RISE OF THE ENTERTAINMENT DISTRICTS

While Minneapolis adjusted to the aftermath of the purity crusade, the madams understood that they had emerged as the victors. At least some of them also grasped that the city was undergoing a transformation that would change how the commercial sex industry was conducted; bordellos were increasingly clustered into established red-light districts, and adjacent to these sex districts, a wider variety of leisure-time activities, such as theaters, concert saloons, and gambling establishments, were becoming available.

As historian Isaac Atwater noted, when the city was first being built up, "its amusements were few and of the simplest kind." The founders were focused on exploiting its natural resources. "But with the rapid settlement of territory [came] a proportionate increase of wealth, and the means to gratify the natural human inclination for diversion and amusement."[42] Although Atwater was writing about theaters, his observations applied to other forms of entertainment, including prostitution.

For example, part of this increased "diversion and amusement" could be found on the west side of the river, where the First Street red-light district was surrounded by many saloons, as well as what the city directory called "theatres and places of amusement," such as the Grand Opera House at Nicollet and Sixth Street, the Pence Opera House at 226–228 Hennepin, or the People's Theater at 20 North Washington.[43]

Some places presented themselves as respectable, even though their exhibits emphasized the sensational. Sackett and Wiggins' Dime Museum at 214–216 Hennepin offered such attractions as a Chinese dwarf, "a curiosity hall," and a "monster museum," all of which "Ladies and Children Can Attend With Propriety."[44]

Theaters like the Academy of Music, which opened at 232–240 Hennepin in 1871, might present serious performers, some of international renown, such as Irish writer Oscar Wilde, who spoke there in 1882. But on occasion, its managers presented coarser fare such as risqué dance. In 1879, the "Hibernian Blondes and female burlesquers" of the Millie Eugene and Maud Santley Company appeared at the academy. Handbills for the show promised a demonstration of the "Parisian Nac-Nac [can-can] dance," according to a newspaper reporter. "However, the reviewer found four badly demoralized virgins,

As Minneapolis rapidly expanded, a range of high and low urban amusements became available. The Palace Museum, shown here in 1896 on the corner of Washington and present-day Marquette Avenues, was a vaudeville theater that exhibited various "illusions, mechanical wonders [and] curiosities." Another entertainment was the minstrel show at Theatre Comique (shown here in 1884), featuring white male performers in blackface and female performers in short skirts. Photograph of the Palace Museum by Arthur B. Rugg; photographs courtesy of the Minnesota Historical Society.

vergin' on fifty, [who] cracked out an occasional song and took such steps as their rheumatic anatomy would allow."[45]

The Theater Comique, a variety theater at 219–223 First Avenue South (present-day Marquette Avenue), was notorious almost from the day it opened in 1879. An 1881 account described one performer there, Miss Libbie Maretta, who drew "storms of applause" as "she bounded onto the stage in a costume which consisted principally of a fan and a pair of slippers." Moralists often claimed that innocent young girls were inveigled into a life of sin there, while scantily clad waitresses tempted men into buying excessive amounts of alcohol. One reporter noted that men as well as small boys were admitted to the theater, where they could "listen to suggestive vulgar talk." Beer was easily purchased there on Sundays, despite closing laws, and the box seats in the darkened Comique were veiled with lace curtains, which allowed the occupants a view of the brightly lit stage, but obscured any activities within. The reporter included a sketch of a half-dressed woman seated on the lap of her male companion in one of the box seats.[46]

Variety theaters, as one newspaper observed, were only a short step, both literally and figuratively, from brothels. One newspaper observed, "The doors of the latter [brothels] are opened after the lights of the former have vanished." In describing a variety theater, a reporter commented that neither the theater house nor the stage was notable, as patrons required only "plenty of beer and beauty." While the customers are generally "of the lower classes," there were some "to whom the best parlors of society are open." The theater's program was "marked by a refreshing lack of conventionality—and clothing." Meanwhile, all-night restaurants might cater to the respectable such as railroad workers, as well as "bands of revelers just drunk enough to be hungry and too drunk to eat."[47]

The entertainment districts offered gambling, although it was prohibited by law. As early as 1873 there were "gambling saloons," such as that of Daniel Brown on Second Street, between Nicollet and First Avenue South. By the 1880s there seemed to be several established gambling dens that catered to a broad range of customers. One place, located on the second floor of "Paul's Saloon" on Nicollet near Second Avenue, was furnished with Brussels carpets, marble-topped tables, and gas chandeliers. It offered roulette wheels, poker, and a faro table, "the most 'aristocratic' and intricate game common in gambling rooms." The "Gentlemen's Club Rooms" on the upper floors of the Merchant's Block (39–49 Washington Avenue South) was so exclusive its members were issued pass keys. The reporter could not gain entrance, but he believed its members to be professionals, businessmen, and men of leisure. At the other end of the spectrum was Flannigan and Sullivan's at 114 Washington South, "the pioneer gamblers of Minneapolis." In this place "there is no exclusion on account of age, sex, color, or previous condition of servitude"; all customers were welcome so long as they were willing to part with their money.[48]

Meanwhile, any number of drinking establishments could be found across the river on or near the Main Street red-light district. By 1885 buildings at 2, 9, 11, 13, and 17 Main Street Northeast housed saloons, and more bars were located on the other side of present-day East Hennepin at 9, 13, 25, and 401 Main Southeast. Frank Pracna ran a saloon at 117 Main Southeast, and when it burned down in 1889, he replaced it with the brick-and-stone building that stands there today. While the Main Street area lacked the concentration of nearby theaters found around the First Street red-light district, it did have some popular attractions. During the mid-1870s, Mannasseh Pettingill's resort at Chalybeate Springs offered Saturday evening band concerts, ice cream, a dance pavilion, and tours of Chute's Cave. For a dime visitors "can take a seat in a boat, with a flaming torch at the bow, and with a trusty pilot sail up Main Street a distance of 2,000 feet, between walls of pure white sandstone, and under a limestone arch which forms the roof."[49] In 1886 the mammoth Industrial Exposition Hall was built near Main Street to house fairs and exhibitions.[50]

THE LIQUOR PATROL LIMITS

Faced with a stinging defeat by the failed war on the madams and growing entertainment districts that often offered alcohol and other temptations, reformers had to find another way to control, if not eliminate, vice in the city. The solution seemed to be the Liquor Patrol Limits.

At the close of 1881, the Minneapolis elite staged their annual New England Society Dinner, putting on an elaborate party to reassure themselves that they remained in control of the city despite the failed purity crusade and the attempt to change the city charter. One newspaper account called it "the most brilliant society event in the city's history," noting that 250 people had gathered at the Nicollet Hotel to listen to the Danz Orchestra and admire the dining room decorated by artist Peter G. Clausen. The society's president, Dorilus Morrison, Governor Pillsbury, Mayor Rand, and University of Minnesota president William Folwell, among others, spoke after the meal. One speaker recalled the first society dinner in 1857, noting how prosperous its members had since become. He bragged that New England exerted its influence across the country: "Nearly all the great movements which mark the upward progress of American ideas and independence, had their inception in the New England states."[51]

But their assertions did not describe the changing social landscape. In 1880 Minneapolis became the flour milling capital of the world. Flour milling and the manufacture of lumber had generated, and would continue to generate, immense wealth, but these industries had attracted hordes of newcomers in search of fresh opportunities. Many of the recent arrivals were foreign-born, and in time the flood of immigrants would dilute the concentration of those with New England roots. By 1880 the city's foreign-born residents constituted 32 percent of the population. Ten years later that number was 36 percent. In fact, one writer observed that by 1890, only one-third of Minneapolis's population had native-born parents; the rest were either foreign-born or of foreign-born parents.[52]

Many of the newcomers had their own ideas about public morality. The struggle between these two views played out during the 1880s on the question of alcohol. The debate was as old as the city itself. Franklin Steele, the founder of St. Anthony, regularly dispensed liquor in his Fort Snelling store, and frequently served it at social or business gatherings.[53] By contrast, John W. North, whom Steele had recruited to the fledgling village, worked to ban alcohol entirely. By the 1880s both Steele and North had passed from the Minneapolis scene, but others had taken up similar positions in the city. The prohibitionists tended to be Republicans, Protestant, and have ties to the New England states, while the "wets" were more likely to be Democrats, Catholics, or recent immigrants.

The events that led to the establishment of the Liquor Patrol Limits illustrate the split in civic thinking. Having served two terms as mayor by 1882, Rand decided to return to private life. The Republicans, who hoped to place more restrictions on alcohol, nominated Charles M. Loring as their candidate, while the Democrats chose Albert A. "Doc" Ames as theirs. Meanwhile, a group of prohibitionists, who advocated a complete ban on liquor, put up William W. Satterlee, the Methodist minister who had earlier railed against the proposed city charter amendment regarding prostitution. The *Minneapolis Journal* supported Loring and worried that Satterlee would split the temperance vote, thus handing Ames an easy victory. One article warned that Loring was challenged by "radical temperance" supporters, who do not expect to win the election but nonetheless "boast of their ability to poll 1,500 votes," and on the other side by "the most compact and formidable organization that ever sought to gain control of the city for its own purposes."[54]

Years later journalist Lincoln Steffens described Ames's appeal to ordinary voters: "He was the 'good fellow'—a genial, generous reprobate. . . . 'Doc' Ames, tall, straight, and cheerful, attracted men, and they gave him votes for his smiles. He stood for license. There was nothing of the Puritan about him."[55]

Backed by liquor interests, Ames was able to purchase a regular column on the front page of the *Journal,* despite the paper's endorsement of Loring. The column enumerated Ames's qualifications, such as his "fine personal appearance," steady manner, and support among the working class. Satterlee was described as an "honorable competitor," but by contrast, the Republicans were characterized as hypocrites who "pander to everything which they profess to hold in utter abhorrence." The writer claimed, "Four years ago there were 137 saloons in the city," but "now there are 270."[56]

Ames won with more than 54 percent of the vote.[57] Part of the Democrats' victory could be attributed to powerful liquor interests and the three-way race. But the failed purity crusade, which had unwittingly spread prostitution across the city, probably played a role as well. A vote for Ames could be seen as a reaction to the mishandled Republican-led war on the madams.

During Ames's second term as mayor the struggle between the "wets" and the "drys" continued. Some temperance advocates came out in favor of higher liquor license fees, which would reduce the number of saloons while providing revenue for the city. Partisans of prohibition refused this approach, arguing, in much the same manner as the earlier purity crusade, that no compromise should ever be made with vice. Apparently, the prohibitionists preferred a complete loss to a modest gain. In 1883, temperance advocates proposed raising the annual fee for a liquor license. The *Journal* argued that if the supporters of higher fees had been willing to compromise, perhaps Mayor Ames would have gone along. But instead they insisted on imposing a $1,500 yearly fee, which Ames vetoed, and thus the cost of a liquor license remained "at the ridiculous sum of $100."[58]

Ames was not reelected in 1884. Instead, Republican George Pillsbury, another New Englander like his nephew, Governor John Pillsbury, became the mayor.[59] A few days later, the *Minneapolis Journal* reprinted Mayor Pillsbury's speech to the city council (which also saw Republican gains) in which he promised to support higher fees for liquor licenses as well as geographic restrictions on saloons. Outsiders, in the new mayor's view, were at least in part to blame for the city's troubles. Pillsbury explained that more restrictive liquor laws in other cities had led to the explosive growth of Minneapolis saloons. He noted that many saloon operators "come here, and before their character or qualifications are known, and before they have had time to acquire citizenship, open up a saloon wherever they wish." Pillsbury's linking of immigrants and saloons was a hint that the city was being changed and challenged by outsiders who did not necessarily share the New Englander's worldview.[60]

Within a month of taking office, Pillsbury and his allies on the city council raised the fees for liquor licenses from $100 to $500.[61] The boundaries of the Liquor Patrol Limits were soon established and included all the existing red-light areas. Saloons were limited to both sides of the central riverfront area, from Twenty-First Avenue North to Nineteenth Avenue South and several blocks back from the river on the west side of the Mississippi, plus a generous section of the Cedar–Riverside neighborhood, all of which encompassed a large, foreign-born population. On the east side of the river, the limits stretched from Sixth Avenue Southeast all the way up to Twenty-Ninth Avenue Northeast.[62] The large section of Northeast Minneapolis was home to a substantial immigrant population. The Republicans drew the boundaries to accommodate those immigrant groups, such as the Germans, who had a long tradition of integrating alcohol into everyday life.

The Liquor Patrol Limits remained in place for ninety years, reshaping the city's urban geography. Unlike the rest of the city, churches, schools, and residential blocks within the patrol limits could have bars as nearby neighbors. The limits were reinstated after Prohibition ended in 1933 and later expanded to include more of downtown. The idea that vice could be confined to a particular area did not die easily, even if people no longer understood the original arguments. By the mid-twentieth century, one newspaper explained that the limits were a quaint relic of the pioneer days, when the city fathers hoped to confine lumberjacks and their hobnailed boots to the riverfront, lest they inadvertently destroy all the wooden sidewalks. When the Eleventh Avenue sex district was formed in the 1890s, it too was contained within the patrol limits. While the patrol limits kept liquor away from

Edward Shelland's saloon at 116 Hennepin Avenue, 1905. One effect of the Liquor Patrol Limits was to concentrate the number of liquor establishments primarily along the Minneapolis riverfront, as evidenced by Shelland's neighbor, the Grand Saloon, which featured Golden Grain Belt Beers. Photograph courtesy of the Minnesota Historical Society.

most residential neighborhoods, they also helped to create entertainment districts by clustering sex workers, saloons, gambling dens, and theaters together.[63]

During the 1880s, reformers, who would have preferred to ban liquor entirely, settled for the imposition of the Liquor Patrol Limits. During the same period, the Sisterhood of Bethany changed its mission from trying to save fallen women of all types to concentrating on unwed mothers and their children. Bethany Home, as it turned out, was not equipped to reform prostitutes, but it did serve as a good, and sometimes the only, alternative for unmarried mothers. In one instance, the *Minneapolis Journal* noted, "The patrol wagon was summoned to Lyndale and Twentieth Avenue North this afternoon by the announcement that a Scandinavian servant girl who had been ejected from the residence where she was employed, was lying on the sidewalk and that she was about to become a mother. The girl, whose name was not learned, was removed to Bethany home."[64]

THE MADAMS RETURN

Once they were pardoned in 1881, Kate Johnson and Nettie Conley came back to Minneapolis and resumed their businesses, but apparently Sallie Campbell did not. Campbell does not appear in accounts of municipal court after 1880, nor is she listed in city directories. At age forty, Campbell may have been ready to retire from the sex trade. Kate Johnson moved back into her bordello on First Avenue South and seems to have remained in the business into the mid-1880s. One newspaper article from 1886 mentions that "the notorious dive of 'Swede Kate' on First Avenue South has been reopened." Another report suggested that Johnson had become successful enough to delegate the management of her brothel to another woman, when she, along with other leading madams, was indicted on charges of renting out houses for purposes of prostitution.[65]

After being in prison with other madams, Conley's business practices changed. While established madams like Kate Johnson profited from the city's prosperity during the 1880s, the truly ambitious and well capitalized ones like Nettie Conley rose to meet the changing market. Conley understood that her competitors were not only the local madams but also those from other cities who were attracted to the rising fortunes of Minneapolis. Once Conley returned to the city she began the transition from serving rough lumberjacks to wealthier clients.

To accomplish this Conley remade her operation, changed her professional story, and established another house on the west side of the river. In July 1882, she purchased a building at 205 First Street South (now occupied by a parking ramp) in the heart of the First Street red-light district, for four thousand dollars from Melville D. Hooker. The First Street South red-light district included High Street (now Robert Fisher Drive, which provides truck access at the rear of the main post office), and parts of First, Second and, Third Avenues South.

In all likelihood, Conley's First Street building already housed a brothel, given the change the area was undergoing.[66] Prostitution had been part of the neighborhood dating back to at least the early 1870s, when other madams operated High Street establishments.[67] By relocating her business to the First Street red-light district, Conley severed her connection to the rowdy Main Street saloon where she got her start and joined the group of more successful madams.

Once Conley had established a base on First Street, she turned her attention to remaking her Main Street business. In December 1882 Conley purchased the lot at 27 Main Street Southeast from brothers Richard and Samuel Chute.[68] The Chutes, natives of Ohio, had deep roots in New England. Richard had served as an officer of the St. Anthony Falls Water Power Company and Samuel as a director of the company. From there, the two had branched out into the real estate business. There was some attempt to keep the purchase secret—a newspaper reporter complained that the registrar of deeds had decided the information was "not for publication." Upon learning of this, the reporter proceeded to tell all.[69]

In the summer of 1883, Conley began construction of her own brothel, hiring contractors to erect and outfit her new place.[70] No original building permits exist for her Main Street bordello, making it difficult to determine its exact size or which architect designed it, although one newspaper listed its worth as ten thousand dollars.[71] The few surviving photographs provide only partial views. Still, there are a few documents such as mechanics liens and insurance maps that describe its appearance. It was a three-story masonry building with natural light on four levels and about six thousand square feet of interior space. It had the appearance of a substantial commercial building. An 1899 photograph of Main Street shows the three-bay facade of Conley's brothel and what appears to be a decorative band of white brick on the parapet and above the central bay of windows and the front door.[72] Conley's contract with Heffner Brothers specified that the furnace would maintain the building's heat at a constant sixty-five to seventy degrees even when the outside temperature was forty below zero. Every room, including the basement and hallways, had radiators. This expensive heating system allowed the brothel inmates to dispense with much of their clothing, even in the depths of a Minnesota winter.

Conley's business had literally and metaphorically risen from its former lowly position as a street-level saloon. Her new Main Street building required clients to ascend a flight of high stone stairs to reach the front entrance. A later newspaper reported that an inebriated William Ames fell about fifteen feet to his death onto the sidewalk below as he was heading into Conley's bordello. Unlike the ordinary lumberjacks who patronized her place in the 1870s, Ames was a successful lumber dealer with an office in the Lumber Exchange.[73] By 1885 eight inmates lived in Conley's new Main Street establishment, ranging in age from twenty to thirty-five.[74]

One of the remarkable aspects of Conley's new building was the lack of newspaper coverage it received. Normally editors were eager to note any building project as it reinforced the idea that Minneapolis was a thriving community, worthy of investment. In 1875, when Thomas Lowry and Clinton Morrison built their three-story commercial block that still stands at the corner of Washington and Second Avenues North, the *Tribune* frequently reported on the building's progress, starting with the excavation for its foundation, to watching the walls rise, and finally noting it was ready for the roof.[75]

Conley's brothel, like the Lowry–Morrison Block, was a midsize commercial building that presented an attractive facade to the public, but it was not considered newsworthy. The most obvious explanation is that Conley's survival and success were a continuing embarrassment to the respectable citizens of Minneapolis. More than a year after her new place was completed, a newspaper acknowledged Conley as "the wealthy proprietress of a pretentious resort overlooking the river."[76]

Once her Main Street operation had been transformed, Conley turned to her First Street venture. In 1884 she upgraded the property, taking out a six-thousand-dollar mortgage with John S. Bradstreet, William R. Tillinghast, and Dexter Thurber of the firm of Bradstreet and Thurber. Bradstreet and Thurber were not bankers but rather sellers of furniture and decorative accessories, suggesting that Conley gave the firm a mortgage on her First Street brothel in exchange for furnishings and interior design expertise.[77] The Bradstreet firm was a perfect choice to refurbish her First Street property. John Bradstreet was already on his way to becoming an enormously influential tastemaker, and he would later design interiors for the Chester Congdon mansion in Duluth, as well as the Charles Pillsbury and William H. Dunwoody residences in Minneapolis, among others. One scholar noted, "Bradstreet created some of the most memorable aesthetic interiors ever produced in the Moorish style, which was extraordinarily popular throughout the country in the 1880s." Conley repaid the Bradstreet loan within two years.[78]

If Conley hoped to draw wealthy customers, what better way to do so than to usher them into an elegantly furnished house that would look similar to their own homes, or perhaps even better? If the setting was slightly exotic or avant-garde by midwestern standards, it added to the feeling that Conley offered unique entertainment. Bradstreet could provide whatever dramatic effect Conley hoped to convey as he had well-established connections to the stage. A few years earlier he had taken part in amateur theatricals as a member of the Island Club, and he had also decorated the stage of the Academy of Music for a production of *Above the Clouds*.[79]

Conley chose another woman, Mattie St. Clair, as the madam of 205 First Street. Conley's ability to delegate responsibility and pick competent managers for her brothels was another indication of her business skills, and it allowed her to expand her business beyond Main Street.[80]

About the same time that Bradstreet held the mortgage on Conley's First Street brothel, he was decorating the newly formed and exclusive Minneapolis Club. A club historian noted, "These quarters were handsomely furnished, Mr. Bradstreet being responsible for their good taste, and here such men as Governor John S. Pillsbury, Messrs.

The showroom of the interior design firm Bradstreet and Thurber. Influential tastemaker John S. Bradstreet provided madam Nettie Conley with a six-thousand-dollar loan for her bordello on First Street, likely for furnishings and design expertise. No interior views of Minneapolis bordellos exist from this period, but this photograph from 1891 depicts the atmosphere that owners of higher-end bordellos sought to cultivate. Photograph courtesy of the Minnesota Historical Society.

Charles M. Loring, Eugene Wilson . . . A. [Alonzo] C. Rand and others, foremost in the life of the town, habitually forgathered."[81]

Although there is no direct evidence, Conley may have even used Bradstreet's expertise for her Main Street brothel, with an eye to her particular needs as well as the customers she hoped to attract. Bradstreet, as a direct descendant of William Bradford, who arrived on the *Mayflower* and was governor of the Plymouth Colony for many years, was well connected to the Minneapolis elite.[82] He could have provided Conley with an entrée to a new group of customers that he was already serving. Respectable firms like Bradstreet and Thurber would never openly advertise a notorious madam as their client, but that was hardly necessary, as her customers would certainly recognize Bradstreet's influence in the elegant furnishings.

During the early 1880s, Conley made other real estate purchases as well, buying rental property with no connection to prostitution in several residential neighborhoods.[83] Conley's investment in real estate diversified her holdings, suggesting she was thinking about a future beyond the sex trade.

About the same time that Conley purchased the Main Street property, another male companion came into her life. The Chutes sold the remaining portion of the lot, which adjoined Conley's Main Street building, to Henry U. Seelye, and a later mortgage on the property identifies Conley as Seelye's wife.[84] By 1885 Seelye was living with Conley at 27 Main Street.[85] Seelye apparently worked with horses in some capacity for most of his life. He received brief mention in a horseracing column: "Much interest is manifest in sporting circles as regards the trotting match to occur May 17th between trotters owned by Pat Sullivan and Henry Seely[e]. Both of the owners are confident of coming out ahead, and it will be a race for blood."[86] By 1893 he was the manager of the Minneapolis Turf Exchange.

Like Frank Gillette and John Knox, who had earlier fought over Conley's favors, Seelye was willing to indulge in public displays of violence. A short piece in the *Pioneer Press* slyly noted, "Henry Seelye and Henry McCrossen indulged in a pistol and knife performance [fight] at Theatre Comique on Thursday night, but no arrests have been reported."[87]

Whatever other attractions Seelye may have had, he possessed enough capital to buy real estate. In addition to buying the property adjoining Conley's on Main Street, Seelye also shows up as the co-owner on two of the residential properties Conley purchased late in 1882. In some transactions, Conley is identified as married to Seelye, while in other documents she is listed as unmarried. The two are characterized as married on several mortgages on their Main Street holdings, even though the properties were held individually. There is no record that the couple ever legally married or divorced in Hennepin County. When they did split up in the 1890s, Conley bought out his share of the Main Street property.[88]

Although it is impossible to determine just how much income Conley's business generated, the number of and dollar amount of mortgages on the Main Street property indicate that lenders thought either Conley or the property was a good risk. She paid off her loan to the Chutes in four years.[89] Starting in 1884 Conley and Seelye mortgaged their lots on Main Street several times, borrowing almost twenty thousand dollars.[90] These mortgages were paid off by the mid-1890s, just about the time Conley and Seelye parted company. From that point forward, the Main Street property was debt free, suggesting that Seelye had been an expensive habit for Conley.

MORE PROMINENT MADAMS SETTLE
ALONG THE RIVERFRONT

Just as the city's increasing wealth had caused Conley to transform her business, it also attracted a new set of sophisticated competitors to the riverfront sex industry. In 1883 St. Paul madam Mary J. France bought the property at 201 First Street, next door to Conley's place, for twelve thousand dollars from John W. and Johanna S. Anderson. Anderson was a building contractor and also served on the city council. France had operated one of the finest brothels in St. Paul from 1875 to 1883.[91] France may have left St. Paul as a result of Mayor Christopher O'Brien's short-lived crusade against tolerated prostitution, but more likely she decided the Mill City offered her more opportunities. The *Pioneer Press* noted France's move: "Madame France, unfavorably known in St. Paul, has purchased property on Second Street [Second Avenue]."[92] France's first Minneapolis bordello proved a success, and within a few years she expanded her operation across the street to 220–222 First Street South. While France apparently did not own this property, she was listed as the owner on the building permits.[93]

Some of the competition came from farther afield: madams Jennie Jones and Edna Hamilton relocated from Chicago, while Ida Dorsey may have come directly from her native Kentucky. All had prior experience in the sex trade and came to Minneapolis to work as madams. These three were hardly the only madams to arrive during the 1880s, but what distinguished them were their long and successful careers.

Jennie Jones, born Isabelle Black in 1852 in Ballymacall, county Tyrone, Ireland, was raised in an Anglican family of ten children. At age seventeen she married neighbor John Colvin, who was twelve years her senior. The couple departed for America shortly after their wedding.[94] By 1870 the Colvins were living in Wayne County, Indiana.[95] The couple separated around 1874, and at some point, Jones entered the prostitution business. She traveled around the United States, going from Indiana to St. Louis to Kansas to Missouri, finally ending up in Chicago in 1881. There she met Edna Hamilton while they were working in the same Wabash Avenue brothel. Typical of the other Minneapolis madams, Isabelle Black Colvin had a variety of aliases during her career. Louise Robbins, Jennie Padgett, Blonde Ella, and Ella Jones were some of the names she used. Her professional identity in Minneapolis was mainly as Jennie Jones, although Louise Robbins, an identity she assumed in Chicago, is the name that appears on her real estate documents and burial record.

Edna Hamilton was born Josephine Matilda Dale on March 10, 1861, in La Porte County, Indiana. She was the first child of Alfred G. Dale and Elizabeth A. Walt.[96] Elizabeth Walt Dale died at age forty in 1879, and that event apparently dispersed the family. By 1880 the widowed, thirty-five-year-old Alfred Dale was working as a laborer and boarding with a family in Michigan City, Indiana.[97] By that time, the teenaged Hamilton was no longer living with her father. She may have married or perhaps already entered the sex trade and was living under a new name.

Chicago would have offered Hamilton and Jones a chance to acquire many refinements and important contacts. It had a variety of brothels ranging from low dives to elegant mansions. By the time Hamilton and Jones arrived there, the city had survived a devastating fire in 1871 and was almost completely rebuilt. Like Minneapolis, Chicago was a collection center for lumber, grain, and meat processing, as well as having superb railways. But Chicago, older, bigger, and richer than Minneapolis, could support a much larger sex trade. One writer, Herbert Asbury, claimed that following the Great Chicago Fire, "prostitution became the biggest and most profitable business of the Chicago underworld." Furthermore, Chicago's demimonde had regular press coverage, which provided it with advertising. These accounts might chronicle that a certain brothel had attractive new inmates or that one prostitute was feuding with another.[98]

At some point, Jones and Hamilton relocated to Minneapolis. During the summer of 1883, Jones started to appear regularly in newspaper accounts of prostitutes who were charged with occupying houses of ill fame.[99] The following year, Jones took over the brothel previously owned by Della White at 228 South First Street.[100]

White had purchased the property from Amos C. Berry, a member of the Minneapolis police force, and his wife, Jennie, in August 1883 for $8,125.[101] White began construction of her bordello but ran out of money; the subsequent mechanic's liens indicate she owed for labor and such items as bricks, a mantle, hearth, and grate for a fireplace, two dozen window pulls, porcelain knobs, clover leaf moldings, a screen door, stained glass, and numbers painted on the transom.[102] When White lost the property in foreclosure, it reverted to Berry, who held the mortgage. A partial view of 228 First Street is captured in a photograph dating from the early twentieth century. Although long past its glory days, the brick building still retained a simple elegance and symmetry suggestive of the Italianate Revival style. Originally the front door opened directly to the sidewalk and was flanked by tall, shuttered windows. The door and the windows were topped with carved stone lintels, and a parapet with decorative brickwork rose above the low-pitched roof. This is the bordello that more than one newspaper characterized as a "gilded palace of sin."[103]

It is not clear how Jones became the successor to Della White. She may have worked for her and had the ready capital to take over White's operation and debts. Either Berry or the subsequent owner, Hiram Truesdale, gave Jones a lease on the property. Although the lease was never recorded, it is mentioned in the document that transferred ownership for the stated price of "one dollar" from the respectable Truesdale to someone named L. J. Gage. The deed, however, was "subject to a lease to Louise Robbins [Jennie Jones] until the 30th day of April 1886."[104] By 1885 Jones was living there with six other women, including Edna Hamilton.[105] Jones retained control of the property until at least 1893.[106]

In 1887 a newspaper provided a glimpse into Jones's bordello when Connie Burton, a twenty-one-year-old prostitute, died there. The newspaper observed that her death "marks the close of a life whose later years were spent in the sin which society cannot pardon in women."

Her fellow inmates supplied the casket and "a beautiful pillow of roses." Showing a fair amount of sympathy for prostitutes, the reporter compared Burton's situation with that of poorly paid but respectable workingwomen, who might end up in "potter's field" if they died among strangers. By contrast, Burton "had no claim upon her former companions other than those of sympathy."[107]

Jones chose to bury Burton in Jones's own plot at Lakewood Cemetery.[108] Lakewood, with its park-like setting overlooking Lake Calhoun, was then on the outskirts of Minneapolis. It was, and remains today, the final resting place for the city's elite, such as the Pillsburys and Washburns. By honoring Burton in death Jones demonstrated to her employees that she saw her as more than just a creature that existed for her enrichment. Perhaps it was a cynical act or it could have been that Jones was genuinely attached to Burton. Jones also made a long-term commitment to her former employee when she became the guardian of Burton's infant son, although this fact would not become known until many years later. Jones's plot received another occupant when six-week-old Albert Sharp, who died of cholera on September 16, 1887, was buried there. His place of death was listed as being between First Street South and the St. Louis and Milwaukee tracks, strongly suggesting that his mother lived in the First Street district.[109] Albert's relationship to Jones is unknown, but it would not be surprising if he were the offspring of another of her inmates.

By the mid-1880s the First Street district had segued into a red-light area that catered to an elite clientele with less toleration for disorderly public behavior. One newspaper account reported an incident involving First Street madam Jennie Wilson, one of her attractive blonde boarders, and a man who left a restaurant about midnight. The very drunk Wilson began talking so loudly as to disturb the neighbors, and the police promptly arrested the trio. The reporter remarked that the incident reminded the cops "of the old wide-open days."[110]

IDA DORSEY ARRIVES

First Street South was not the only location on the west side of the river where a successful madam could be found. Ida Dorsey managed to attract attention from the local press and patronage of the elite during the whole of her life in Minneapolis—unlike most other madams, Ida

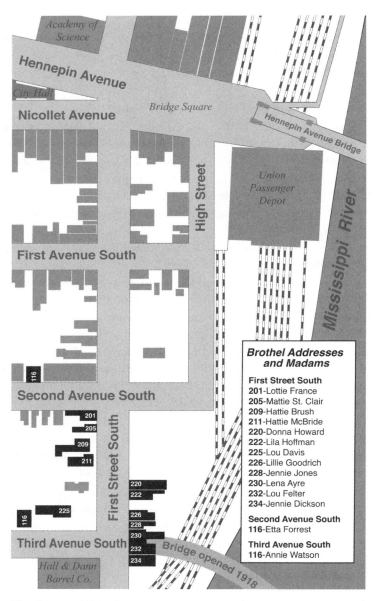

Academy of
Science

Hennepin Avenue

City Hall

Nicollet Avenue

Bridge Square

Hennepin Avenue Bridge

High Street

Union
Passenger
Depot

Mississippi River

First Avenue South

Second Avenue South

116

First Street South

**Brothel Addresses
and Madams**

First Street South
201-Lottie France
205-Mattie St. Clair
209-Hattie Brush
211-Hattie McBride
220-Donna Howard
222-Lila Hoffman
225-Lou Davis
226-Lillie Goodrich
228-Jennie Jones
230-Lena Ayre
232-Lou Felter
234-Jennie Dickson

Second Avenue South
116-Etta Forrest

Third Avenue South
116-Annie Watson

201
205
209
211

220
222

225

116

226
228
230
232
234

Third Avenue South

Bridge opened 1918

Hall & Dann
Barrel Co.

First Street red-light district, 1886. The sex trade on the west side of the
river started to coalesce around First Street in the mid-1870s. Madam
Anna Carnahan owned lots there by 1878. The present-day Third Avenue
Bridge did not yet exist, and the future bridgehead was occupied by a line
of bordellos that stretched across Third Avenue South. This district was in
close proximity to the Union Depot and Bridge Square.

Dorsey was African American. While Dorsey was not the first African American madam to operate in the city—Mary Evans did business on High Street in the 1870s—Dorsey was far and away the most prominent.[111] Over the span of three decades, Dorsey ran brothels in at least four locations along the riverfront. Her property at 212 Eleventh Avenue South is the lone surviving bordello from the era of tolerated prostitution in Minneapolis.

Ida Mary Dorsey was apparently born on March 7, 1866, in Woodford County, Kentucky. Her birth name was Ida Mary (or Marie) Callahand (or Callahan in some sources). Dorsey reverted to a version of this name toward the end of her life. Dorsey's mother was Marie Turner, an African American woman who was probably born into slavery. Her father was John Callahan, who probably was white.[112] Marie Turner was born in Woodford County in 1842 to William and Ann Turner.[113] Marie Turner had two children with Callahan, Ida and her sister, Roberta, who were consistently described as "mulattos," while their mother was described as "black."[114] The relationship apparently ended by the mid-1870s. Although her parents remained in Woodford County, Marie Turner left for a new life in neighboring Fayette County. Somewhere along the way, she met and married George Burkes, an African American (depending on the source, the name is spelled Burke, Burk, or Burkes). By 1880 the couple was living in the city of Lexington in the neighborhood known as Goodlowtown, characterized by writer John Kellogg as "the largest Negro residential area in Lexington."[115] Forty-nine-year-old George Burkes worked as a farmhand while his wife, Marie, was a homemaker. At this point, the Burkes had five children living with them: Ida, Roberta, Moses, George, and James. Neither of the parents could read or write, but the older children were literate, indicating that their parents had the means and inclination to provide them with an education. Greater employment and educational opportunities in Lexington may have been the factors that spurred the Burkes to relocate there.[116]

This is where Ida Dorsey would have received the primary schooling that would carry her to a better life. She was not the only upwardly mobile member of her family. By 1870, only five years after the close of the Civil War, their grandfather William Turner had gone from being property to owning property.[117]

What else the Burkes children learned in Lexington can only be

conjectured. The Kentucky legislature laid the foundations of a segregated society by retaining the language of the old slave codes in the
state laws, even though slavery was officially illegal. Public records such
as tax rolls and marriage records were kept separate by law, interracial
marriage was banned, and public accommodations were divided by
race. Violence from the Ku Klux Klan provided further intimidation
to black Kentuckians and underlined the "innate" inferiority of blacks
in the minds of many whites. In this atmosphere, it is not surprising that the out-migration of blacks, which had started in the waning
years of the Civil War, continued afterward.[118]

One lesson Ida Dorsey likely learned as a young girl in the South
was the peculiar and convoluted standard of sexual behavior to which
African American women were subject, one of the many legacies of
slavery. Most of this knowledge would have been gained by her everyday existence in a hierarchical and segregated society. Regardless
of what their inclinations might have been, Maria Turner and John
Callahan were forbidden by law to regularize their relationship and
marry. The fact that Callahan is listed as Dorsey's father on her death
certificate is an open acknowledgment of this strange system.

In a much later newspaper account, Dorsey claimed to have operated a bordello since she was sixteen years old, although she did not
specify where this career began.[119] Somewhere in her journey from
Kentucky to Minnesota, Ida Burkes became Ida M. Dorsey, but this
may have been only one of her names. She was certainly known as
Dorsey by 1885, when she was living in St. Paul with a young African
American man named John Hershfield.[120] By 1886 Dorsey was operating a brothel at Fifth and Jackson Streets described as "a very tough
place" that catered to "colored soldiers."[121]

Dorsey soon relocated to Minneapolis, likely attracted by its growing wealth and the possibility that there she would draw a notably different clientele. Dorsey seems to have made her debut in the Minneapolis press during the summer of 1886, when the *Minneapolis Journal* ran
a series of articles investigating various forms of prostitution, which
included a detailed description of her first brothel in the present-day
Warehouse District. "A shabby weather-beaten frame house stands at
125 Second Street north. The visitor is met at the door by a smart looking mulatto [probably Dorsey herself]. Once the threshold is passed,
the shabbiness of the house disappears. The hall is handsomely car-

peted and its wall covered with costly paper. Mirrors, soft portieres [curtains hung across a doorway] and plush upholstered furniture give an air of richness to the rooms." Dorsey offered more than just a lush setting for her operation. She was selling her clients interracial sex and other forbidden delights. The reporter continued, "Seven or eight negro girls, ranging in color from coal black to a blonde whiteness, in gaudy dresses which reveal as much as they conceal, entertain the guests with the can-can, the 'shadow dance' and other foul orgies that only an abandoned negress can descend to."[122]

Can-can dancing had been banned in Minneapolis after the chief of police deemed it indecent, but customers could find it at Dorsey's bordello.[123] The reporter did not explain what a "shadow dance" was, but one dictionary defines it as "a dance shown by throwing the shadows of dancers on a screen." If this is what Dorsey was offering, the performers behind the screen could have mimed all manner of risqué poses and actions. The "other foul orgies" doubtless referred to some variety of striptease and live sex shows. Scholar Timothy Gilfoyle recounted a show in New York witnessed by reformer Anthony Comstock in 1878 in which three inmates removed their clothing and then proceeded to engage in oral sex with one another.[124] "Violet," one of the survivors of the Storyville district in New Orleans, described her regular participation in these shows, which she called "circuses."[125]

After describing Dorsey's bordello, her employees, and services, the reporter finally got to the heart of why her operation was both so objectionable and attractive to the citizens of Minneapolis:

> There is something so weird, so wild and abandoned in the revels of these dusky beauties that the fast men of the city and others who are becoming so, are drawn in large numbers to the place. Married men with sweet, pure wives at home, and pale young men whose dissipations are breaking, perhaps an old mother's heart, come here to gratify an unnatural craving for new and darker forms of vice. Business men of high social standing have been known to visit the place, securely lock the house against intrusion and give themselves up to a night of revelry.[126]

Dorsey introduced a particularly irresistible and dangerous form of abandonment to the sex trade that brought out the worst in those who were supposed to be the city's best citizens. She was not selling a few moments of pleasure to migrant lumberjacks but rather targeting the city's elite, who would return again and again over the years.

If the newspapers used prevailing racial stereotypes to characterize Dorsey and her inmates, then Dorsey masterfully turned those images to her advantage. She was in competition with the other madams for rich white men, and she was winning this contest, despite her skin color. Or viewed from another angle, her success was based in part on her race. Bordellos were strictly segregated by race, as illustrated by one of the charges laid against Mrs. Hertogs, who was accused of placing an African American prostitute, who formerly worked for Dorsey, in a white bordello. Hertogs told the madam that the woman was "Spanish" and a dancer "who would sell a great deal of beer."[127] Other madams such as Nettie Conley or Jennie Jones could only offer their clients white sex workers. By contrast, Dorsey offered a range of very dark or very light-skinned prostitutes, appealing to whatever racial stereotype might tempt the customer. Each of Dorsey's inmates, even those who appeared to be white, would be "an abandoned negress" capable of "foul orgies," and this was a fantasy for which Dorsey's clients paid handsomely.

At one point Dorsey apparently attracted the ire of the local African American community, which circulated a petition calling for the closure of her brothel. One newspaper asserted that "the moral and churchgoing element of the colored people of the city have always considered it a shame that Ida Dorsey should be permitted to run a colored bagnio in this city."[128] But there was another distinct constituency in this campaign, specifically African American men who objected to Dorsey's whites-only policy.[129] One of these men, Jack Morris, described as a professional gambler, menaced Dorsey's life. When arraigned in municipal court, Morris admitted that he threatened Dorsey "because colored girls were kept there for the use of white men exclusively."[130]

Dorsey also attracted the attention of Judge Young. While most Minneapolis reformers had backed away from outright attacks on the commercial sex industry, Young apparently retained the same views he held before sending the three madams to prison. Starting in mid-1886, Young again got a grand jury to issue indictments against the leading madams of the city and continued his campaign against prostitution into the following year. Among the first to be indicted was Ida Dorsey.

Her appearance in court was described in several newspapers: "Ida Dorsey the proprietress of the 'coon' dive on Second Street North," was described as a "pleasant looking mulatto" and charged with running a house of prostitution and selling liquor without a license. She was indicted as "Mary Coon."[131]

Judge Young presided at Dorsey's trial, and when the jury found her guilty, Young said that he neither wished her harm nor wanted her money, as "it would be an outrage to take it." The judge expressed the hope that "she would become a useful woman to her people," and then sentenced her to ninety days in the state penitentiary. Dorsey was evidently not expecting this result, as she started weeping, "rocking to and fro in her grief," sobbing "until it seemed as though her slim body could no longer stand," and according to another witness, "swooned dead away and did not recover for over an hour," after which she was taken to prison.[132]

Dorsey believed she had secured the permission of the relevant city authorities to operate her business and was blindsided by the verdict and harsh sentence. She began serving the term immediately and was released after seventy-six days, having been given time off for good behavior. Stillwater records describe her as twenty-two years old, five foot four inches tall, married, a nondrinker, but someone who "used tobacco."[133]

JUDGE YOUNG'S CONTINUING WAR ON THE MADAMS

During 1886 Judge Young managed to convict several other madams of various prostitution charges, but these white madams merely paid large fines, whereas African American Dorsey went to prison. The alcohol charge against Dorsey seemed dubious, as a St. Paul newspaper noted that "the grand jury, which assumes to be an ultra reformatory institution, more than anything else, . . . indicted Ida Dorsett [Dorsey] for selling liquor without a license," even though she had contributed for a liquor license.[134] The newspaper's characterization of the grand jury, coupled with Judge Young's remarks, hints that Dorsey was the casualty of an ongoing purity crusade waged by the judge; it was also a slap at the current mayor.

A few months before Dorsey was indicted, "Doc" Ames had been elected to his third term as mayor. Just before the April election, the

Journal reported that many believed Republican George Pillsbury would be reelected.[135] The voters again rejected the reformers, however. Once the ballots were counted, even the Democrats were surprised by the size of their victory. The city as whole and some reliable Republican districts had chosen Ames, giving him approximately 59 percent of the total votes cast. Democrats also saw gains on the city council.[136]

In a move that took a swipe at the largely Republican reformers and the Sisterhood of Bethany, Ames began his own system of issuing liquor licenses to brothel keepers. The *St. Paul Daily Globe* noted that Ames had imposed "a new order of things" for brothel keepers. Instead of the city charging the madams what Ames termed "blackmail of $52.50 per month," which was divided between the city coffers and Bethany Home, he instituted another plan. Ames explained to a *Globe* reporter that he had no idea if sex was purchased at "these houses," but was very certain that alcohol was. To combat the illegal liquor trade, Ames planned to charge each madam $50 a month until she had paid $500 into the city treasury and a liquor license would be issued to her. He predicted, "There will be a great howl when this becomes known for the reason that it will cut off the revenue of Bethany Home."[137]

It is not surprising that Ames cut off Bethany Home because most of the Sisterhood and its supporters were Republicans, toward whom Ames harbored an old grudge. Ames had been a Republican when he was elected to the city council in 1875. In 1876, he fought hard to be the Republican nominee for mayor, but his party instead chose George Brackett. At the same time, the party endorsed Charlotte Van Cleve, president of the Sisterhood of Bethany, as one of their nominees for the school board. Instead of quietly dropping out of the race, Ames angrily claimed the nomination had been stolen from him and announced that he would run for mayor as a Democrat. The *Minneapolis Tribune* endorsed Brackett and noted that Ames had campaigned for the Republican nomination by traveling from saloon to saloon, buying drinks for potential supporters. Still, Ames triumphed over Brackett and was sworn in to his first term as mayor.[138]

In 1886 Ames, now in his third term, exacted revenge against the Republicans. He denied funds to Bethany Home and redirected the fines into his own pocket, as his handpicked chief of police, not the municipal court, collected money for these special liquor licenses.[139]

A reporter later noted, "During the third term there arose such odors of corruption in the city government that no one could well doubt the guilt of the mayor."[140] For a time Ames did succeed in diverting city funds from Bethany Home. The annual reports for the years 1887 and 1888 allude to the terrible financial strains that Bethany Home suffered. After the end of Ames's third term, when Republican E. C. Babb replaced him, a newspaper editorial assessed Ames's treatment of Bethany Home and the city's treasury, observing, "it would be a feat worthy of the ex-mayor's untiring devotion to the public's interests" to demonstrate how either the public or Bethany Home had benefited "by his illegal and abandoned scheme of issuing saloon licenses to the keepers of houses of ill fame."[141]

Meanwhile Ida Dorsey returned to operating a brothel, this time at 119 Second Street North, which she leased from Carrie Moore. Moore had run a bordello there, but the police shut it down in June 1886.[142] By December 1886, Dorsey again was charged with keeping a house of ill fame in a wave of grand jury indictments against many of the established madams, including Lou Felter, Mattie St. Clair, Hattie Brush, Kittie Williams, Jennie Jones, and Nettie Conley. Judge Young particularly admonished the first four women for having "stood with the [Ames] administration." Carrie Moore was indicted on charges of renting her house to Dorsey, who in turn used it for prostitution.[143] Judge Young, in presiding over the court where the madams entered their pleas, issued public statements on prostitution, saying the laws were not made to regulate brothels but to eradicate them, and adding that "to acknowledge anything else is to acknowledge that crime is stronger than law."[144]

The madams used their court appearances as an opportunity for free publicity and to display their finery. One newspaper observed there was a large audience in the courtroom, ranging from businessmen to rough characters. "The women attracted considerable attention, but seemed entirely unaffected by the glances cast at them. They were all dressed in the height of fashion," and most of them "treated the whole matter as a big joke, to be smiled at and dismissed."[145] In this round of indictments the madams were found guilty and paid large fines ranging from $200 to $350, but none drew prison sentences. Mayor Ames might divert money for his special liquor licenses from the city, but

Judge Young could impose large fines on the madams that were paid directly into the district court coffers, beyond the reach of Ames.

Judge Young never wavered in his belief that the city was a sink-hole of lawlessness, estimating that "25 percent of all crime" committed in the United States occurred in Minneapolis, even though the city constituted less than 1 percent of the nation's population. He singled out bordellos as "breeders of crime" that served as meeting places for outlaws, "yet there is no crime in respect to which society and municipal governments are so tolerant." After eighteen years on the bench, Young left for private practice in 1891.[146]

By 1887 Dorsey moved her operation to the established First Street district, settling in a bordello where madam Etta Forrest had operated since at least 1885, and just across the street from Mary France and Nettie Conley's establishments.[147] By the late 1880s she was frequently in the news, either because her brothel was raided, or because she was again found guilty of prostitution and paid a $350 fine to the district court, or because a man decided to smash in her door, or because her younger sister, Roberta Burkes, sometimes called "Birdie Berts," had joined the business. One newspaper reported that "the colored women from Ida Dorsey's bagnio, at 116 Second Avenue south were before Judge Mahoney yesterday to answer to the charge of occupying apartments in a house of ill-fame, the two Dorsey women being charged with keeping such a house." Another account noted, "Birdie Berts, the dusky representative," paid the monthly fee of $80.[148]

By the end of the decade, neither prison sentences nor hefty fines had decreased the number of public women in Minneapolis. The imposition of Liquor Patrol Limits had confined saloons to designated areas, but at the same time entertainment districts that offered everything from theaters to bordellos had coalesced in and around the patrol limits, making vice all the more visible. During the 1890s, the public women of the city would become even richer and bolder as they built grander "palaces of sin" and established a completely new red-light district with the acquiescence of the municipal authorities.

THREE

Red Lights along the Riverfront
The Madams Make Their Move

The Sixth Ward people will not submit to having the
"scarlet sisterhood" located in their midst. . . . They
do not want their property values depreciated; they do
not want their best business streets encroached upon
by houses of ill-fame; . . . they do not want their wives
and daughters compelled to elbow on the street and the
stores, the devotees to a life of shame.

—"VERY LARGE RED 'NO,'"
ST. PAUL GLOBE, FEBRUARY 10, 1891

The 1880s had been a time of opportunity for Minneapolis madams; as the city grew in wealth and population, so did they. During this decade, a rough balance was reached between the forces of reform and those representing vice. Neither liquor nor prostitution could be eradicated, but both could be contained within designated geographic areas. Periodically, especially large fines would be levied against some madams, and occasionally one would be sent to prison. Still, from 1881 to 1890, only two Minneapolis madams served any time at Stillwater penitentiary.[1] The arrangement allowed reformers the appearance of being in control, while the madams were free to conduct business and accumulate ever-larger bankrolls. It was only a matter of time before the successful madams would seek to advertise their wealth and expand into larger, more elegant bordellos that suited their particular needs and tastes, as Nettie Conley had done earlier. To accomplish this the madams would have to become real estate owners.

THE FIRST STREET RED-LIGHT DISTRICT DECLINES

Even before an 1891 newspaper predicted the end of the First Street red-light district, some of its most prosperous madams were making plans to move away. A reporter stated with conviction that "the notorious houses of ill fame on First Street and vicinity" would be removed. An unnamed "committee," hoping to close down the district, persuaded the Northern Pacific Railway to refuse any more rents from their tenants on the eastern side (river side) of First Street South and stated that "the priestesses of vice" would soon be gone. As for the other side of the street, the writer opined that if the property owners did not evict "the objectionable tenants," they would be driven to do so by unfavorable publicity. Just how property owners like Nettie Conley or Mary France would be embarrassed by public exposure was not explained, but the reporter forecast that soon many of the current First Street residents would be relocated across the river.[2] A year later Main Street did have more bordellos, but while First Street lost much of its luster, brothel-based prostitution continued there well into the twentieth century.[3]

Madams with higher aspirations and more capital recognized that First Street was becoming a less desirable place to conduct their business. The area was turning into a magnet for lumberjacks, agricultural workers, and other transient laborers who gathered to rest between jobs or scour the employment agencies to find their next assignment. The 1890 city directory lists twelve employment agencies, all in the Bridge Square area. By 1892 the first "cage hotels" made their appearance in the neighborhood. As the name suggests, a cage hotel offered small cubicles with locking doors and chicken wire over the top that allowed for air circulation, but kept other guests from climbing from one cage to another, providing a modicum of security for a low price.[4] These were hardly the sort of men who could afford to patronize the parlor brothels run by Nettie Conley or Jennie Jones. Bridge Square was remembered by a Minneapolis policeman who patrolled the area during the 1890s as "a hot old place," with crowds on the street until 4:00 a.m. "A policeman on the Bridge Square beat didn't think he was working unless he broke up a half dozen fights a night." For their part the lumberjacks "didn't seem to feel right when they were full of liquor unless they used their fists."[5]

As the city grew away from the riverfront the central business district shifted away from Bridge Square, and important businesses ranging from shops and banks to high-end bordellos moved to other locations. In 1879 nine of the ten banks in the city were located on or near Bridge Square. By 1900, however, Minneapolis had thirteen banks, but only two were left in the Bridge Square area. In 1879 the Bridge Square area had six book and stationery stores, as well as the Minneapolis Athenaeum, precursor to the Minneapolis Public Library. By 1905 there were only two bookstores there, and the Athenaeum had moved into the new public library building at Tenth Street South and Hennepin Avenue in 1890.[6] Cheap lodging houses and employment agencies replaced the banks and bookstores, serving a transient population that increasingly dominated the neighborhood. By 1900 there were at least sixteen employment agencies in the Bridge Square area, whereas twenty years earlier none of the city's five employment offices were in that location.[7]

The exodus of the leading madams from the First Street area opened opportunities for other madams. Very soon, the bordellos formerly operated by Jennie Jones and Ida Dorsey were under new management. Successful madams such as Mary France and Nettie Conley never entirely deserted the First Street district, however. Perhaps they had a sentimental attachment to the location, but it is likely there were practical considerations as well. By 1890 France was over fifty years old and probably ready to retire. She had been gradually turning the business over to her daughter Charlotte (Lottie) France, and by 1887 Lottie was in charge of her mother's First Street bordello.[8]

For whatever reason, Nettie Conley retained ownership of her First Street real estate until nearly the end of her life. Both France and Conley continued to spend money on their First Street properties, even as the neighborhood declined. Between 1892 and 1908, France spent over $1,200 on her house at 201 First Street South, and Conley more than $1,000 on her building at 205 First Street South. By contrast, the house at 107 First Street South received only $622 worth of improvements between 1896 and 1907.[9] Occasionally, old buildings were recycled rather than replaced by more expensive new structures. In 1906, a bordello formerly owned by Sarah Carnahan, dating from the late 1870s, was moved from 221 First Street South to 107 First Street South, as an addition to an existing wood-frame brothel.[10] The formerly desirable First Street district was no longer worth serious investment and received just the minimal maintenance that kept it tottering along its slow decline.

By the first part of the twentieth century, the First Street red-light district was whittled away by neglect and respectable redevelopment. A photograph taken sometime between 1906 and 1913, together with contemporary insurance maps, illustrates the decline of the area. The solid line of bordellos that formerly stretched across the bridgehead of the present-day Third Avenue Bridge was gone by 1906. Instead of a three-story bordello between 228 and 220 First Street South, there is only a vacant lot. An older bordello at 218 First Street South is two stories high and exhibits some aspirations to style with a false front, shuttered windows, and decorative cornice. By contrast, the new bordello at 210–212 First Street South is a plain, squat, concrete-block building. Meanwhile, across the street, a hardware warehouse owned by Janney, Semple, and Hill has supplanted the two bordellos formerly owned by Sarah Carnahan.

By 1915 First Street madams were treated almost as figures of fun compared to those who had earlier been demonized as "priestesses of vice." When May Schultz was caught in a raid and charged with operating a house of prostitution at 207 First Street South, one newspaper reporter described her as "an old time hooker" who was just "trying to make an honest dollar or two" servicing lumberjacks.[11] That same year, the row of brothels stretching from 201 to 211 First Street South was razed and replaced by a massive addition to the Janney, Semple, and Hill warehouse. Meanwhile, across First Street, the remaining six bordellos were slated for demolition.[12] The rest of the First Street sex district would be completely obliterated by the 1930s, but its reputation as a symptom of urban decay would linger on into the mid-twentieth century. Its gritty history would spur the city fathers to work even harder to remake the Bridge Square/Gateway area landscape.

JENNIE JONES BUILDS A PLACE OF HER OWN

Although it was not immediately evident, Jennie Jones was the first to plan her move away from the First Street district. Jones's pursuit of bordello ownership reflected her audacious, yet careful, business practices. On August 20, 1890, Henry T. Welles, a wealthy man and the first mayor of St. Anthony, leased two Main Street lots to Hugh Butler, a hotel clerk. The lease stated the annual rent was one hundred dollars, but the renter would pay all property taxes and assessments.[13] Six months later, Butler's lease was assigned to lawyer Frederick Cook. On the same day, Cook reassigned the lease to Louise Robbins, more commonly known as Jennie Jones. Further clouding the arrangement, the lease was not recorded at the county for another five years. Butler had served as a "straw man" on the lease, putting some distance between the respectable Welles and the tainted Jones.[14]

In April 1891 Jones started construction of her bordello at 25 Main Street Northeast, which one newspaper described as "the costliest and most notorious resort of its kind in the northwest."[15] By building at a location outside of an established red-light area, Jones extended the boundaries of the Main Street district across present-day East Hennepin Avenue. Thus Jones's new brothel represented one boundary of the Main Street sex district, while Nettie Conley's place at 27 Main Street Southeast was the other. Using the name "L. Robbins," Jones took out a permit to build a brick "clubhouse" trimmed with brown sandstone. The three-story building enclosed more than 8,500 square feet and cost in excess of $16,000 to construct.[16] The term "clubhouse," instead of "hotel" or "boardinghouse," as other bordellos were described on building permits, conveyed exclusivity, suggesting membership and steep dues. All these clues pointed to a private retreat where a client's wildest fantasies could be safely indulged.

Jones chose architect Harry G. Carter to design her new place. He was experienced in this type of building, having designed at least one other bordello, that of Sadie Terhune at 228 Eagle Street in St. Paul in 1889. The *Improvement Bulletin* noted that he was "the only architect in the Northwest making a specialty of theatrical architecture. He is the architect of the handsome new People's theater, Minneapolis, the Minneapolis Bijou and many others." Another advertisement for Carter subtly cemented the connection between general entertainment venues and the bordello: "Plans of opera houses, theaters, rinks and all places of amusement made."[17]

One newspaper article characterized Jones's bordello as a place "where once courtesans held forth[,] where champagne flowed and ribald laughter was heard all night."[18] An inventory of her estate suggests she offered several types of entertainment, including a library with books by William Cullen Bryant, John Greenleaf Whittier, Robert Burns, and Sir Walter Scott, as well as a copy of *Samantha in Europe* by Marietta Holley, who was called by some the female Mark Twain. There was also a copy of John Milton's *Paradise Lost,* illustrated by the famous French artist Gustave Doré. The presence of the Doré book offers a hint regarding how Jones presented her operation to the world. Doré was known to have had love affairs with two famous courtesans: Cora Pearl and Alice Ozy. Perhaps, by stocking her library shelves with literature, Jones would convey the idea that her employees were not mere prostitutes who could be purchased by anyone, but more akin to the opulently attired, and often cultured, *grandes horizontales* of nineteenth-century France, who had careers as companions to prominent men and became legends in their own right.[19]

Jones's crew could demonstrate a lively sense of fun. For example, inmate Camilly Deforest told a census taker that she was an "art embroider," and Jesse Perry was listed as a "typewriter." Beatrice Benedict called herself a "schoolteacher"; Edna Hamilton, a "governess"; Gertie Roberts, a "music teacher"; and Jennie Jones, a "housemaid."[20] As sex workers, these women played any number of roles and probably taught their clients some things along the way, but it was certain that Deforest did not bloody her fingers with sewing needles, nor did Jones scrub any floors. Ordinarily brothel inmates were recorded as "unemployed" or "whore" or "prostitute" by census takers, but in this case, the enumerator played along with the joke that Jones was operating a respectable boardinghouse for young women.

While it must have been amusing to tease the census taker in private, for the most part, Jones kept a low profile and had a keen sense of what she could get away with. Only occasionally did she go "too far," and then her connections to the local power structure became apparent. By 1893 another bordello had sprung up on Main Street Northeast near Jones's place, and this development disturbed the neighborhood. One newspaper noted that First Ward citizens and the mayor had reached an agreement regarding the two brothels: "One house is to move away and the other, in the big brick building [belonging to Jones], is to remain, provided the front windows are kept closed and the girls do not make a show of themselves on the street."[21] The two madams had presumably committed similar offenses, but Jones received a mild rebuke while the other brothel keeper was forced to relocate.

Less than a year after her bordello was built, Jones again commissioned Harry G. Carter to design a one-story brick addition to the rear of the house. Her business seemed to be recession proof. In 1893 and 1896, when much of the country was suffering from the financially devastating Panic of 1893, she took out building permits for more improvements to her property.[22] By 1895 Jones owned the land on which her bordello stood, having purchased the property from H. T. Welles for "$1.00 and other valuable consideration."[23] Apparently Jones paid for everything with cash, as there is no record of a mortgage on the property during her tenure there. Perhaps she had a private arrangement with Welles or some other patron that allowed her to acquire the property and erect a showy bordello, or perhaps she was very successful at providing her clients with exactly what they desired.

Jennie Jones's inmates were probably among the group of prostitutes who nearly caused "a catastrophe that might have split Minneapolis society wide open." The occasion was the 1894 grand opening of the women's apparel store Young-Quinlan Company; Elizabeth Quinlan recalled the story many years later: "All the carriage trade that the firm hoped would come to the opening of the store did come. The wives of the lumber kings, the flour kings, the wheat kings, the banking kings. Everyone a real 'lady.'" Other shoppers, however, were not welcome—"beautiful, bold, overdressed women from 'Main Street.' They streamed in, the big pockets of their long, voluminous skirts heavy and bulging with cash." Quinlan turned to her business partner, Fred Young, and told him that if the respectable customers learned "who those girls are," they would desert the store permanently. The unflappable Young told Quinlan, "'You sell to the carriage trade, Elizabeth, I'll sell to "Main Street." And never the twain shall meet!'" While the story may have been embellished over time, Quinlan understood that the "real ladies" and the women who worked in the sex trade were competing for the same wealthy men and that, as a merchant, she had to serve both groups, albeit discreetly.[24]

Jennie Jones died in 1899 at age forty-seven, and her passing produced only a brief mention in the local newspapers.[25] However, once the many stories told by and about Jones converged in a dispute over

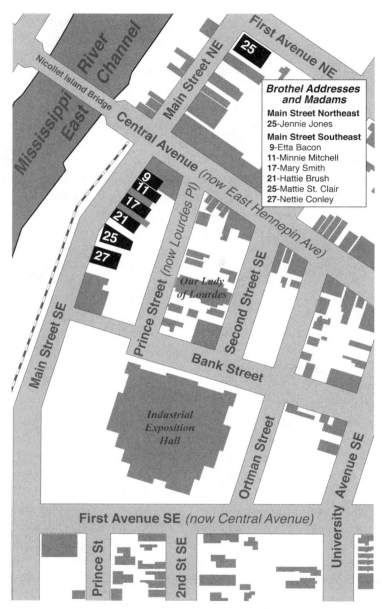

Brothel Addresses and Madams

Main Street Northeast
25-Jennie Jones

Main Street Southeast
9-Etta Bacon
11-Minnie Mitchell
17-Mary Smith
21-Hattie Brush
25-Mattie St. Clair
27-Nettie Conley

Main Street red-light district, 1895. This neighborhood was possibly the city's first sex district; Nettie Conley was doing business there by 1872. By 1895 the Main Street red-light district extended on either side of present-day East Hennepin Avenue. Main Street was flanked by railroad tracks on the riverside.

her considerable estate, newspaper reporters found plenty to write about. Three parties were vying for the Jones estate, as she had apparently died without leaving a will.[26] One was a man calling himself William Colvin, who was supposedly a long-lost son that Jones had by a prominent St. Louis businessman.[27] Another was fifteen-year-old William Burton, Jones's so-called adopted son and the child of Connie Burton, who had worked for Jones in the 1880s. After Burton died, Jones assumed responsibility for William, placing him in the care of a woman called Anna Cobb.[28] Finally, Jones's nine siblings claimed they were entitled to her property.[29]

Some of the confusion over the estate seems to have been generated by Jones herself, as several witnesses testified that she told them she had a son. Perhaps she was referring to Burton, and her audience construed him as her natural child. Or perhaps Jones was telling stories to entertain clients. The suggestion that she had a love child, fathered by a wealthy man, might have been just the right tale to generate sympathy and fascination, or what a reporter called a "romance of shame and fortune." This story would explain her fall from grace as well as intimating that the rich and powerful found her attractive. In this narrative Jones was a fallen woman, but not a heartless one who abandoned her child. Instead she turned to prostitution to support her son but distanced the innocent creature from his origins, or in the words of one newspaper, "for years the mother concealed her relationship and her occupation."[30] Or at least that was what gullible customers might believe.

The Jones probate proceedings unfolded over the summer of 1900. Edna Hamilton, described as "a handsome middle-aged woman . . . wearing a dark skirt, a white shirtwaist and sailor hat," took the witness stand. She never lost her calm demeanor under cross-examination, even when attorneys representing William Colvin and the Blacks accused her of stealing Jones's property.[31] Hamilton explained that the diamond jewelry and other items in her possession were gifts from Jones. She also produced a bill of sale for half of the furnishings in the bordello as well as a lease signed by Jones just before her death, granting Hamilton lifelong use of 25 Main Street Northeast with the rent set at an unvarying fifty dollars per month.[32]

In the end Probate Judge Harvey ruled in favor of Jones's siblings. William Colvin's claims were dismissed because, among other reasons, at age thirty-six he was too old to have been born to Jones. William Burton had no legal claim on the estate because there was no will naming him as an heir. The judge believed the testimony of Dr. W. W. Kimball, who said Jones never told him she had a child. Harvey also gave weight to an inscribed Episcopalian Bible that was found among the dead woman's possessions. Jones's brothers William and Edward Black testified that the family Bible listed her true name and birth date. Edward, a Presbyterian missionary in South Dakota, added that he had received several letters from Jones over the decades, but never been able to reunite with her since he had last seen her in Ireland.[33]

The estate included almost $17,000 in certificates of deposit and the Main Street brothel, valued at just under $15,000. The Blacks now jointly owned what should have been a valuable piece of real estate, but their only income from it was a token rent for the foreseeable future. By year's end the Blacks had sold the property to Edna Hamilton for $7,000.[34] The fact that Hamilton paid less than half the appraised value is not surprising. The lifetime lease had lowered the building's value, and realistically she was the only buyer. Hamilton retained the property for the rest of her life, and along with the brothel she kept the connections Jennie Jones had established with the local power structure. When the city closed down the entire Main Street red-light district in 1904, Hamilton was somehow able to keep operating there for another year.

THE MAIN STREET SEX DISTRICT EXPANDS

Even before Jennie Jones decided to move across the river, the Main Street red-light district was growing. Main Street, which had started out as the town of St. Anthony's first commercial street, was coalescing into two specialized sectors. There was an industrial area starting near present-day 125 Main Street Southeast and stretching several blocks downstream. It was home to industries such as foundries, flour mills, sawmills, furniture makers, and blacksmiths. The other sphere, serving what might broadly be termed an entertainment industry of saloons, restaurants, and brothels, was centered near the intersection of Main Street and present-day East Hennepin. The bordello-building boom on Main Street may have begun as early as 1886, when a group of Minneapolis businessmen erected the Industrial Exposition Hall, designed to host various events and exhibitions. Looming over Main Street, the vast warehouse-like structure stood between present-day Central Avenue Southeast and Bank Street Southeast. This development probably inspired saloon keeper Joseph Lyons to erect a three-story brick-and-stone "boarding house and saloon" at 25 Main Street Southeast to serve the hoped-for throngs who would visit the hall.[35] After the initial interest subsided, however, the Exposition Hall did not generate the level of commercial activity that civic boosters predicted. Regardless of whatever clientele Lyons had originally envisioned, his hotel–saloon became a bordello, and by 1889 madam Anna Wright was operating a house of prostitution there.[36]

Even if the Exposition Hall did not attract much business, Main Street provided the commercial sex industry a hospitable environment

The Main Street red-light district as seen from the St. Anthony Falls horseshoe dam on April 30, 1899. This unusual view of Main Street shows, from right to left, Levin Brothers Furniture (29–41 Main Street Southeast) and Nettie Conley's bordello with the white trim and awnings (27 Main Street Southeast) next door to Mattie St. Clair's place (25 Main Street Southeast). Jennie Jones's three-story bordello (with the prominent parapet) at 25 Main Street Northeast can be seen on the left side of the photograph. Photograph by the Schadde Brothers; courtesy of the Hennepin History Museum.

for expansion during the late 1880s and 1890s. Nettie Conley had been operating there since the 1870s, and if the First Street district was to be shut down, the sex trade would have to go somewhere. Three-story brick bordellos, often designed by local architects, replaced the older wooden buildings along this stretch of the street. Madams who deserted the First Street district moved into these newer, more spacious quarters. For example, Grace Holmes, formerly of 117 Second Avenue South, purchased the newly built brothel at 21 Main Street Southeast for thirty thousand dollars in 1892.[37] That same year a three-story brick bordello sprang up at 11 Main Street Southeast.[38] By 1895 Main Street hosted at least eight brothels. The district offered accommodations ranging from Jennie Jones's luxurious establishment to the modest, one-story wooden building at 15–17 Main Southeast. By the mid-1890s, two African American women were living there along with a mulatto man who served as a waiter. This establishment likely represented the low end of the Main Street price spectrum.[39]

The expansion of the Main Street sex district was driven by several circumstances. The exodus of madams from First Street as it declined from the premier red-light district was one factor. Another was that a group of madams had the means to buy more substantial brothels, and Main Street property owners were willing to sell to them. The location of Main Street itself proved very important. Late in 1891 the Republican Party announced it had chosen Minneapolis as the host city and Exhibition Hall as the site for their national convention, which would open June 7, 1892. One estimate placed the expected number of convention visitors at around fifty thousand, all of whom would need food, shelter, and entertainment of all sorts during their stay.[40]

Anticipation of the national convention may have spurred an offer by an eastern gambling syndicate to buy the "palatial building at 25 Main Street Northeast," the brothel owned by Jennie Jones, and turn it into a private "gaming house on mammoth portions." The syndicate planned to attract the wealthy, who would no longer have to go "to Europe to see a paradise arranged to order for the knights of the green cloth." The one-hundred-dollar entry deposit would bar "small fry" because "they will not have sufficient money to make the deposit and play as well."[41] Jones, who was possibly the source of this news item, decided not to sell her bordello. However, she and the other Main

Street madams certainly benefited from the publicity, as a gambling palace located in the midst of a red-light district would clearly expand the entertainment possibilities. If Minneapolis developed a reputation for offering a generous quantity and quality of amusements, then all the entertainment districts would thrive. If the millers could make Minneapolis the flour milling capital of the world, the madams would put the city on the map in their own manner.

Some Main Street madams erected new, purpose-built bordellos; others remodeled existing buildings. In at least one case, it is possible to follow the conversion of an existing building into a brothel. During the 1870s John Thielen built an Italianate Revival–style brick-and-stone building at 9 Main Street Southeast that housed his grocery store.[42] In subsequent years it was expanded and used as a barbershop and saloon.[43] By 1892 contractor Nels Peterson was the building's apparent owner, and he in turn sold the property to Minnie Brewer. The purchase agreement with Brewer stipulated that Peterson had to remodel the property to her specifications by April 1, 1892, or be subject to daily fines, a deadline clearly driven by the approaching Republican convention. The plans, drawn up by well-known architect Edward Stebbins, called for new room partitions, additional toilets, bathtubs, and new floors, as well as interior decorating in the form of painting and gilt wallpapers.[44] The short deadline for the repairs and the fees assessed for nonperformance assured Brewer plenty of time to prepare for the horde of visitors that would soon descend upon the city. Brewer and other madams doubtless hoped that a national convention would revitalize the Exposition Hall and draw other attractions to it in the future.

As the conventioneers began to arrive in Minneapolis, newspapers from across the country published stories on the event. A *New York Times* reporter noted there was "a moving mass of humanity" marching six abreast as far as the eye could see on Hennepin Avenue. Meanwhile, across the river at the Exposition Hall, railroad sleeping and dining cars served as "the temporary abodes of organizations from the East, West, and South."[45] Local newspapers reprinted what out-of-town papers had to say about the convention. The *Indianapolis Sentinel* gushed, "Minneapolis has thus far taken care of the visitors in excellent style." A. C. Thomas of the Associated Press exclaimed,

A rear view of several Main Street Southeast bordellos from the Exposition Building looking toward Nicollet Island, about 1910. Nettie Conley's place, at 27 Main Street Southeast, is the three-story building with the back porch next to Levin Brothers Furniture. The next bordello at 25 Main Street Southeast was once operated by Mattie St. Clair. The shadow of the steeple of Our Lady of Lourdes Church can be seen at far right. Photograph by Charles Hibbard; courtesy of Minnesota Historical Society.

"Minneapolis is a winner. She has handled this convention as no convention has ever been handled before." Meanwhile the *Chicago Post* hinted that not all of the delegates spent all of their time at the convention, noting, "The prevailing social sentiment of the place is eminently puritanical, but there is a dash of continentalism, which expresses itself in Sunday saloons and Sunday matinees at the lower class theaters."[46] The madams had been wise to upgrade and expand their brothels in anticipation of the national convention.

FRENCH BALLS

Along with expanding red-light districts and purpose-built bordellos, the commercial sex trade was taking up more public space in other ways. The so-called French Ball was a form of public display that had appeared in other large cities for several decades. Madams often sponsored these balls as advertisements for their services. Scantily clad public women attended the masked balls, as did a wide swath of respectable society. Historian Timothy Gilfoyle characterized French Balls as "probably the most significant public forum for testing the boundaries of urban sexual behavior." At New York balls, "one could find everyone from Wall Street businessmen to prostitutes and gay drag queens in masquerades."[47] But New York was not the only city offering this type of entertainment.

Minneapolis may have seen its first French Ball in January 1891, when a group calling itself the "Minneapolis Theatrical Union" sponsored one at the Turner's Hall at 500 Washington Avenue North. The *Minneapolis Tribune* described it as "a great affair for the elite of First Street and other similar retreats. Members of the Minneapolis demimonde turned out in large numbers in costumes as scant as their reputations." The behavior at the ball was apparently so outrageous that the two policemen who had been assigned to keep order shut it down. The police chief announced that the series of future balls planned by the union would be canceled.[48]

Despite the police chief's declaration, the 1891 event was hardly the last French Ball sponsored by the Theatrical Union. In 1896 the union again held its "annual masquerade ball" in Turner's Hall. The following year the ball took place in the Normanna Hall. The *Minneapolis Journal* called the 1901 ball, which ended at dawn, "one of the most disgraceful orgies in the history of the city": "several hundred residents of the Minneapolis tenderloin, together with their friends from St. Paul," joined with "the usual slumming parties," all of whom engaged in a cacophony of yelling, swearing, dancing, and drinking. After the brothels closed for the evening, "those inmates who had been unable to get away earlier, flocked to the ball." While gorgeously costumed prostitutes plied their trade, several policemen stood by "watching the fun," making no move to put an end to the festivities.[49]

Despite the description of these events as being grand parties for the benefit of outlaws, French Balls also enabled pairings between all sorts of people, be they gay, straight, white, black, young, old, rich, or poor. If the balls had simply been an opportunity for social deviants like prostitutes to debauch each other in private, few respectable citizens would have noticed. But these events were open to the public, or at least members of the public willing to buy a ticket, and represented an open affront to the carefully constructed social castes. Respectable society was both fascinated and repelled by French Balls and patronized them for years.

French Balls also served as yet another form of advertising for the madams, allowing them to display their "wares" beyond the geographic boundaries of the red-light districts, not unlike modern-day trade fairs. Without entering the established sex districts, potential customers could view and interact with a variety of brothel inmates. At a French Ball, a man might become acquainted with a particular prostitute or learn that a certain madam offered the type of services he preferred. If he liked what he saw at the ball, he could easily become a regular customer.

A NEW RED-LIGHT DISTRICT MIRACULOUSLY APPEARS

Only weeks after the police chief declared the cancellation of all future "Minneapolis Theatrical Union" balls, a brand-new red-light area popped up in the city. Seemingly overnight the area on Eleventh Avenue South between Second Street South and Washington Avenue South and Second Street South from Tenth to Twelfth Avenues South was transformed from a humdrum neighborhood of modest hotels serving the Milwaukee Depot, lumberyards, and small commercial ventures such as laundries and grocery stores into a concentrated sex district.[50] The Eleventh Avenue red-light district was sandwiched between the huge flour mills of the West Side Milling District and heavily traveled Washington Avenue, where streetcars rumbled along in both directions, day and night. In February 1891 the local newspapers took notice of this new sex district, after First Street madam Hattie Cole purchased the Sexton Hotel and another parcel with plans to open a brothel. One newspaper noted that the relocation of First Street brothels to the new area "has gone further than anyone supposed."[51]

Newspapers predicted that the surrounding neighborhood would not allow this development to go forward. One article stated that prominent residents such as Jacob Stoft, a former Sixth Ward alderman and current park board commissioner, would lead the fight.[52] Mayor Phillip Winston, who received many indignant letters on the subject, promised to attend a protest rally. The mayor maintained, through a spokesman, that "he has not allowed himself to be mixed up in the question in any way." Still, Winston gave himself a way out when he noted that "if the Sixth Ward protests with sufficient energy," the new sex district would be shelved.[53] Another newspaper reported that the large Scandinavian population was "highly incensed that their homes are to be surrounded by houses of ill-fame 'under police protection.'" The reporter was certain that no city official had approved such a plan, and speculated that the idea must have originated with an unscrupulous real estate agent.[54]

An estimated four hundred people turned out for the protest meeting at Normanna Hall, which was chaired by Stoft. The mayor, a Democrat, did not show up. William Gunderson, a Republican, sought to score political points by rhetorically asking who, if not the mayor, did have the authority to remove the brothels? Chairman Stoft quickly silenced Gunderson, saying that this was not the question before the gathering.[55] But in fact, this question had sparked the protest rally into being.

One newspaper article suggested it was the madams who unilaterally decided to establish a new red-light district, noting, "if the madams select a neighborhood that does not excite public outcry, all [is] well and good."[56] If that were true, then the madams were in charge of city policy. In other instances, however, the city had shut down unauthorized bordellos. Lena Leppala's assignation house, well outside the established red-light district, was closed in 1889 after a police raid caught several prominent men, including a St. Paul judge.[57] Even if a bold real estate speculator had initiated the move to the Sixth Ward, the worldly madams would never have bought into such a scheme without assurances from the relevant municipal authorities. Without such promises, a *Minneapolis Journal* article observed, "Hattie Cole will have made a poor investment."[58]

Despite follow-up newspaper accounts that suggested a victory for Sixth Ward residents, the largely immigrant population had neither the wealth nor the political clout to prevent the imposition of a new sex district in their midst.[59] Mayor Winston's statement that the proposed red-light district would be dropped if citizen protests were particularly vigorous really meant that city officials were confident this location would produce the least amount of political damage. Assuming the city had entered into a clandestine agreement with the madams, municipal officials were not in a position to renege on the deal. If their arrangement with the madams came to light or if they allowed prostitution to gain a foothold in other neighborhoods with more powerful constituents, they would be turned out of office.

MORE MADAMS MAKE THE MOVE

Even before the newspapers broke the story, yet another First Street madam, Mabel Baker, began buying up real estate in the emerging red-light district. Early in 1891 Baker acquired a lot at 1019 Second Street South and soon built a three-story brick bordello there. For a few years Baker continued to conduct business at her First Street house, but her Second Street place, characterized as "the most elaborate establishment," and the Eleventh Avenue district in general became her primary focus.[60] She systematically bought properties at 1021 and 1023 Second Street South, giving her significant frontage along Eleventh Avenue as well.[61] Like Ida Dorsey, Baker worked with her sister, Frances Stewart, later known as Frances Myers, an arrangement that allowed them to operate multiple bordellos. The two women were among the major landowners in the Eleventh Avenue district.

A native of Michigan, Baker first appeared in Minneapolis during the 1880s, running a bordello at 220 First Street South. At that point she was in her midtwenties and had married saloonkeeper Robert Bleakie in 1887.[62] Bleakie was described in one account as a young man who came to Minneapolis from Chicago, with eighteen thousand dollars in cash, an inheritance from his parents, which he "lost in gambling and high living."[63] Perhaps Mabel had helped in the dissipation of his fortune. In 1888 she bought a house in South Minneapolis, well away from any red-light district, which she would retain long after she cast Bleakie aside.[64]

Despite Baker's regular acquisition of property and successful business ventures, her disorderly personal life sometimes spilled into public view. Shortly after establishing herself in the new red-light district, Baker, Bleakie, Frances Stewart, and "Professor" (a title typically assigned to piano players in brothels) George Denzel were arrested after a brawl erupted outside her Second Street bordello.[65] Less than a year

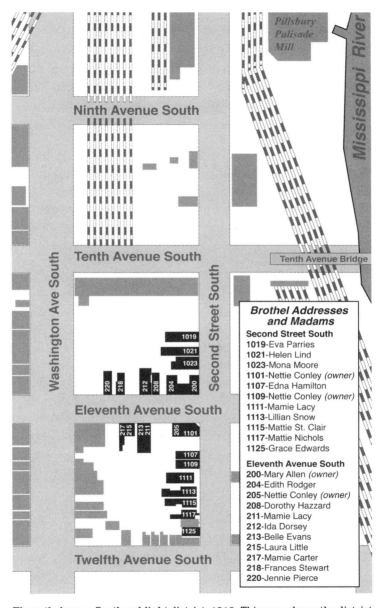

Ninth Avenue South

Tenth Avenue South

Pillsbury Palisade Mill

Mississippi River

Tenth Avenue Bridge

Washington Ave South

Second Street South

Eleventh Avenue South

Twelfth Avenue South

Brothel Addresses and Madams

Second Street South
1019-Eva Parries
1021-Helen Lind
1023-Mona Moore
1101-Nettie Conley *(owner)*
1107-Edna Hamilton
1109-Nettie Conley *(owner)*
1111-Mamie Lacy
1113-Lillian Snow
1115-Mattie St. Clair
1117-Mattie Nichols
1125-Grace Edwards

Eleventh Avenue South
200-Mary Allen *(owner)*
204-Edith Rodger
205-Nettie Conley *(owner)*
208-Dorothy Hazzard
211-Mamie Lacy
212-Ida Dorsey
213-Belle Evans
215-Laura Little
217-Mamie Carter
218-Frances Stewart
220-Jennie Pierce

Eleventh Avenue South red-light district, 1910. This map shows the district at its high-water mark, with more than twenty brothels concentrated in two square blocks. By this time, successful madams such as Nettie Conley owned brothel buildings and rented them to other madams.

later, the two sisters were again in the news when Baker celebrated her wedding anniversary by eloping to Detroit with William ("Montana Jack") Allen, a hack driver. A few weeks earlier, Frances Stewart had traveled to Detroit, along with one of Baker's children, in preparation for a rendezvous with her latest conquest, a Minneapolis printer; they were to be joined by Baker, Allen, and Baker's daughter, who had been living in a convent. Earlier Bleakie had confronted Baker and Allen, whom he found "in a compromising attitude," in the parlor of the Second Street bordello and demanded that Mabel declare herself. She did just that, announcing, "You are my husband, but Jack is my lover." One account described Baker as among "the leaders of the demi-monde" and "a woman possessed of more than her share of the real estate and money of this city." She had thoughtfully planned her departure by reserving a private room on the train and equipping it with, among other things, a half gallon of rye whiskey; she also had notified the stable where her horses were boarded that Robert Bleakie no longer had the right to use them.[66]

Baker's connection with Bleakie did not end with her elopement, however. A few years later, Bleakie was refused entrance to Baker's First Street bordello, so he battered down the door. "Pandemonium reigned for a time," as Bleakie slashed "Montana Jack" with a knife, inflicting serious injuries.[67] After Baker divorced Bleakie, she took on the identity of Mary E. Allen and moved her operation entirely to the Eleventh Avenue district, but Bleakie returned to the First Street brothel, now operated by another madam, where he met up with Mabel/Mary. After she refused to give him any more money, he pulled out a .38-caliber revolver and tried to shoot himself in the heart; he missed and struck a rib instead.[68]

By 1900 Mary Allen had hired the firm of Bertrand and Chamberlin, architects of many other business buildings, to design two adjoining three-story brick bordellos.[69] Instead of orienting her buildings to Second Street South, as she had done in 1891, Allen turned them ninety degrees so that they had addresses of 200–202 and 204–206 Eleventh Avenue South, a clear indication that Eleventh Avenue had become the principal street of the district. In 1905 Allen hired the same architects to design a third, freestanding building at 208 Eleventh Avenue South.[70] Meanwhile Allen's sister, Frances Stewart, served as madam

Mary E. Allen's three-story former bordello at 200–204 Eleventh Avenue South, long after its heyday. By 1939, the building housed the Silent Sales Company, a vending machine firm. Photograph by the *Minneapolis Star-Journal;* courtesy of the Minnesota Historical Society.

and owner of two buildings at 218 and 220 Eleventh Avenue South that had been converted to brothels.[71] For more than two decades, Allen and her sister would operate in the Eleventh Avenue district in one capacity or another: property owners, landlords, madams, and bail guarantors for arrested prostitutes and madams.

IDA DORSEY MOVES TO ELEVENTH AVENUE SOUTH

Whatever agreement the madams and the city had worked out for the creation of the Eleventh Avenue district, it was in place by November 1890, when Ida Dorsey quietly began her move from the First Street district, well in advance of Hattie Cole's very public transition. This appeared to be an opportune time for such an agreement to come about.

In November the Republicans had lost their bid to remain in charge of the mayor's office. Once the new Democratic mayor was sworn into office in January and the new red-light district suddenly appeared, it might not be clear who exactly was responsible for this situation. Both Democrats and Republicans had taken a variety of stands on tolerated prostitution over the years.

The chain of events leading to Dorsey's relocation was similar to that of Jennie Jones's move to Main Street in that it involved secret dealings with members of respectable society. It began with Andrew C. Haugan, a Norwegian immigrant who had served on the Minneapolis City Council and was the cashier at Scandia Bank.[72] He and his wife, Louise, sold the land at 212 Eleventh Avenue South to Carolina Anderson, a person with no apparent connection to the sex trade.[73] Carolina was the wife of Zacharias Anderson, a brick mason. In December Carolina took out a building permit to build a three-story brick-and-stone structure with an estimated cost of well over twelve thousand dollars. Her husband served as the general contractor.[74] The permit describes the building as apartments, but a mechanic's lien filed against the property tells another story. That document states that Ida Dorsey was the occupant of the building and that John L. Anderson was the legal owner of the property. He in turn held it in trust for Carolina Anderson and Ida Dorsey. Furthermore, Carolina had a contract from Dorsey for the purchase of the property.[75]

Haugan was hardly the only solid citizen doing business with Dorsey. Jacob Stoft was one of the incorporators of the Simonson Brothers Manufacturing Company, which supplied lumber for Dorsey's new brothel. When an unpaid bill led Simonson Brothers to file a mechanic's lien against the property, it was Stoft who signed the bill of particulars noting that lumber had been furnished not long after Stoft chaired the meetings protesting the new red-light district.[76] After only five years in Minneapolis, Dorsey had managed to assemble the contacts and capital that allowed her to build her own bordello in a red-light district that did not yet officially exist. Even the well-established Nettie Conley had spent a decade in the business before she owned the real estate on which her brothel stood.

Dorsey's new place provided a striking contrast to her first, "a shabby weather-beaten frame house." The architect-designed, three-

Madam Ida Dorsey's bordello at 212 Eleventh Avenue South. Dorsey was the first madam to build in the Eleventh Avenue district, and her building is now the lone surviving bordello structure in Minneapolis. Photograph by Jerry Mathiason, 2006.

story, brick-and-stone building proclaimed Dorsey's worldly success. Apparently, it was even equipped with an electric alarm that could be used to summon the police in case of emergency, a precaution that would serve to protect both Dorsey and her very well-connected clients.[77]

Dorsey's talent for offering the right mix of forbidden pleasures, and perhaps the suggestion of some danger, in a lush setting continued to attract wealthy customers for the remainder of her career. Nearly thirty years after the account of her first Minneapolis brothel was published, another newspaper reporter complained that unlike the others, Dorsey's operation was never raided because "some pretty big guns would be grabbed there, and the papers would have some great stories."[78]

Dorsey spent, according to one account, another fifteen thousand dollars to furnish her new bordello. She celebrated its completion by mailing out announcements.[79] Pastor T. F. Allen, who along with Rev. G. L. Morrill was working hard to stir up a new purity crusade, declared that he wished he had been there with a "Kodak" to watch the respectable businessmen who had "responded to the nice invitations sent them to attend the opening of that house."[80] The two ministers had the opportunity to attend the festivities, as one newspaper noted that Dorsey sent Morrill two invitations, one of which "came with a special delivery stamp upon it."[81]

Dorsey also continued to be the subject of newspaper articles after her move to Eleventh Avenue.[82] She maintained her whites-only policy, refusing admittance even to Harris Martin, better known as the "Black Pearl," a champion African American prizefighter in the Twin Cities.[83] Early in 1894 two robbers, Pat Crowe and another man known as McKnight, claiming they knew a mutual acquaintance of Dorsey's in Kansas City, managed to gain admittance to her bordello and held her at gunpoint while they wrenched diamond earrings valued at $1,200 from her ears. "Ida fought like a tiger," clinging to one robber as he made for the door and ripping off part of his overcoat; one of her inmates "drew a revolver from her dress pocket" and fired two shots after them. The men got away. Still, Dorsey observed in a subsequent newspaper article, they did not get the $10,000–$15,000 worth of diamond jewelry located in her private room.[84]

During the 1890s Dorsey also brought her widowed mother and half brothers from Kentucky to Minneapolis. She did not house them at her bordello but rather at a nearby apartment building. By 1904 she had purchased a house for the family in South Minneapolis.[85] After her thirty-three-year-old sister Roberta died of cancer in 1898, Dorsey took charge of Roberta's young daughter, Alvah.[86] Going forward Dorsey would refer to Alvah as her daughter and later left virtually her entire estate to the girl.[87] In 1906, when Dorsey formally completed the purchase of the Eleventh Avenue bordello, the deed listed her birth name, Ida M. Callahand, an identity she would increasingly use.[88]

Dorsey made another significant real estate purchase, at 1214–1220 First Avenue South (present-day Marquette Avenue).[89] Like many others who did business with well-known Minneapolis madams, the sellers of this property tried to put some distance between themselves and the end purchaser. In a series of transactions in April 1907 starting with Lucy Cook, who had inherited the property, the parcel was first sold to Joseph and Flora Moore, who in turn sold it to lawyer Louis A.

Hubachek for $12,500. The next day, Hubachek sold the property to Dorsey, who used the name of Mary I. Callahand.[90] The transaction was not recorded at Hennepin County until several years later.

Dorsey probably benefited from the secrecy as well. The property was not associated with the sex trade, as it housed a grocery shop at street level and several families in the apartments upstairs. Dorsey seemed to be diversifying her holdings by acquiring income property, perhaps in anticipation of a life outside of the commercial sex trade.

Finally, sometime in the early years of the twentieth century, Dorsey began an association with Carleton Pillsbury. Born in 1882, Carleton was the only surviving son of Frederick and Alice Pillsbury. His grandfather was George Pillsbury, who had been mayor of Minneapolis; his uncle Charles was one of the founders of the Pillsbury Flour Company; and his great-uncle was Governor John S. Pillsbury, who had been at the forefront of the purity crusade against the madams in 1879.

The contrast between Ida's and Carleton's circumstances was dramatic. Carleton was born into wealth and privilege. He was a member of the 1901 class of Lawrenceville, an exclusive boarding school in New Jersey. He not only stayed in fine New York City hotels, such as the Holland House, but his visits there were noted in newspapers. He had dealings in London, where he kept a fair amount of money that was later inherited by his youngest sister. Although he worked at the Pillsbury "A" Mill for a couple of years, he seemed to have plenty of time to give dinners for his friends such as Gardner Greenleaf at the Minneapolis Club or indulge in automobile racing.[91]

Perhaps Carleton sought out Ida Dorsey because of his interest in music and acting, and because of a certain fascination with African Americans, or at least popular portrayals of them. By 1904 Carleton was one of the members of the all-male Roosevelt Club rehearsing a musical called *Cinderella and the Prince,* which would be staged at the Metropolitan Theater in downtown Minneapolis. This decidedly nontraditional version of Cinderella, in which all parts were played by men, included "a chorus of eight funny Orientals," an Irish fairy godmother, and "three black face parts" that were "among the cleverest and most artistic." Carleton Pillsbury appeared in one of the blackface roles, that of Robinson Crusoe's "man Friday," who sang "two negro melodies of the sonorous, syncopated type for which the Southland is famous." Carleton, dressed in costume and blackface makeup, even posed for a newspaper photograph. Possibly Carleton learned this syncopated musical style, better known as ragtime, while visiting Ida Dorsey's establishment. She certainly provided music for her guests, and it is likely her musician brother, Nebraska Burkes, performed some of it.[92]

Shortly after his performance in *Cinderella,* Pillsbury and several of his friends incorporated the Pillsbury–Dana Company, also known as the C. C. Pillsbury Company, for the purpose of printing and publishing music. Some of the music published by this firm seemed to reflect Carleton's interest in persons of color. One piece was called "Floating Along: A Kaffir Idyll." "Kaffir," a term now considered offensive, referred to black people in South Africa. Another song was "De Cleanin' Man: A Blackville Satire," which featured two African American men on the cover, one dressed as a janitor, the other as a flashy gambler.[93]

That Dorsey had connections to the Minneapolis elite was hardly a secret, but the Carleton Pillsbury liaison broke the rules by being acknowledged outside the confines of her bordello. Their connection was remembered in both the white and the black communities long after the relationship ended. Six years after his death, a white reporter referred to Carleton as "Ida's suicided hubby."[94] The local African American press wrote about "Pillsbury of the Ida Dorsey affair in this city" as another example, not unlike New York millionaire John R. Platt, who kept the light-skinned Hannah Elias as his mistress, of "white men, clandestinely affiliated with Negro women." The writer noted these men were never castigated in any way, "because they followed a custom of their forefathers, fixed by long continuance."[95]

When Carleton died of acute alcoholic dementia in 1910, Dorsey, using the name "M. Callahand," was among the creditors making claims against his considerable estate.[96] Possibly Carleton had provided some of the resources that allowed Dorsey to acquire more real estate beginning in 1904, as by then his money was no longer under the control of a guardian. Perhaps Carleton had promised her support in the future or he may have considered her his wife and entitled to at least a share of his estate. Possibly there was an earlier will that named Dorsey as an heir. The will under which Carleton's estate was probated was executed only nine days before his death, and it revoked all earlier wills.

In 1916, when Dorsey served as the informant on her brother Moses's death certificate, she identified herself as "Mrs. Ida Pillsbury," revealing that she considered herself to be Carleton's widow.[97] Whether Carleton and Ida had entered into a common-law marriage is unknown; there is no evidence that they married in Hennepin County. Whatever the nature of their relationship, it clearly meant something to Dorsey.

THE MADAMS REMAKE ELEVENTH AVENUE SOUTH

By 1897 the red-light district extended along Second Street South as far as Twelfth Avenue South. Albert Johnson, a wealthy eccentric who owned vast tracts of real estate, began leasing some property in the area to several madams. Within a few years, six bordellos were packed onto three city lots. When Johnson died in 1905, his heir, Edna Dickerson, soon sold most of the properties to the individual madams occupying the houses.[98] By the close of this year, women owned almost all the real estate in the Eleventh Avenue red-light district.

By 1901 even Nettie Conley had a presence in the Eleventh Avenue sex district, but not as a madam. This time, she was working the real estate side of the commercial sex industry, as the owner of five lots fronting Eleventh Avenue South.[99] Conley, along with Dorsey, Mary Allen, and Frances Stewart, were the principal property owners in the district. She soon set about erecting her newest bordello, a three-story brick building at 1111 Second Street South. Frank B. Cottom, Conley's latest male companion, was listed on the permit as the owner, although he had no legal interest in the property.[100]

Three years later Conley built a one-story saloon at the corner of Eleventh Avenue South and Second Street South, orienting it to the Mississippi River. While nearby Washington Avenue South offered any number of drinking establishments, Conley's saloon may have catered specifically to the Eleventh Avenue sex district. In 1906 the saloon received a two-story addition to accommodate a bordello above. To underscore its association with the red-light district, this section of the building had a separate entrance on Eleventh Avenue.[101] By 1910 thirteen female "boarders" lived in the building along with three servants.[102]

When the Main Street red-light district permanently closed in 1904, the Eleventh Avenue district experienced another growth spurt. By the summer of 1905, the Eleventh Avenue sex district had eighteen known bordellos.[103]

Finally even the well-connected Edna Hamilton came to do business in the Eleventh Avenue district. Still, having run the most ostentatious brothel in Minneapolis, Hamilton was not going to relocate to just any building. She would require a substantial house built to her specifications, and who better would understand her requirements than another Minneapolis madam? Apparently Nettie Conley was the perfect choice for this undertaking. In the spring of 1905, Conley began building a bordello for Hamilton. The three-story brothel at 1107 Second Street South adjoined another at 1109 Second Street South that Conley had built a few years earlier.[104] Edna Hamilton and her crew moved out of the last openly operated brothel on Main Street and into the new place in late 1905. Five years later twelve prostitutes and Hamilton resided in the Second Street South brothel, as well as six servants.[105]

The madams not only created a new red-light district, they also changed the orientation of the blocks to cement its identity as the Eleventh Avenue district. Prior to 1890 a few modest buildings fronted on the 200 block of Eleventh Avenue, with the more important buildings of brick or stone facing Washington Avenue or Second Street, which offered a connection to the Tenth Avenue Bridge, a railroad station, and the river. The turn toward Eleventh Avenue began with Ida Dorsey's brothel. Mary Allen continued this shift when she oriented her 1899 brothel to Eleventh Avenue. As bordellos were concentrated along Eleventh Avenue, the adjacent real estate gained value if it could be rechristened with an Eleventh Avenue address, and this fact was not lost upon its owners. In reorienting to Eleventh Avenue, the madams had created their own spaces and specialized buildings.

The new Eleventh Avenue sex district was well situated from both the authorities' and the madams' points of view. Because the district was well within the Liquor Patrol Limits, alcohol would neither be introduced to a previously dry area nor impinge on wealthy residential neighborhoods. Some workers from the nearby flour mills, railroads, and other industries would become walk-in customers, while others would arrive via streetcars, trains, or carriages. The neighborhood was well traveled: streetcars ran along Washington Avenue, and there was traffic from the other side of the river from the Tenth Avenue Bridge. Once the Chicago Great Western Railroad erected a freight and passenger depot at the corner of Tenth Avenue South and Washington Avenue South, more potential customers were delivered to the red-light district. All this activity provided a general air of "busyness." Any man seen in the vicinity might have some connection with the respectable businesses there, might be visiting a brothel, or might be in transit.

A sex district that could materialize seemingly out of nowhere underlined the power of the madams, who had expanded their influence to the point of being able to build a neighborhood of their own in an area that had no prior connection to the sex trade. Virtually all the real estate in this sex district was owned by women, be they active madams or those formerly in the business. Like the First Street and Main Street districts, it had good accessibility to public transportation, a bridge across the river, and nearby saloons and theaters. But more important, it offered ample expansion space for those madams who had accumulated enough capital to build their own "gilded palaces of sin." The Eleventh Avenue district would represent the high tide of brothel prostitution in Minneapolis.

For the most part, the Minneapolis reformers appeared powerless to halt either the expansion of red-light districts or the regular occurrence of French Balls that enabled the commercialized sex trade to taunt the respectable with their success and power. It all suggested that the contagion of prostitution was spreading across the landscape and that the madams, not the reformers, were winning the contest for the soul of the city.

FOUR

Reforming the City
Doc Ames, "White Slavery," and the End of an Era

> They objected to the children that are inmates of
> the Home for the Friendless attending the public
> schools. This institution, it seems, is of a charitable
> and reformatory nature and seeks to care for homeless
> children or children whose parents are in houses of
> ill-fame, and who wish their children be brought up
> properly.
>
> —"DRAWING THE LINE,"
> *MINNEAPOLIS TIMES*, NOVEMBER 18, 1891

Late one April morning in 1910, when most inhabitants of the Eleventh Avenue red-light district were likely asleep, the police department began "the biggest and most sweeping raid in the history of Minneapolis." Acting at the request of County Attorney Al J. Smith, they swarmed to the "territory on Second Street between Tenth and Twelfth Avenues and Eleventh and Twelfth Avenues between Second Street and Washington Avenue," enclosing it with "a cordon" of uniformed policemen, while "scores of plain clothes men" started "serving twenty-four warrants on the proprietors. By 1:30 p.m., nineteen were under arrest." Only the madams, not the ordinary inmates, were jailed. Although the "raid was conducted with lightning-like swiftness," a crowd "of nearly 3,000" spectators gathered to watch. Few seemed to realize that this invasion would mark the end of the open red-light district of Minneapolis. The story of how Minneapolis reformers accomplished this apparent triumph goes back two decades.[1]

THE REFORMERS GET ORGANIZED

Nineteenth-century and early twentieth-century America was awash in a number of reform movements, ranging from abolitionists who finally saw the end of slavery to temperance advocates to advocates of universal suffrage. Some of these movements drew strength from one another, even if their main goals were not the same. For example, the Anti-Saloon League allied itself with any group that opposed alcohol for whatever reason, such as nativists, suffragists, and the radical International Workers of the World, and used these alliances to further their cause. The Progressive movement favored, among other causes, a steeply graduated income tax, and in time, this led to the adoption of the Sixteenth Amendment to the Constitution. This reform, meant to redistribute the tax burden based on the ability to pay, also furthered the cause of prohibition, as it replaced the federal liquor-tax revenues once legal alcohol sales ceased. Better and faster communication enabled local reform groups to learn from both the mistakes and successes of similar-minded groups across the country.

In 1891 the madams and the commercial sex trade gained the upper hand in Minneapolis, but the forces of reform did not retreat from the fray. After losing the battle to prevent the formation of the new red-light district on Eleventh Avenue South, the fight shifted to the courts, the school board, and finally the political arena. Over time, Minneapolis reformers who hoped to eradicate prostitution and municipal corruption in general were able to link their cause to broader national trends, lending them a certain legitimacy, as well as providing stories for the national press to disseminate about the progress reformers were making in Minneapolis.

In September 1891, district court judge Thomas Canty urged a grand jury to indict the usual lawbreakers who ran gambling dens and "blind pigs," or saloons that remained open on Sunday. But he placed particular emphasis on clandestine brothels that operated outside the red-light districts, noting that if the sex trade was to be tolerated it must be "quarantined" as you would a "pesthouse," making the separation between the two "as wide and deep as possible." In Canty's mind, the secret prostitutes, who occupied the upper floors of business blocks that were rented out by unprincipled landlords, were "the most dangerous instruments of seduction and debauchery." These women managed to bribe beat cops to look the other way and were "unknown at police headquarters," yet they continued to attract any number of eager clients.[2]

Canty's exhortations revealed a deeply divided city. The judge acknowledged the inconsistency of juries from years past: one might have indicted all the well-known madams but allowed their inmates to go about their business and move into previously untainted parts of town, whereas the next jury refused to indict prostitutes, even if they operated outside the established sex districts. Although Canty pleaded for the law to be applied consistently, he made no attempt to persuade the grand jury that prostitution should be completely suppressed; mere containment was his goal.

The grand jury complied with some of the judge's wishes by indicting Jennie Jones and Catherine E. Lloyd on two counts each. Jones paid fines of several hundred dollars for keeping a brothel and allowing her new building at 25 Main Street Northeast to be used for prostitution. The well-known Jones was hardly operating a secret bordello, but the stiff fines might persuade reformers that the law was making an effort to tamp down the sex industry.

Thirty-seven-year-old Lloyd paid a much heavier price—ten months in Stillwater for keeping a bordello and running a house of assignation. By operating her brothel on the upper level of a building at 126 Fourth Street South, Lloyd was clearly beyond the bounds of the First Street red-light district and was an easy target for the grand jury. Again, Canty condemned assignation houses because they enabled women to secretly work as prostitutes in order to gratify their desires for fine clothing, and then they "go forth into the world as virtuous, honest women; into the homes of respectable families and contaminate everything they touch." The judge also offered Lloyd a reduced sentence if she would reveal who was the true proprietor of her assignation house (her attorney had portrayed her as a mere employee).[3] But Lloyd remained silent on this point. In fact, she may have been the actual owner of the business as she had been paying monthly fines for prostitution for at least two years.[4] Perhaps Lloyd and her attorney were playing on Canty's anxieties about all the hidden vices that seemed to riddle the city. The citizens of Minneapolis seemed powerless to stop the sex trade from taking up more public space, but the

The former bordello at 25 Main Street Northeast
built by Jennie Jones is the dark three-story building
in the center of the photograph, as seen in 1951.
By this time it was a rooming house and few people
remembered its original function. Photograph by
Minneapolis Star-Journal; courtesy of the Minnesota
Historical Society.

judge could make an example of one not-very-well-connected madam
by sending her to the penitentiary.

If the reformers had placed everybody, including customers, landlords, land speculators, and merchants, who contributed directly or
indirectly to the Minneapolis sex trade on one side of the divide and
the saintly on the other, Canty's pesthouse analogy would have broken down. Prostitution in Minneapolis was not some invasive foreign transplant but a local industry that enriched a broad sector of
individuals and was patronized by many. Still, the analogy hinted
that Minneapolis reformers were beginning to take a somewhat different tack in their fight against the madams. By condemning the sex
trade and conflating it with diseases both physical and spiritual, the

reformers could characterize it as a plague that corrupted everyone. If this contagion could not yet be eradicated, then it should be isolated. Reformers of all stripes would increasingly use metaphors of filth and germs to describe various social conditions. In the coming decade, writers like Lincoln Steffens would announce that municipal governments needed to be "cleaned up," as if complex issues ranging from outright municipal graft to prostitution could somehow be simply "disinfected."

"DRAWING THE LINE"

Perhaps the most desperate reaction to the spread of prostitution came from the Minneapolis Board of Education. In a move similar to Judge Canty's quarantine efforts, the forces of reform sought to isolate certain individuals they deemed contaminated. At a special meeting held late in 1891, the board responded to a petition from a group of Lyndale School parents asserting that they had the right to keep their children from associating "with other children who have been raised in an atmosphere of vice and crime," namely, those living in the Home for the Friendless at 3334 Harriet Avenue South. The home offered shelter to orphans, children whose mothers lived in brothels, and others whose parents could not otherwise care for them. Two girls had been expelled from Lyndale School simply because they lived at the home, and the school board backed up this action by ruling that any child living in a "reformatory institution" would be banned from the public schools.[5]

One editorial denounced the school board by saying the decision may have been well intentioned but was still wrong. The piece noted that there were many children who lived in brothels or houses of assignation and regularly attended public schools, but ironically would be denied an education if they were living in a wholesome place like the Home for the Friendless. The newspaper argued that it was acceptable to expel children from schools for bad behavior, but it was unfair to punish them for their parents' sins. Another editorial called the petition "a libel on the Eighth Ward" because only four people had actually signed it and they did not represent the majority opinion.[6]

Unmoved, the school board refused to back down, despite arguments by former district judge John M. Shaw. A pro bono attorney for the home, Shaw noted that state law required the public schools to admit anyone between five and twenty-one years of age living within the city, regardless of color, social circumstance, or nationality. The president of the school board, A. T. Ankey, maintained that the Lyndale School was at capacity and could not admit any more pupils. Shaw countered that no one had mentioned overcrowding when the two were expelled, only that they had no right to attend the school. He also observed that the school could not be that packed as it had admitted children from Richfield and other localities, even though it had no legal obligation to do so.[7]

The reformers had somehow managed to enlist the school board in their fight against prostitution, and the board refused to budge. A furious Shaw asserted that the school board not only opened themselves up to fines and imprisonment if they continued this course of action, they also put in "peril and jeopardy" the state funds that in part supported Minneapolis schools; worst of all, their actions "made a murderous and suicidal attack upon the system of free schools in this country." The school board and their supporters apparently felt so overwhelmed by the powerful sex industry that they allowed fear to trump their duty to provide education for all.[8] Unable to halt the expansion of the sex districts, taunted by triumphant madams with their French Balls, and harboring the guilty knowledge that many of their own members patronized the sex trade, some reformers reacted by lashing out at a group of unfortunate children.

DOC AMES: THE REFORMERS' UNWITTING FRIEND

While the early 1890s had witnessed triumphs for the madams, the end of the decade saw changes to the Minneapolis prostitution industry that would reverberate into the twentieth century, and contribute to the demise of the quasi-licensed brothel system. In 1897 municipal court judge Andrew Holt decided to raise the usual monthly fines for brothel keepers from sixty to one hundred dollars. In most cases, monthly fines for ordinary brothel inmates were discontinued. The superintendent of police objected, saying the higher fines would cause some of the thirty-six openly operated bordellos to close and their inmates, "instead of being together in houses under surveillance," would scatter, making them much more difficult to control. But Judge Holt's decision stood.[9]

Although it was little noticed at the time, the municipal authorities were altering their long-standing, if unwritten, contract with bordello boarders. On the face of it, exempting ordinary boarders from fines reduced their business expenses. But it also meant they no longer had the unwritten protection of the law to engage in prostitution, placing them at odds with their employers, the madams. Even if the madams had to pay more each month, the law still protected their business dealings, while their inmates now occupied a legal shadow land. As in earlier purity crusades, when reformers tried to distinguish the "pitiful" prostitutes from the "exploitative" madams, the change allowed municipal authorities to maintain that they had no wish to punish the ordinary sex workers, only the madams.

A reform pushed by Minneapolis progressives in the mid-1890s resulted in an unforeseen and certainly unintended consequence, namely, the election of Doc Ames to a fourth term as mayor. Historian Carl Chrislock noted, "Minneapolis opinion makers began to advocate legislation limiting the use of money in politics and other measures designed to curb bossism. One tangible accomplishment of this activity was the establishment of the direct primary in Hennepin County by the 1899 legislature, a step taken at the request of Minneapolis leaders."[10] The direct or open primary system allowed any voter, regardless of party affiliation, to vote for any candidate in the primary. The top vote getter in each party would advance to the general election. In 1900 Ames, who had won three terms as a Democrat, filed as a Republican candidate for mayor. Despite vehement editorials opposing his candidacy in the *Minneapolis Journal* and *Tribune,* Ames narrowly won as the Republican nominee, helped in part by a three-way race against two relatively unknown and inexperienced candidates as well as a loyal Democratic base instructed to vote for him despite his new status as a Republican. In November Ames won handily against Democrat James Gray and Independent W. J. Dean, helped in part by endorsements from leading Republicans and even one of his opponents from the primary, as well as the very long coattails of presidential candidate, William McKinley.[11]

Ames and his lieutenants understood that his reign as mayor would be short and worked to plunder the city as quickly as they could. Shortly after taking office in early 1901, Ames appointed his brother,

Fred, chief of police and then fired over one hundred police officers. He replaced them with his own men, announcing that the police force would all be Republicans on his watch.[12] Ames appointed as chief of detectives professional gambler Norman King, who commenced to organize poker games run by card sharks. King and his assistants lured out-of-town visitors into rigged games in which the victims were effectively robbed and then threatened with arrest if they complained.[13]

Ames quickly expanded the executive branch at the expense of the judicial. On the tenth of the month, the usual date when prostitution fines were assessed, often totaling $3,500–$4,500 per month, a police representative informed the madams that they need not appear in municipal court. Ames had acted so abruptly that not even Judge Dickinson, who was expecting to preside over the regular hearings, had been notified. The police chief told the reporter that he was simply carrying out the orders of the mayor. In a later interview, Judge Dickinson said he had "the impression from a talk with Mayor Ames that the latter proposes after this to regulate prostitution without the help of the municipal court."[14] A few days later, Mayor Ames told a reporter that "the regulation of the social evil is strictly a police prerogative" and that "the Minneapolis resorts are taxed too high." Ames thought fifty dollars a month was the right amount, and "as for the opinion of the municipal court, he doesn't care a straw. It does not concern the court in the least."[15]

The madams soon found themselves in an impossible position. On one hand, they were threatened with indictment by a grand jury investigating municipal corruption, but on the other, they faced retaliation by Ames if they or their employees gave evidence. Many madams decided to leave the city in the hopes the situation would somehow be resolved. One reporter observed that by "Friday all of the houses of the 'red light' district were dark."[16] With the brothels closed, there was "a noticeable increase in the number of loudly or flashily-dressed women . . . who have heretofore seldom appeared in public . . . now promenading Nicollet Avenue sunny afternoons and in the evenings the downtown streets."[17]

In one sweeping move, Ames halved the amount of fines going into the municipal coffers and rejected the authority of the courts. Apparently the mayor collected the usual fines of one hundred dollars from madams on the off months, with the money going directly into his coffers. A subsequent investigation showed that Ames had imposed his own private system of "fines" on prostitutes who did not work out of established brothels within the designated sex districts, and it was these "fines" that would eventually lead to his conviction for bribery. One of Ames's former cronies, Irwin A. Gardner, later testified that Ames ordered him to compile "a list of these women who were running suspected houses of assignation in other than the regularly licensed district." For example, Addie Mills paid Gardner fifteen dollars for the privilege of operating a "cigar store" at 900 Third Street South.[18]

"Cut-rate licenses" were not the only services available from the Ames administration, however. Gardener also collected money from established madams in the rapidly declining First Street district, noting, "these ladies that were paying the money complained that the street walkers [in front of their bordellos] were interfering with their business." Gardner apparently promised that policemen would keep the street prostitutes away, lest clients' appetites were sated before they had a chance to enter a brothel. Ames had at last instituted the policies he had failed to impose during his third term as mayor: the direct payment of fines into his pocket.

Ames had other schemes to increase his personal wealth. In March 1902 he declared that a system of weekly inspections of brothel prostitutes for venereal disease would be instituted. City physicians would conduct these examinations and charge one dollar per exam. Reaction from one outraged newspaper declared the scheme "illegal, immoral and absolutely useless as a preventative measure against disease."[19] The article went on to explain that for such a system to be effective it would have to be thorough and free, and would require the services of at least six doctors and two or three bacteriologists. Since the new rule applied only to inmates of brothels, not other sex workers or much less their customers, the system had no chance of working. It also placed the city in the absurd position of certifying some prostitutes as safe and disease free.

By the spring of 1902, the regular district grand jury was convened. Wealthy Minneapolis businessman Hovey C. Clarke became the jury's foreman, and he, in turn, persuaded the jury to investigate Mayor Ames. Clarke used his own money to hire investigators loyal to him and gather evidence against Ames. He also offered deals to Ames's cronies to turn state's evidence. Soon, Ames and several members of his administration were indicted by the grand jury.[20]

By June the medical exams of bordello inmates were stopped, and the following month the two physicians who had conducted them and collected the fees were dismissed under protest. "Both Drs. Clark and Cohen insist that as Mayor Ames was president of the Board of Corrections and Charities they had no option in the work as in the line of their duties. Once public sentiment finally condemned the system, they abandoned the work voluntarily."[21]

The end of the Ames administration came when Ames and his brother Fred slipped out of town in July 1902. By August Mayor Ames, still on the run, had submitted his resignation. Fred Ames was apprehended and returned to Minneapolis for trial. He was found guilty and sentenced to a term in Stillwater state prison.

REFORMING THE CITY

Once Ames resigned, Alderman David P. Jones, president of the city council, became the acting mayor and served out the remainder of the term. A newspaper listed the things Jones would and would not do as mayor, such as reorganize the police department and remove "disreputable characters" from the residential neighborhoods; he would not "spy out men who wish to drink a cocktail on Sunday."[22] By September 1902, the Jones administration began to roll out the new rules regarding prostitution. The boundaries of the red-light districts were redefined. Women who operated outside the new boundaries were told to "get near the river" and move "into the 'red light' district or go out of business by October 1." The new red-light district was to be confined to a strip between the river and Washington Avenue South running from Nicollet Avenue to Twelfth Avenue South.[23]

There were other rules as well: newly appointed Police Superintendent Edward Waite decreed that bordellos could not sell liquor. Additionally, "no music will be tolerated [in brothels] on Sunday nights," and "inmates will not be allowed to stand in the doorways and hold conversations with persons passing." Nor would any minor of either sex be allowed inside bordellos, suggesting that any children living with their prostitute mothers would have to be sent away.[24]

The new rules were brave talk by an administration bent on reform, but enforcement was another matter. The new administration
intended to eliminate the Main Street red-light district, but the actual shutdown would not occur until several years later. Customers
expected to drink in brothels, and madams depended on liquor sales
for a large part of their profits. It was unlikely they would quit selling
liquor without a fight. The ban on Sunday night music put the city in
the curious position of sanctioning commercial sex but not music on
the Sabbath.

Spurred on by the desire to distance itself from the corrupt Ames
administration, the Jones administration's next move was to eliminate the monthly fines for madams. In early October a newspaper announced that the Board of Levy approved the mayor's plan to drop the
system of fines. In one summary action, Mayor Jones recharacterized
decades of Minneapolis history by declaring the "fines to be nothing
less than a piece of 'municipal grafting,'" arguing "the city should not
stoop to such a source of revenue."[25] At least one person noticed this
declaration as a form of revisionist history. In a newspaper article,
former mayor William Eustis objected to Jones's description of the
old system, even though he was in favor of trying out the new rules.[26]
Jones's reinterpretation of local history accused all former administra-
tions of being corrupt and diverting prostitution fines from the municipal treasury to their own pockets. A few days later the same newspaper praised the mayor's action, observing that it was "a long step
forward in the morals of local government in Minneapolis." While
admitting that the city had for years managed and controlled prostitution, and noting that the municipal court "has been collecting $40,000
a year from the keepers of the vile houses," it condemned the fact that
"court fines have been used not as a means of punishing or extermi-
nating crime, but as a means of licensing and protecting it."[27]

Unlike the reformers who waged war against the madams in
1880, Mayor Jones did not propose to completely suppress prostitution in the city. His go-slow approach was likely based on practical
considerations—one account noted that "citizens rarely, if ever com-
plain against these places [brothels]," and the initiative for dealing
with the issue rested with the police. The same source quoted an alderman who said that while he did not believe saloons should be legal,

he did not think either bordellos or saloons could be eliminated.[28] Nonetheless, the system of tolerated prostitution was gradually coming to an end. Once the monthly fines stopped, the unwritten but long-standing contract between the city and madams started to unravel. The brothels had gone from being a "necessary evil" that protected the virtue of well-behaved women to "a vice considered so dangerous to public morals that the laws of Minnesota make it a felony."[29] Jones did not seem to notice that keeping a brothel had been a felony for all the years that prostitution was considered necessary.

Meanwhile, momentum for municipal reform had further quickened when journalist Lincoln Steffens's article "The Shame of Minneapolis" appeared in the January 1903 issue of *McClure's Magazine,* the first of a series on municipal corruption around the country that was later collected into a book called *The Shame of the Cities.* Minneapolis reformers, like many others across the country, hailed this as a brilliant exposé on urban ills, but the story was a bit more complicated.

Many years later, Steffens explained in his autobiography that editor McClure had "dictated the title and thesis of the article I was going to write on Minneapolis before I left New York." McClure believed American democracy itself was the source of the evil and that "one man has to run a city just as one man has to run a business to make it a success." Steffens claimed that, by contrast, he hoped to "search like detectives for the keys to the mystery," but McClure "would not have it so." Steffens lost the fight and "what I went to Minneapolis to write was that democracy was a failure and that a good dictator was what is needed."[30]

Steffens glorified Hovey Clarke while equating Albert Ames with genuinely powerful city bosses, such as Boss Tweed of New York. A later study of city bosses, by contrast, painted Ames as handsome and "in personality exceedingly winning because of cordiality," but he "lacked self-control" and "was remarkably vain." Ames was "one of the easiest of easy bosses" but he "did not possess power over the entire government of Minneapolis," only over the police department, whereas other departments were under the direction of the city council. This is hardly the picture of a disciplined leader who could ruthlessly and efficiently run a big city for any length of time.[31]

Still, the embarrassing Ames administration and the Steffens ar-

ticle turned out to be great boons to Minneapolis reformers by allowing them to redefine the fight against prostitution and reinterpret
local history. In this view, the presence of successful madams and sex
districts was simply a local manifestation of the national problem of
rotting urban areas and bad government. There was an undercurrent
that suggested both corrupt elected officials and sex workers could
be driven from town by extralegal measures, such as Hovey Clarke's
hiring his own detectives. Reframing the question in this manner allowed reformers to ignore the many drivers of the commercial sex industry as well as the fact that it was a reform measure that had opened
the door for Ames to become mayor for the fourth time.

It was in this atmosphere that Ames was finally tracked down
and returned to the city for trial. In May 1903 he was convicted of
taking bribes from prostitutes and sentenced to six years in the state
prison.[32] One editorial declared the guilty verdict "an acquittal for
Minneapolis" and said that even though the town was "saturated with
personal sympathy for Dr. Ames," the jury had done the right thing.
The piece concluded that heroic public prosecutors "come by chance,
but the juries of the people are with us always." The Doc Ames story
did not end there, however.[33]

CLOSING DOWN THE MAIN STREET SEX DISTRICT

By 1903 Democrat James C. Haynes was elected to replace acting
mayor Jones. For the remainder of the era of regulated prostitution
in Minneapolis, Haynes and Jones would be elected to alternating
mayoral terms. Haynes continued the policy of gradually ending the
system of regulated prostitution. In the summer of 1903, a campaign
to shut down the Main Street red-light district gathered steam. Police
Superintendent E. J. Conroy announced he was "ready to turn his police loose" if nearby residents "make it known that they want Main
Street cleared of its evil resorts in order to secure the improvement of
the exposition ground as a park." But Conroy added that he did not
want "to go after them too fiercely for it is only right that they have a
few days in which to gather up their belongings and move away," as
by then some of the brothels had been in place for thirty years.[34]

Another account reported that East Side businessmen would be
glad to see the red-light district close, as the prostitutes did not make

many purchases in their stores. Perhaps shuttering the bordellos would wreak economic hardship on the building owners who lost their tenants, but the speaker was confident that when the sex trade was gone, these buildings could serve as hotels or decent boarding houses, since "the location is very central and accessible," and once "the exposition grounds have been transformed into a pretty park, which will attract people, then business will derive considerable more benefit from this district than it has for several decades."[35]

Opinion makers once again pinned their hopes for a Main Street revival on the Industrial Exposition Hall. After its brief glory as the site of the Republican national convention, the building had gone into bankruptcy. With more than seven acres under its roof, the building was simply too large for most uses. Marion Savage, best known as the owner of the racehorse Dan Patch, bought the hall for use as a warehouse for his mail-order business. At a public meeting, Savage seemed to promise to turn the Exposition Hall grounds into a public park if the city would shut down the Main Street red-light district. At another public rally, the Chute Brothers Real Estate Company offered to add their property near the Exposition Hall to the proposed park. Organizers of the rally "expect to have Main Street cleaned out in the course of the next month or two."[36]

After a few weeks had passed, the reformers' passion for closing the Main Street district cooled. Mayor Haynes stated that while he personally favored shutting down the East Side red-light district, he wanted to make certain there was sufficient public support, apparently aware that closing down the district would not be universally popular. Marion Savage then announced that he had never offered to donate land for a park, or in the words of one reporter, if anyone held the idea that "the city of Minneapolis would obtain a park by purifying and fumigating and deodorizing East Main Street it is news to M. W. Savage." Savage did state that he planned to make landscape improvements to the Exposition Hall and that the public would be welcome to use the grounds, but he would retain ownership. Still, one editorial proclaimed, "the dives are doomed" because they "disfigure the most conspicuous part of the finest river aspect in the center of the city." The writer suggested, however, perhaps inadvertently, that the public outcry against the red-light district had a somewhat artificial, manipu-

Two buildings that were formerly bordellos at 9 and 11 Main Street Southeast, about 1948. By this date, the Main Street red-light district had been closed for more than forty years. Photograph courtesy of the Minnesota Historical Society.

lated quality: "It was only needful to arouse public opinion on this head to stimulate energetic official action."[37] The red lights of Main Street burned on through 1903.

Early in 1904, Mayor Haynes announced that the Main Street district would close no later than April 1.[38] As the authorities worked to close one red-light area, there were hints that their actions would have widespread repercussions, as no one could agree where the commercial sex industry should be relocated. One report observed, "Hennepin Avenue is much stirred up over the theatrical invasion of the red-light denizens from the East Side." The story continued with comments by businessmen such as Thomas Voegeli, who thought that prostitutes should be concentrated somewhere else given that "Hennepin Avenue is destined ultimately to become a street catering to the higher class of trade." W. C. Badger of Hennepin Avenue Properties thought, "The evil ought to be kept down south [on Eleventh Avenue] with the rest of this class of people." A man identified only as a leading East Side citizen said, "The clearing of Main Street was not a matter for the Eastside alone to approve, but something that affected the whole city."[39]

The deadline was not met, but a few weeks later, Main Street was described as "dark." Although some brothels were still occupied, "the music and dancing has ceased, and the absence of the hacks [taxi-cabs], which formerly were to be found standing in front, emphasizes the fact that the women have taken the mayor at his word."[40]

Not every Main Street bordello had gone out of business. In his earlier announcement that "when the order comes to close the disreputable houses on the East Side, it will include every place on Main Street, northeast as well as southeast," Mayor Haynes was referring to Edna Hamilton. Her bordello was described as being "at the very portals of the East Side and was the most conspicuous on account of its magnificence." Its presence "was a disgrace and constant source of pollution."[41] Still, shutting down Hamilton's brothel would prove difficult, because like her predecessor, Jennie Jones, she served a very wealthy, well-connected clientele. For example, a "prominent politician" communicated to one of the organizers of the public rallies to shut down Main Street that "one house at least should be allowed to remain, since its record was fairly good."[42]

Hamilton's bordello was still in operation a year later, with six young women living there who carried on the tradition of giving misleading answers about their occupations. This time, a seamstress, laundress, sales lady, nurse, domestic, and dressmaker occupied the house. Or at least, that is what the census taker was told. That same year, Hamilton and five of her workers were arrested for being a "disorderly house at 25 Northeast Main Street."[43]

At some point it became clear that this was no short-lived purity crusade. The red lights on Main Street would be permanently extinguished, and Hamilton would have to move her operation. Having run the most ostentatious brothel in the city, Hamilton would not relocate without a suitable replacement. She would require a house built to her specifications, and former madam Nettie Conley was the perfect choice for this task. In the spring of 1905, she began building a three-story, brick bordello for Hamilton at 1107 Second Street South, next door to the one she had built a few years earlier at 1109 Second Street

South. Conley again hired architects Bertrand and Chamberlin to design the new bordello.[44] Hamilton and her crew moved out of the last openly operated brothel on Main Street and into the new place late in 1905. By 1910 twelve prostitutes lived there as well as six servants.

Late in the year, a newspaper obliquely noted that Hamilton had finally vacated her old bordello by reporting that some businessmen hoped to buy the property and turn it into a hospital. The reporter asserted, "East Siders see the hand of fate in its transformation." The luxurious bordello would be cleansed of its former associations, and "angels of mercy will alleviate the misery of the unfortunate and still the cries of pain."[45] The writer expressed confidence that a subscription plan would raise enough money to purchase the building and remodel it as a modern hospital. Reformers may have hoped to eradicate the contamination of prostitution from the bordello by turning it into a hospital staffed by well-behaved women instead of the brazen variety who sold sex, but "the hand of fate" evidently did not raise enough money for the purchase price: Hamilton owned the building for the rest of her life.

WHITE SLAVERY

As early as the 1890s, Minneapolis experienced a rising public hysteria over what would be called "white slavery," currently known as human trafficking. Although there was little hard evidence of its being a genuine problem in the city, popular outrage over white slavery would play a role in ending regulated prostitution in the city. Fear of this supposedly widespread problem persisted long after the era of tolerated brothel prostitution ended.

Certain public arenas, such as saloons and dance halls, were identified as recruiting grounds for those who would lure or kidnap innocent young women into prostitution. In one account of the Jumbo Saloon, on Washington Avenue South, a reporter described the "four blank beer-stained walls" as a place where "the hopes and happiness for the here and the hereafter of many young lives are bartered away . . . daily." Although most of its patrons were male, a few women ventured in. As the reporter saw it, they were mostly not prostitutes but rather "young unhappy girls of the poorer and more ignorant classes, unfortunate and deserted wives, working women whose hard lives and dismal homes make the glitter, the excitement and the free love-making of the place a fascination and a solace."[46] The reporter described how these women unfortunately met unsavory characters, namely, "the professional recruiting agents of the regular established places [brothels] about the city." Or possibly worse, the victims "are deceived with false promises," filled with liquor, and made insensible to their frightful dangers as the recruiters trick them into going "to the vile dens at Hurley [a Wisconsin lumbering center] and other places of that description."[47]

By the turn of the century, campaigns against white slavery were gathering strength across the country. Historian Timothy Gilfoyle has noted that "with European immigration on the rise, Americans grew more concerned with growing problems of prostitution in American cities."[48] These concerns were often manifested in the belief that the commercial sex industry was dependent on a steady supply of white slaves forced into the life by shady foreigners or racial minorities. And there was the enduring belief was that corrupt officials either ignored the problem or derived profit from forced prostitution. In 1901 a New York district attorney detailed the workings of the "infamous cadet" (pimp) system "by which young girls are lured into disorderly houses and kept prisoners there. The police, he said, would quickly find and release such girls from their horrible fate if they did not know that by doing so they would incur the displeasure of the district leader."[49] A report of the Committee of Fifteen, a citizens' group formed in 1900 to fight vice in New York, concluded that prostitution threatened to overrun the city.[50]

Reformers, who believed Minneapolis was rife with white slavers aiming to prey upon young women and force them into prostitution, gathered ammunition from two incidents that occurred in 1904. In one instance, at least two newspaper articles broke the news that police believed they had uncovered "a practical reproduction of New York's 'Cadet System' in this city," complete with a customary victim who was "homeless and an orphan," who had come from the country to earn her living.[51] One newspaper stated that Louis Herschowitz (or Herschovitz in some accounts) had drugged a sixteen-year-old girl and then tried to "sell her bodily into a life of shame."[52] As the story unfolded, however, that narrative became less clear. The young woman worked as a waitress in a restaurant where Herschowitz often ate. He persuaded her to come out with him after work and then gave her alcohol to drink, after which she lost consciousness. Herschowitz next made arrangements with a madam, Clara Larson, to have the victim enter her brothel as an inmate.

Larson became suspicious, though, and laid a trap for Herschowitz, telling him to return with the girl. "As he started away from the resort, after taking the girl there, Sergeant Fred Johnson stepped out and arrested Herschowitz." Larson told the police that "she would be only too glad to prosecute a man who would deliberately ruin a young girl's life and, true to her word, she appeared before the grand jury this morning." At this point, it appeared as if the intended victim had been rescued by a representative of the very industry supposedly bent on her destruction.[53]

Within a few weeks a very different story emerged, as various newspapers had carried the story back to the young woman's hometown. After Herschowitz was convicted on a charge of abduction, the "orphaned" girl's father came forth as a witness to her incorrigibility. Calling the girl "the terror of her town," one account claimed, "in the face of her escapades in the little country town in which it appears no youth was safe from her wiles," it seemed fair that the evidence against Herschowitz be reexamined. The district attorney decided the evidence did not support the conviction and set Herschowitz free.[54]

Another account of trafficking in teenage girls followed close on the heels of the Herschowitz story. This time four men of Chinese ancestry were charged with "enticing girls into chop suey restaurants and paying them to pander to most bestial lust." Sensational headlines followed that characterized it as the "most revolting crime in [the] history of the city," along with assertions that detectives "believe they have secured evidence of the most elaborate and debased system of organized vice ever exposed in Minneapolis." A subsequent editorial excused racial hatred because "that sort of thing breaks out wherever there is a Chinese quarter." Another editorial reasoned that because the Chinese face discrimination, "the result is that they are little more than parasites on the community" and hold "few scruples about preying [on other people] in any way that their passions suggest." Adding fuel to the fire, the *Minneapolis Tribune* carried a story from Philadelphia that claimed a national ring supplied white slaves to Chinese men after several young women were found imprisoned in Chinatown.[55]

A few days later a Minneapolis newspaper announced that "the inherent depravity of the Chinese was again brought to the attention of the police" when John Leon, a Chinese immigrant with a white wife, was accused of molesting his fourteen-year-old stepdaughter. At first it was difficult to tell from the newspaper account if Leon was in more trouble for marrying a white woman or for allegedly abusing the girl. Described as a "wily Chinaman," Leon had won the affections of a young widow and married her, just a few years after arriving in the United States. Even if their neighbors described the couple as living seemingly "happily at their home at 3560 Snelling Avenue" along with their three other children, or that Mrs. Leon had no reason to mistrust her husband, the police declared they "have a solid case against Leon." Within a few days, however, the story changed dramatically. Apparently, "the accounts of the Chinese outrages" (i.e., the story of the Chinese men who were supposedly trafficking in young girls) "inflamed the mind of Anna Leon, who has been tormented more or less for years with having a Chinaman for a father with a desire to get even with him." According to her parents, Anna had been "a most notorious liar ever since she was a little girl," and had even accused her mother of consorting with other men. Charges against John Leon were dropped, and Anna was sent to the state training school for girls.[56]

Despite articles and editorials pressing the idea of Chinese immigrants as threats to the general community, it would have been difficult to identify a genuine "Chinese quarter" within Minneapolis, as there were fewer than 100 people of Chinese ancestry living in the city in 1900. By 1905 a census revealed a total population of 261 Chinese, largely male, in the entire state with only 86 of those residing in Minneapolis. Many of these individuals worked in laundries or restaurants, although there was at least one store at 1217 Nicollet that specialized in Chinese goods. That same year, the population of the city was pegged at well over a quarter of a million. Meanwhile, contemporary city directories reveal about fifteen laundries with identifiable Chinese names scattered around the city whose proprietors, and possibly employees, lived on-site. There were three Chinese restaurants, two on the 200 block of present-day Marquette Avenue and another on nearby Nicollet Avenue, and these may have served as the cultural center of the tiny Chinese community.[57]

Meanwhile, the four men in the white slavery case were charged and taken off to jail; their bail was set at an extraordinary five thousand dollars apiece. To shape public opinion, one newspaper used Louis Herschowitz and the four Chinese men as examples of "the dangers lurking in the city for young girls." It was reported that the Humane Society was planning to employ someone "to watch over young girls in the street, and now that public sentiment is at its highest pitch and parents can see the danger that threatens their daughters, a definite crusade will start at once."[58] A few days later another story appeared, detailing a conference of the Woman's Christian Temperance Union at which the municipal authorities were condemned for not taking action. "The purpose was to decide what could be done to protect young girls and to arouse interest in driving out the social evil." Underlying was the threat of vigilante or extralegal action by a committee, "to see that the matter is properly presented to the grand jury, taking the matter into its own hands if the police authorities fail to handle it satisfactorily."[59] This account was followed by another that asserted "public sentiment has been deeply stirred on the question of the protection of young girls from the vices that beset the feet of the ignorant and wayward," while enumerating the various sources of these dangers such as public dance halls, saloons, and exposing young girls to either too little or too much sex education.[60]

From the very start, the story of the Chinese men who supposedly coerced teenage girls into prostitution did not quite square with the popular white slave narrative. The men had neither kidnapped nor drugged the girls, but rather offered them jobs, with the consent of their parents, who were glad to have the additional weekly income of four dollars. One mother, a widow, explained that she thought her daughter was working in a factory and used "the pittance which my daughter took home to buy bread and clothing for the other little ones at home."[61] Whether this mother was telling the truth or hoping to generate sympathy, and thus deflect blame, is difficult to judge. Soon, the seemingly clear-cut case against the four men deteriorated. During the trial of R. Sing, testimony was given that some older girls had led the younger ones into "consorting with the Chinamen" after telling them "how easy it was to get money." Despite his denials of guilt, Sing was convicted and sentenced to ninety days in jail.[62] Moy S.

Jim, described in one early account as "the king bee of Chinamen in Minneapolis," was acquitted, and shortly thereafter the two other men, Gee Lee and Jim Lee, were set free. Unlike the lurid allegations that made front-page headlines, this news was buried deep in back pages of the newspaper, which observed that releasing the men "practically makes a fiasco of the whole list of sensations on the alleged 'yellow peril' in Minneapolis." But this was hardly the end of the white slavery scare in Minneapolis.[63]

MORE TRIALS FOR DOC AMES

Meanwhile, late in January 1904, the Minnesota State Supreme Court overturned Doc Ames's guilty verdict. The matter might have been dropped at that point, as Ames was out of office and unlikely to harm the reputation of the city any further. However, the former mayor was subjected to another four trials over the course of the year, all of which ended with hung juries. During Ames's fifth trial, one newspaper commented that although the locals had lost interest, tourists flocked to the courtroom, "because the 'Ames trial' has become an institution in Minneapolis, and, as one woman from St. Louis put it, 'I want to say I've seen it, you know.'"[64]

At the close of the fifth trial in December, not only was Ames free but charges against some of his former companions in crime were dropped as well. Newspapers reacted with angry editorials. One observed, "We shall not be able to excuse ourselves here in Minneapolis for this result." Another theorized that despite careful jury selection intended to root out any with sympathy toward criminals, "the fact that so much remains must be evidence that the poison is widely diffused in the community," stating that the "object of these trials" was less to punish Doc Ames than "to purify the community and vindicate it before a scornful world." The only comfort the writer could find was that "we share this taint with every American city of considerable size. The record of American lawlessness is growing big and ominous."[65]

Perhaps the jurors did not find the evidence against Ames convincing, or perhaps they were reacting to how the forces of reform were directing the latest purity crusades within Minneapolis and the collapse of the white slavery trials a few weeks earlier. One scholar noted, "Ames possessed few of the puritanic qualities of his father." This might explain his four terms as mayor and why the juries chose to side with Ames in the same way that the populace had voted for him earlier in reaction to reformers who had gone too far in imposing Liquor Patrol Limits on the city or sending madams away to the penitentiary. As the campaign to shut down the Main Street district unfolded, it was clear that rich men would still have easy access to commercial sex, while bordellos at the opposite end of the economic spectrum were being increasingly restricted. The scolding editorials that followed the last trial suggest the city was not of one mind about Albert Ames, or what constituted municipal corruption, or even if there was a "Shame of Minneapolis."[66]

HOPING TO CLOSE THE FIRST STREET DISTRICT

After having more or less successfully shuttered the Main Street red-light district, reformers turned their attention to the west side of the river, starting with the First Street district. Late in 1904, the superintendent of police announced that a portion of the First Street district, along Second Street South from Nicollet to Third Avenue South, would be closed down within a few days.[67] After this deadline passed without results, the city then declared that the brothels on Second Street South would be closed by February 1. Described as a "festering region" and "one of the poison spots of the city," the area was "exceptionally objectionable" as it was in full view of people going to and from the train station. If Edna Hamilton's establishment was "conspicuous on account of its magnificence," the First Street district was offensive for being too gritty and racially mixed. Between High and First Streets South, many "tumbledown frame shacks" were inhabited by prostitutes "of all nationalities and color. Negroes and whites occupy buildings side by side, while a bagnio filled with Japanese women has been recently installed."[68]

The end of the First Street district had been proclaimed in 1890, and the 1905 announcement proved premature as well. The denizens of this red-light district and their customers were more tenacious than the city's enforcement mechanisms. One madam, May Schultz, who had been operating a First Street red-light district since at least 1905, was still in business there when she was caught in a 1915 raid.[69] Instead of closing down, the First Street district experienced a minor building boom once the red-light district across the river was shuttered.

The First Street South red-light district as seen from the Hall and Dann Barrel Factory on Third Avenue South, ca. 1907. The two-story brick building (228 First Street South) on the far right was built by madam Della White but later taken over by Jennie Jones. By this time, the First Street district was in steep decline. The squat building two doors down (210–212 First Street South) was built in 1905 after the Main Street district closed. Across the street, a couple of former bordellos had already been removed and replaced by the Janney, Semple, and Hill warehouse. Photograph by Charles J. Hibbard; courtesy of the Minnesota Historical Society.

In 1905 architect William S. Hunt was hired to design a three-story brick "dwelling" behind the bordello run by madam Schultz at 207 First Street South. An insurance map clearly identifies this as a "female boarding house," so there is little doubt as to its function. But unlike the grand bordellos of Eleventh Avenue, this one was modest, costing less than $3,700 to complete. More striking is the address of 211 First Street South, even though the building fronted the alley behind First Street South and looked out on a stable.[70] Unlike the other First Street bordellos built in the 1880s or those in the Eleventh Avenue district that openly faced the principal road, to welcome in visitors, this one was hiding from the greater world. Across the same alley, another "female boarding house" lurked with the ostensible address of 222½ Second Street South, but like the other house, this too apparently faced the alley. Another bordello went up at 210–212 First Street South; it was described on an insurance map as a female boarding house of "artificial stone" and cost about $1,200 to complete. Apparently, this most basic of buildings even lacked indoor plumbing. This structure was not a parlor bordello, but more akin to the poor quality "cribs" found in the Storyville district of New Orleans, where individual prostitutes worked out of tiny rooms, often renting them by the hour.[71]

Just as the grand bordellos of Ida Dorsey and Jennie Jones reflected their aspirations and the clientele who supported them, this cheap concrete-block building reflected the quality of customers in the First Street district of the late nineteenth and early twentieth centuries. As the neighborhood increasingly became the home base of migrant workers, First Street madams no longer entertained a wealthy clientele as they had in the 1880s, but rather the seasonal workers who rode the rails back to Minneapolis to wait for the next job, which might be harvesting wheat in the Dakotas or working in northern Minnesota lumber camps.

By 1908, municipal officials were again announcing a "cleanup" of the Bridge Square area by removing the brothels and saloons and replacing them with a public park. This plan was part of a determined campaign of civic improvement, which one report noted, "It now appears that concerted action, so much lacking in previous attempts, will insure the consummation of the plan."[72] Perhaps these events were inspired by earlier efforts on the other side of the river to build a new park if the city shut down the Main Street red-light district. The ambition to radically transform the appearance of the riverfront had been around since at least 1906, when architects John Jaeger, C. B. Stravs, C. E. Edwins, and F. E. Halden unveiled a new plan for Minneapolis called "City Practical, City Beautiful." Although never realized, the plan called for remaking the city's birthplace with a diagonal street grid that would be laid over existing roadways. Two monumental "public concourses" would be placed on either side of the river, requiring the wholesale destruction of many blocks and obliterating much of the city's built history.[73] Rewriting the city's past in architecture seemed to be the goal of more than one plan. When a possible site for a new post office was under consideration that same year, one newspaper recounted both innocuous and lurid highlights of the favored site's history. Instead, the article advocated building the post office at a nearby location on Washington Avenue South where the "famous Jumbo Saloon was located" and where, over the years, many crimes had been committed, one "finally ending with a murder." That block had also been part of the red-light district, and, the writer concluded, "as a wiping out of memories, the taking of Block 40 would be a better sponge than the block selected by the public-spirited men of the city."[74]

Mayor Haynes declared that all brothels between the Union Depot near the Hennepin Avenue Bridge and the Milwaukee Depot at the corner of Third and Washington Avenues South would be closed by the first of May. As madams investigated relocation to the Eleventh Avenue district, the neighbors predictably voiced their objections. Henry F. Burt of the Pillsbury House asserted that bordellos were "a notorious menace to the morality of the young people of the district" and that "our final aim is not to resist an increase in the number of these resorts, but to eliminate them altogether from our midst."[75] The city also hoped to remove the saloons in the First Street district and, by extension, their patrons. A subcommittee of the city council proposed that liquor licenses for several Bridge Square saloons would be renewed only for one year; that gave the proprietors time to relocate, even though they had not broken any law. Citing the "noisome sights and offensive odors," one newspaper stated that the "saloons that crowd both sides of the square are principally responsible for this condition of affairs. They are mostly low groggeries that attract the street loafer and the expectorating transient." The writer predicted that once the saloons were gone, the old city hall razed, and a park built, Bridge Square's character would immediately improve, drawing new businesses that would offer goods and services aimed at the carriage trade.[76]

Late in 1908 several architects published their proposals for making over Bridge Square in the *Western Architect*. Their designs were variations on the theme of an expansive public plaza surrounded by monumental buildings based on European models. The accompanying text claimed that Minneapolis's planning for public spaces had not kept pace with the city's private residences in terms of cleanliness and refinement. The author admitted that, at least in theory, "interesting structures and such natural contours as will lend themselves readily to the preservation of sentimental association" should be retained. The plans showed, however, that all the standing buildings surrounding Bridge Square would be demolished. The author observed that "clay is clay even though once a Caesar, and in its unsanitary condition must be removed. Thus it is with most of the structures in this country that in their time made history and the ravages of time have made dust heaps." Better that a city "is beautified by modern architecture and engineering science," while those who wish to study a city's history could read the written accounts or paintings, rather than examining the actual buildings and streets where that history took place. Architect Edwin Hewitt noted in his plans for Bridge Square that a "fitting memorial" to the old city hall, which he proposed to demolish, would be "an inscription." As political leaders rewrote the history of the city, architects and planners proposed to accomplish a similar feat through demolition and recasting the built environment after European models.[77]

CLOSING THE ELEVENTH AVENUE DISTRICT

The campaign to permanently close the Eleventh Avenue red-light district may have begun as early as 1907. While some outraged citizens might gather in mass meetings to call for the closure of bordellos, another group of reformers took a different approach. Accompanied by a reporter and police escort that would allow them visit brothels without a subsequent blot on their reputations, Mrs. Norah E. R. Perkins of Milwaukee, representing the Mutual Rescue Alliance, led her followers on a tour of the bordellos that ranged "from the meagerly furnished to the most sumptuously appointed." One newspaper observed, "At a time when the people were pouring out from the theaters and the cafes uptown last night, unusual scenes were witnessed in the underworld." Going from door to door, the party of "pure women" were in each instance "invited into the dance room," and "mingled with the scantily garbed or gaily bedecked inmates." Kneeling alongside "women sodden in sin and novitiates of the half-world life," the alliance workers prayed for the salvation of the inmates.[78]

According to the reporter, the rescue workers were treated as honored guests at every stop. "At the first resort the visit was a surprise and the inmates were clad in accustomed negligee garb, but at other resorts the word had gone ahead by telephone and the inmates appeared in their best parlor gowns." At another brothel, the piano player, "a genial man," offered to play accompaniment to the hymn singers. At the final visit, the African American madam said, "'Come again. You will be welcome anytime.'"[79] The reporter did note that the word "sure" seemed to be "the invariable response" to any question asked by the visitors, whether they requested entrance into a bordello or wondered if the inmates wanted to change their current situations. Apparently, the reporter took the answer at face value: "It was a hopeful, even wistful response and was never given flippantly or inconsiderately."[80]

During 1908, when most municipal efforts concentrated on closing down the First Street district, the campaign to shut down Eleventh Avenue was most concerned with where to relocate the red-light district, rather than how to suppress prostitution completely. Reporting on a meeting of South Minneapolis citizens, a newspaper observed: "If some one will point out a place in which to transplant the South Side red light district he will have gone a long way toward solving the problem now confronting Mayor J. C. Haynes and the South Side citizens' committee."[81] The article suggested the underlying threat of vigilante action. While the committee understood that it would be difficult to simply shut down the long-established red-light area, business owners "all stand firm for the eradication of the plague spot, and they rather expect the co-operation of the mayor. They do not want to do anything without the mayor, but if he doesn't act, they will."[82]

The year 1909 opened with a new purity campaign led by the Civic Federation of Minneapolis, a collection of temperance societies, churches, and other civic groups formed earlier in hopes of reforming the city.[83] Deeply disturbed by a private, ticketed, New Year's dance that apparently featured a gambling room and inebriated men and women, federation member Dr. C. E. Burton of the Lyndale Avenue Congregational Church accused the police force of being blind to evil. Police Chief Frank Corriston replied to the charge by saying, "You are a set of cranks. You don't want results; you want blood." Burton countercharged that the only blood drawn was "by that monster, police-protected vice— the blood of our fairest women, of our most hopeful young men."[84]

The federation also railed against saloons, immoral literature, drugs dispensed by "lax druggists who sell the drugs without question," cigarettes, and burlesque theaters. One newspaper mockingly noted that the reformers were shocked to learn that even choirboys clandestinely lit up. Still, by June the federation claimed to have pledges from 116 employers not to hire boys who smoked. By year's end, the

A temperance parade in Minneapolis in 1910, featuring a wagon filled with children and bearing a banner that proclaimed, "For the protection of innocence and virtue, stop the liquor traffic." Photograph by Edward D. Mayo; courtesy of the Minneapolis Collection, Hennepin County Library.

federation's "purity squad," working in conjunction with the police department, was given credit for more than five hundred arrests on charges that included public drunkenness, prostitution, operating an illegal saloon, gambling, selling opium, and vagrancy.[85]

If some viewed the Civic Federation's efforts as ridiculous, others took seriously another concurrently conducted campaign, namely, the growing concern over white slavery. The *Minneapolis Journal* urged the legislature to approve two measures that would "seek to stamp out the infamous 'white slave trade.'" One bill outlawed soliciting young women coming to the city into prostitution, while the other prevented madams from holding their boarders' personal property as security for debt.[86]

The anxiety over white slavery was not limited to Minneapolis. After several years, the simmering national campaign against white slavery reached a boiling point by late 1909. Minneapolis newspapers regularly carried articles on the "national white slave war" that was being conducted in big cities such as Chicago and New York. The *New York Times* provided extensive coverage of the campaign as reformers maintained the evil was spreading throughout the country, while spokesmen for groups that were targeted as human traffickers, such as immigrants and Jewish communities, vehemently denied the charges. *McClure's Magazine* featured articles such as "The Daughters of the Poor," which named New York as the "leader of the world" in the white slave trade, and baldly stated that Russian and Hungarian Jews were directing this trade. Editor Sam McClure told a large audience of New York reformers that the shocking articles he printed only hinted at the true extent of the problem. "The horrors of white slavery have scarcely been opened to the public."[87] Late in November, Illinois congressman James Robert Mann, who was chairman of the House Committee on Interstate and Foreign Commerce, began drafting legislation that would bear his name aimed at stopping the white slave trade.[88]

Meanwhile, by 1910 the Minneapolis campaign against human trafficking intensified even as any evidence for it remained elusive. The Reverend T. W. Stout called for a crusade against organized white slave traffic even though he admitted he had no personal knowledge of it, at the same time insisting that "there is, nevertheless, far more activity of this nature than the public dreams of," and asserting that "not one girl in fifty would come alone in safety to this city from these hired thugs." He urged the city not to wait for actual cases to surface, but to "take the initiative and ferret out all there is here without waiting for popular clamor."[89]

Around this same time, the Minnesota Federation of Women's Clubs distributed pamphlets statewide warning parents about traffickers who preyed upon young girls in the cities. The clubwomen claimed that they did not want to interfere with employers nor have their efforts mistaken for a crusade to keep all women from seeking employment outside the home. Still, they claimed that every year thousands of girls were taken by "white slave traders who have reduced their art to a national and international system," with "ramifications from the Atlantic seaboard to the Pacific Ocean, with clearing houses or distribution centers in nearly all the large cities." As an afterthought, Mrs. C. G. Highbee, president of the state federation, said the Minnesota clubs were not prepared to declare if such white slave traffic actually existed in the Twin Cities, but would nevertheless distribute the pamphlets as a preventive measure.[90]

Reformers' belief in a well-organized white slave trade was so strong that it did not matter that no one could find any proof of its existence in the state. As women's clubs sent out warnings, a government investigator and former New York City detective named Mr. Freimuth failed to find any evidence of white slavery in Minnesota. He concluded that the inmates of Minnesota bordellos took up that life by choice.[91] The persistent belief in a large-scale, internationally operated system of human trafficking would soon have repercussions for the commercial sex industry in the city. Meanwhile, by February two versions of the White Slave Traffic Act, more commonly known as the Mann Act, received approval in both houses of the United States Congress. By June the House and the Senate resolved the differences between the two bills, the final version passed, and President William Howard Taft signed it into law.[92]

It was in this atmosphere that Minneapolis citizens launched their final campaign against the Eleventh Avenue district, despite a warning by Police Chief Frank Corriston. Corriston, who favored segregation (officially designated red-light areas), argued that "it is the only way to handle this sort of thing. Wherever in other cities these districts have been wiped out, they have invariably been established again after two or three years." Hundreds of citizens attended a mass rally on

February 14, 1910. Speakers declared that the brothels of the Eleventh Avenue district would be vacated by March 1. The Reverend W. E. Paul, pastor of Riverside Chapel, asserted, "The sentimental idea of segregation is all wrong." He claimed that "there are 300 inmates of these places, but there are 3,000 more who are there. If we drive these 300 out it will mean only that the city will begin to notice the 3,000." Despite the fact that no one could actually find any white slave traffic in the city, Paul flatly stated, "This district is the hub of the white slave traffic. Knock out the hub and the ribs and spokes will fall in." Frank Nelson, president of Minnesota College, announced, "It is a righteous cause and it cannot fail."[93]

Although it did not quite meet the stated deadline, the South Side citizens' campaign did achieve its objective on April 10. Nineteen madams were arrested in a morning raid, among them Ida Dorsey and Edna Hamilton. One newspaper attributed the raid to the citizens' campaign to close the district that had begun two years earlier. The raid was precipitated by yet another mass rally held ten days earlier at which the mayor had been denounced for failing to carry out his promise to close the district. The citizens then went to a district court judge to have him appoint a special attorney who would issue arrest warrants for the madams. A few days before the raid, the county attorney announced that all brothels would be closed permanently. Interestingly, no warrants had been served on any of the First Street brothels, even though it was common knowledge they were still operating. No mention was made of the police uncovering any white slaves during the raid.[94]

As the South Side citizens' committee reported "elation" over the removal of the red-light district from their midst, spokesman Henry F. Burt admitted that "no particular thought had been given to the ultimate disposal of the evil," believing it should be left "to the mayor and the city council to wrestle with the problem." James Peterson, attorney for the Sixth Ward activists, believed that "most of the women [prostitutes] will move to Chicago, St. Paul or some other city. Those who remain will probably get some honest work to do." The problem of "what to do with the inmates" remained, however. To prevent the brothels from reopening, police patrolled the Eleventh Street district as the inmates of those brothels went uptown to work the cafés and restaurants.[95]

Police matron Sarah Schaeffer proposed paying the fares of the bordello inmates who agreed to return to their homes, claiming that this would help the prostitutes as well as prevent them from scattering about the city. "This action will get these people out of the city and results that would naturally follow the breaking up of the segregation plan, will to large extent be eliminated." Speaking on behalf the Sixth Ward movement, Henry Burt seconded Schaeffer's plan and offered to provide money for the prostitutes to leave town. No one asked the most basic question of whether the displaced inmates had a home to which they could return or how they would earn a living once they got there. Meanwhile, Nick Smith, captain of the Minneapolis detectives, worried that "one hundred secret places will spring up in place of the twenty three just closed."[96]

In addition to the inmates who were now working all over the city, the madams charged the authorities were arbitrarily depriving them of their livelihood and destroying the value of their property. One un-identified madam was quoted as saying, "We had to pay high prices for the property and are not going to sell it for nothing," noting a rumor that the red-light district was being eyed by railroad interests for new railway terminals or other businesses that hoped to buy their property cheaply. She continued, "If that is the power back of the movement, we will fight it. We do not have to sell."[97]

It is difficult to say if the railroads truly wanted the Eleventh Ave-nue district properties. At the grand jury examinations after the raid, the madams' defense attorneys brought up possible links between the South Side citizens' campaign and railroad interests. When quizzed by a defense attorney, Henry Burt denied being employed by the Great Western Railway. But he was less certain when asked if the railroad was connected to the citizens' committee. When asked if officials of the Great Western had ever talked about getting rid of the Eleventh Avenue bordellos, Burt said some railroad officials attended a meeting of the citizens' committee, but he denied receiving any payments from the railroad for promising to shut down the red-light district. When asked by a defense attorney, "You understand, though, that money was paid?" Burt replied, "What I may say on that point is hearsay. I never saw any money given to anyone, but I heard that the Great Western gave money to this committee." Burt's testimony further revealed that the committee had received five hundred dollars from the railroad to hire an attorney. In response to the county attorney's objection, the judge ruled this point irrelevant to the proceedings.[98]

By linking the South Siders' purity campaign with predatory rail-road interests, the madams' lawyers hoped to discredit the citizens' group, suggesting their motives were not to protect the public welfare but to collude in an ill-disguised attempt to seize the madams' hard-won real estate. If the madams' property could be devalued or seized, then other property holders were at risk too. Whatever the outcome, the madams were not going to meekly acquiesce and close up shop.

Two weeks after the raid, D. C. Pierre, characterized as a taxpaying property owner in the Sixth Ward, presented the county attorney a petition signed by 624 other Sixth Ward businessmen and residents. The petition requested that the grand jury drop all charges against the Eleventh Ward madams because the madams were looking to re-locate to other Sixth Ward neighborhoods. "The businessmen," Pierre said, "feel that segregation is the solution, and as the conditions have been allowed to grow up under the systems in that part of the city, cer-tain merchants are now injured." The petition asked that the brothel proprietors be allowed to remain in the designated red-light district. Apparently the petitioners did not like the results of the campaign, as business owners noted that "their respective trades [have] been on the decrease at an alarming rate" since the raid and laid the blame on police measures that were "forced by the South Side committee," all of which suggested that opinion in the Sixth Ward had never been solidly in favor of closing the red-light district, despite the reformers' claims.[99]

A few of the madams caught in the April raid simply forfeited their bail and left town, but the majority of the indicted madams paid hundred-dollar fines. None were sentenced to the penitentiary. The judge and other elected officials were reluctant to impose harsh penal-ties on the madams at this point, hoping no doubt that the April raid would serve as a warning that the old rules had changed. Open brothels would no longer be tolerated; if the authorities could not end prostitu-tion, at least they could make it less visible. The predictable result was that it was also harder to control. Some madams would retire from the business, while others would continue in the business that they knew best, albeit less openly. The era of tolerated prostitution was officially over in Minneapolis, but closing the Eleventh Avenue red-light district abated neither the commercial sex trade nor the white slavery hysteria.

FIVE

Vice Report
After the Bordellos Closed

Once the Minneapolis city fathers made the decision to suppress rather than segregate prostitution, there was a demand (ironically, perhaps) that the entire issue receive serious study. In July 1910, fifty-seven prominent men petitioned Mayor James C. Haynes to conduct an investigation of what they termed the "Social Evil."[1] Soon a fifteen-member commission headed by Marion Shutter, a Universalist minister, was investigating how law enforcement, saloons, dance halls, economic conditions, home discipline, and "the influx of a new type of foreign element" that has "without question, tended to lower the social and morals stands of the community," related to prostitution.[2] The commissioners ranged from officers of the court such as Judge Edward F. Waite and probation officer Edward J. Davenport, professors John H. Gray and David H. Painter, physicians Dr. Herbert O. Collins and Dr. Mabel S. Ulrich to business and union representatives such as Charles M. Way and Nicholas C. O'Connor. Their findings were published in the 1911 *Report of the Vice Commission of Minneapolis to His Honor, James C. Haynes, Mayor.*

The commission did its best to maintain a nonpartisan position and steer clear of assigning blame or uncovering corruption in its investigation of the roots of prostitution in Minneapolis. Many of the commissioners grudgingly admitted favoring the system of regulated prostitution at the beginning of the study, but once their work was completed most of them had changed this position. Perhaps they had come to this conclusion as a result of their investigations, or perhaps the commissioners sensed a shifting political reality and understood the old-style red-light districts would never return.

The vice commission pursued a vigorous course of research, sending out approximately 350 letters in a representative sampling of Minneapolis citizens from a wide variety of businesses and professions. They interviewed madams who kept brothels and police officials who had enforced a variety of policies on prostitution over the years. Although none of the madams were named, it is quite likely Nettie Conley, Ida Dorsey, and Edna Hamilton provided testimony, given their prominence and years of experience in the business. The commission corresponded with authorities from other cities, and traveled to other municipalities to investigate how they approached the problem of public prostitution.[3]

The commission briefly recounted the history of how the city dealt with prostitution, stating, incorrectly, that the system of fines had begun in the early 1880s and making no mention of the crusade against the madams that had sent three of them to prison. The report then moved on to the current situation. Considering the arguments for legalizing prostitution, the commission quoted several writers who presented rationales for a system that would put the commercial sex trade on the same footing as liquor, allowing the city to confine it to certain areas and exercise control through licensing. One suggestion was to locate a sex district on Nicollet Island under city ownership, while another thought the Eleventh Avenue area was as good as any. Instead of the old system of monthly fines that acknowledged prostitution was indeed a violation of state and city laws, legalization would end the hypocrisy and recognize that prostitution would never be completely eradicated, only regulated. The report affirmed that this argument was "theoretically logical and consistent" but impossible in any practical sense. "Legalizing and licensing prostitution is a method foreign to the sentiments and feelings of the American people and repugnant to their moral sense." The report concluded that the electorate would never elect state representatives who would repeal current prostitution laws nor a city council that would enact similar ordinances.[4]

In the end, the commission favored strict enforcement of antiprostitution laws, citing a "new spirit abroad in the land, and particularly in our cities, so different from former indifference and assumed helplessness, that it is called a Civic Awakening." This new idealism manifested itself in a determination to eliminate political bossism and partisan politics, and make cities better through beautification and slum clearance.[5] The commissioners reported that never within their collective memory had prostitution been under better control than since November 1910, "when the police department put into effect the drastic order prohibiting saloons from harboring prostitutes and directing the police to pursue a vigorous policy for the elimination of disorderly houses."[6]

When writing about this "new spirit," the commissioners revealed what they believed were specific causes of and solutions for prostitution. Their agenda was much broader than the question of whether prostitution should be tolerated or suppressed. The commissioners declared that the public was becoming less tolerant of prostitution because white slavery was the cause, not merely a side effect, of the commercial sex trade. Despite finding no evidence of white slavery in Minneapolis, the commission concluded that unnamed syndicates stimulated the sex trade because "there have not been found women enough to go readily into Public Prostitution, nor men enough to go out of their way to seek the public houses, to make the business pay. Supply and demand has been created by artificial methods."[7]

The commission envisioned a society in which all sex would be within the bounds of wedlock and primarily used for the creation of healthy children. They declared that the old belief that sexual release was necessary for men's health had no scientific basis: "there is no physical reason as there is no moral one, for maintaining two standards as regards chastity, one for men and the other for women." The commissioners encouraged harmonious "family life on which the security of the race and the progress of civilization depend," noting "the promotion of masculine chastity will be the most powerful means of checking prostitution."[8]

This group seemed to be fighting human nature itself as well, revealing their anxieties on the subject of "race suicide"—the fear that racial minorities might produce more offspring than whites. Unlike earlier reformers, the commissioners were less intent on vilifying prostitutes and madams and more concerned with domesticating sex itself, and they concluded that there were not enough men to patronize brothels on their own and that the white slavers had somehow created an unnatural demand for sexually available women. If only the human sex drive could be rationalized and human beings educated to practice "normal" sex, then, the commissioners believed, other problematic forms of sexuality could be eliminated as well. They advocated a policy of prevention that would not only suppress the commercial sex trade "but will tend to eliminate all other forms of Social Vice—those illicit sexual practices in which public prostitutes play no part, and which constitute such important elements in the entire problem."[9]

The "illicit sexual practices" that so worried the commissioners would include homosexuality and masturbation, which was believed at the time to cause a host of illnesses ranging from blindness to insanity. In their own words, these seemingly aberrant practices could not be blamed on prostitution, as men seeking male partners or men who only engaged in autoerotic acts were unlikely to become customers of the likes of Ida Dorsey or Nettie Conley. The commissioners reasoned that these unnatural sex practices must have their roots in ignorance on the part of those who participated in them.

Not surprisingly, the commissioners advocated education as the answer to these problems and their report offered a grab bag of solutions: teach the young about the horrors of venereal diseases through a carefully controlled sex education program that would emphasize wholesome family living. It called for other measures: more playgrounds, lest children be tempted into pool halls or rowdy theaters; censorship of plays and motion pictures; an ordinance banning female ushers in theaters; and censorship of suggestive postcards and billboards. The commissioners also requested more sanitary working conditions, especially for young people, as anything that endangered health would weaken resistance to evil. While such goals as providing parks, playgrounds, better housing, and improved working conditions were admirable on their own, it is difficult to see them as remedies to prostitution. Censorship might make forbidden plays, books, or theaters more attractive; barring women from legitimate employment might lead them into less savory ways of earning a living.

The report's emphasis on white slavery pointed to another social ill that worried the commissioners: unchecked materialism. Not only did the sex industry exist for the sole purpose of profit, it also tempted daughters of the poor into prostitution as an easy way to gain wealth. The vice report freely acknowledged that female workers were often underpaid and overworked in the broader economy, which might contribute to their descent into prostitution. But aside from a few vague hints for employers to pay fair wages, the report asserted that women should not work outside the home unless it was absolutely necessary. The report acknowledged that people should earn a living wage but said they should be less concerned about acquiring material wealth, evidence that the commissioners were hoping to create a new type of citizen, free of unwholesome vices and desires, with a single-minded focus on health, race purity, and advancing civilization. The report also recommended the establishment of a permanent Moral Commission to monitor and suppress prostitution, and generally direct matters concerning public morals. The proposed commission would investigate citizen complaints and refer them to the appropriate municipal department.

If the sponsors of the vice commission believed the study of prostitution would somehow make it go away or quell public fears of it, they must have been very disappointed in the results. Just prior to publication of the report, a rumor floated around town that the Eleventh Avenue red-light district would be reopened. Although Mayor Haynes denied the story, the South Side Citizens' Committee swung into action with strong protests.[10]

Once the vice report was published in July 1911, public debate on prostitution did not subside but seemed to grow more intense. After conceding the commission was handicapped by the lack of funds with which to conduct research, the *Minneapolis Journal* asserted the report was "a sermon rather than an investigation, an argument rather than an effort to come at the facts scientifically." The commission, the writer claimed, should not have simply taken the word of the police force that since the policy of segregation of the red-light districts had ended, public morality had improved. "The slightest penetration beneath the surface of things would have revealed the fact that the trade of prostitution was never more widely or insidiously plied in Minneapolis than at this moment." In the months following the publication of the commission's report, the *Journal* kept its focus on what it viewed as a breakdown of public morality, charging that both prostitution and illegal liquor sales were invading the whole city; at one point the *Journal* claimed that the old Eleventh Avenue district was again in operation "and, in addition, two or three hundred resorts [brothels] as far West as Forty-eighth Street," all the while blaming Mayor Haynes for allowing or even encouraging this to happen.[11]

The *Journal's* attacks on the mayor prompted Commissioner Marion Shutter to write a long letter to its editor in which he conceded the newspaper had a right to find fault with the vice commission's report as much as it liked, but had no basis in concluding that the commission "was a creature of Mayor Haynes" or that the report was written to support some preconceived conclusions. Shutter charged that the *Journal* "has a controversy with the mayor," and while it was acceptable for the paper to have as many differences with the mayor or any other public official "as will satisfy its appetite for war," it was not right that the paper mischaracterize the commission's work.[12]

By contrast, the *Minneapolis Tribune* found little fault with the commission, noting "we shall wait long for a higher example of good citizenship than the report of the vice commission." The *Tribune* concentrated on exposing the conditions the writer believed led to prostitution and proposing solutions, among them: "put an end to the conscription or the false allure of the recruiting agent; remove aphrodisiac spectacles and amusements that are the tools of trade. Unmask the [parts] of it that deceive the innocent." If the marketplace dictates that women workers are not paid enough to support themselves, "point out, if you cannot change, the thronging of young women from homes to shops that makes this possible."[13]

Others rejected the vice commission's conclusions as well as the charges that the mayor was too lenient in regards to the commercial sex trade. In a letter to the editor, Howard Hall reported that he, like the Minneapolis commissioners, had recently visited Des Moines. But unlike the vice commission, which judged there had been a general decline in that city's "crime and disorder" since the closing of the red-light districts there, Hall stated that he had not walked three blocks "of their clean innocent city, before I was hailed by one their scarlet women." He concluded that it was "true, they have no district in Des Moines, for the simple reason that they have made the whole city the district." Hall advocated a return to the old designated red-light districts that would be under the control of an elected commission, as a "certain percent of the population of our city is composed of a vicious element which we cannot eliminate, but which we can control."[14]

By 1911 the leaders of Minneapolis had shifted their fight from closing openly operating brothels to reforming public morals in general. While they had triumphed over the madams, there remained the problem of finding an effective means of shutting down clandestine bordellos. Meanwhile, the group of once-powerful madams began to fade from sight, rarely appearing in newspaper stories. Each madam responded to the changing times in her own way.

EDNA HAMILTON

Edna Hamilton, one of the madams arrested in the April 1910 raid, retired from the sex trade and began operating her old brothel on Main Street Northeast as a legitimate boardinghouse. During the first year as a boardinghouse keeper, she was listed under her old professional name of Edna Hamilton. But by 1912 Edna Hamilton had disappeared from the city directories and been replaced by "Mrs. Josephine M. Dale," a variant of her birth name. Still the sly storyteller, Edna/Josephine often listed herself as the "widow of John," even there is no evidence that she ever married (Hamilton had clearly been involved with many "johns" over the course of her long career).[15] She renamed her property at 25 Main Street Northeast as well. By 1914 her former bordello was retitled the Hotel Du North. This vaguely French name might have suggested elegance or perhaps it was just another of Hamilton's plays on words. For the first few years, Hamilton left the day-to-day management of the Du North to a woman called Ethel Wilson while Hamilton lived elsewhere. By 1917 she was back on Main Street, renting out furnished rooms to working-class men[16]

Hamilton lived there with William Wolverton. Born in Minneapolis in 1862, Wolverton was the only son of Evalyn (Olmstead) and Jacob Wolverton, a successful real estate dealer. In 1890 William Wolverton married Lydia F. Barrows, but after fathering two daughters, he deserted his family.[17] Lydia was forced to rely on her parents for support and filed for divorce in 1899. In the court documents, Wolverton was described as an abusive drunk, "a man of peculiar habits and temperament and indifference to his children, and to domestic duties generally."[18] Perhaps Wolverton had reformed by the time he began living with Hamilton or perhaps she was willing to overlook his faults. Hamilton certainly did not rely on him for financial support, remaining in control of her real estate and money to the end of her life.

Sometime during the 1920s, Hamilton and Wolverton moved out of the Hotel Du North and into an apartment at 1515 Stevens Avenue. Hamilton did not live with Wolverton during her last years, but he did reside nearby. Around 1928 Hamilton moved into the Imperial Flats at 22 Grant Street, along with her housekeeper, Hester Jackson. The Imperial was an elegant, three-story, Beaux-Arts-style building designed by Harry W. Jones that was clearly intended for prosperous middle-class residents. Hamilton had survived thirty-some years in the sex trade, managing to provide herself with a comfortable retirement and with enough to leave a small estate to her friends and family. She died in 1932 at age seventy-one and was buried at Hillside Cemetery. Her chief asset was the property at 25 Main Street Northeast; the rest of her estate consisted of clothes, dishes, and cash. The real estate was appraised at $5,000, but its value was reduced by the $3,500 mortgage it carried. Hamilton's will directed that her estate, which totaled about $1,600, should be split three ways. Her younger brother, Walter Dale, received one-third; Hester Jackson, described as her maid and friend, and Mary King, another friend, split a one-third share; and William Wolverton received one-third.[19] Walter Dale, born in Michigan City, Indiana, in 1883, was the child of Alfred Dale and his second, wife, Jenny Wilcox. Even though Walter was born after Hamilton had left home and started her career as a prostitute, the family ties were strong enough for Walter to relocate to Minneapolis after his father died in 1897.[20] Far from being shunned by her family as a result of her life in the sex trade, Hamilton, like several other madams, drew family members to Minneapolis.

William Wolverton outlived Hamilton by five years. Interestingly, his martial status on his death certificate was listed as "widowed," with his wife's name given as "Edna." The informant, Lucia Camp, clearly knew of Wolverton's relationship with Hamilton and considered them the equivalent of a married couple, and she also knew of Josephine Dale's other identity as Edna Hamilton.[21] Hamilton's boardinghouse at 25 Main Street Northeast survived her by another forty years. Used as a residential hotel for many years, the Hotel Du North's colorful history and owners were long forgotten by the time it met the wrecking ball in 1974.

NETTIE CONLEY

Nettie Conley retired from actively running a bordello in 1901. A newspaper noted she had "been the proprietress of a disreputable house in Minneapolis for the past 25 years" and had been charged with running a place of prostitution; "the indictment was only a makeshift to punish her for the practice of having girls under 16 years of age in her resort." Conley entered a not-guilty plea and her trial commenced. The charge grew out of an incident in which Samuel Hines, a business school student, escorted the willing Dolly Taylor, age fifteen, to Conley's place "for immoral purposes." On other occasions, Hines had taken other young women to Conley's brothel, and at least two of them became inmates there. As a defense Conley stated that all the girls swore that they were eighteen before she let them into her house. Her attorney, the former Judge Mahoney, argued that Conley kept one of the best-run brothels in the city. Judge McGee agreed: "It was true that there were worse places than the Conley woman's. One place masqueraded under the name of a theater that perhaps started more girls and boys on the road to ruin than did such places as run by the Conley woman."[22] While the jury was deliberating, Conley changed her plea to guilty. She was then handed a thousand-dollar fine in lieu of two years in the workhouse. Conley paid her fine and apparently quit the business, which likely heartened the forces of reform. Already in her fifties, Conley may have been ready to leave the day-to-day responsibilities of running a brothel. She had to be aware that prostitution was undergoing changes, such as the rise of "call girls" that would eventually render old-style brothels and madams obsolete. However, Conley did not abandon the sex trade completely, but rather moved into buying real estate in the Eleventh Avenue district, building bordellos, and lending money to other madams.

When prostitution was formally outlawed, Conley was living quietly in the residential neighborhood adjacent to downtown Minneapolis with her much younger companion, Frank Cottom, who died of heart failure in 1911. She still actively managed her real estate holdings that were largely prostitution related. Conley owned her First Street property until 1915 and held mortgages on several residential properties that had no known connection to the sex trade.[23] Like those of Edna Hamilton and Ida Dorsey, much of Conley's family had relocated to Minneapolis over the years. Her brother William Angle was the first to arrive in the 1870s. He had started out working in Conley's Main Street establishment, but later settled in Northeast Minneapolis and worked as a flour packer. Conley's oldest sister, Julia, came to Minneapolis to live with her daughter in about 1918 after being widowed.[24] Conley's younger sister, Ella (in some sources Ellen), Ella's husband, William Mack, and son, William Junior, relocated to Minneapolis about 1886. When Ella died of cancer at age sixty-five, she was living with Conley at her home at 1704 Fifth Avenue South.[25]

Nettie Conley died at age sixty-nine of what was called "chronic morphinism" on her death certificate. The secondary cause of death was a hip fracture that had occurred ten months earlier. Defined as chronic intoxication due to the habitual use of opium, Conley's morphinism may have been the result of physician-administered drugs that alleviated the persistent pain of her broken hip. Or Conley, with her well-established connections, may have been a long-term user of opium and medicated herself.[26]

Although she had been living as Mrs. Frank Cottom for nearly two decades, her considerable estate was probated under her professional name, Nettie Conley. The inventory of Conley's property placed its worth at over $50,000, or well over $600,000 in 2010 dollars.[27] Conley's real estate included her homestead at 1704 Fifth Avenue South, 27 Main Street Southeast (by then known as the Riverview Hotel), and her holdings in the Eleventh Avenue district. Her large array of household goods ranged from multiple bedroom suites to books, paintings, and fur coats, as well as her extensive collection of fine jewelry. Conley's estate was apportioned among her surviving relatives: her siblings William Angle, Julia (Angle) Buckley, and George Angle (a half brother), and nephew William H. S. Mack, the son of the deceased Ella Mack. Conley's former brothel at 27 Main Street Southeast continued as a boardinghouse, but was torn down in the 1970s when the revival of the riverfront was just beginning, its original owner and function long forgotten. Her residence at 1704 Fifth Avenue South, along with large portions of the central city, was razed to make way for I-35W in 1963. Her First Street establishment, along with several other brothels, was razed when construction on the Janney, Semple, Hill Company warehouse was started in 1915. Her holdings in the Eleventh Avenue district met a similar fate in the late 1980s, when her former brothels were cleared to make way for surface parking lots.[28]

IDA DORSEY

Ida Dorsey actively continued her life in the sex trade after the era of tolerated prostitution ended in Minneapolis in 1910. At this point, she was in her forties and apparently not quite wealthy enough to retire. After being arrested at her Eleventh Avenue brothel in 1911 as part of a vice raid, and faced with an increasingly hostile environment in Minneapolis, Dorsey decided to move her operation to St. Paul. During testimony in a high-profile graft trial that eventually sent St. Paul's chief of police, Martin Flanagan, and chief of detectives, Fred Turner, to the state penitentiary, Dorsey recounted her move to St. Paul. Negotiations for the bordello at 151 South Washington Street owned by Nina Clifford, St. Paul's most famous madam, began in August 1912 and continued into the following year. Dorsey revealed that she had met with Chief Flanagan to tell him she "wanted to open a disorderly house here and run it on the square," offering him references from Minneapolis officials.

In subsequent testimony, Nina Clifford corroborated Dorsey's story, saying that Dorsey had paid her four thousand dollars to relocate to St. Paul—one thousand dollars went to Clifford for the house. The remaining three thousand dollars was to be distributed among various officials and members of the city's underworld, who in turn would allow Dorsey to conduct her business.[29]

Dorsey opened her new operation on March 7, 1913, but despite her careful preparations her St. Paul venture closed a few months later when the chief of police ordered all the city's sixty-two known brothels closed.[30] Dorsey testified that her friends had advised her against the move, and afterward she "felt like a dummy" for making it, as she had never before paid protection to open a new business.[31]

In addition to trying to survive the changing political and social climate, Dorsey seemed to be spread too thin and facing too many challenges after 1910. In her 1914 testimony, she said she also owned brothels in Duluth and Superior, Wisconsin. Moreover, she suffered several personal losses during this period, along with the death of Carleton Pillsbury. Her brother, twenty-eight-year-old Nebraska Burkes, died of tuberculosis in 1912. Two years later another of her brothers, Moses Burkes, died of heart disease. In 1918 Henry Burkes Bailey, who was somehow related to Dorsey, succumbed to tuberculosis.[32]

Finally, a newspaper editor relentlessly dogged Dorsey to her last days. Howard A. Guilford arrived in the Twin Cities in about 1912. After a brief stint in St. Paul, Guilford moved to Minneapolis and founded a newspaper called the *Twin City Reporter.* The *Reporter* concentrated on exposing graft, corruption, and selective enforcement by public officials, with particular emphasis on prostitution. Although racial and ethnic slurs often appeared in print at that time, Guilford's paper was unusually forthright in its racism. Guilford did not hesitate to refer to Dorsey as a "nigger wench," or imply that she spoke a parody of Black English such as "Friday (dat am some unlucky day, Ida, doan yo' know it)."[33] In another instance, Guilford asserted that the building at 1216 Marquette Avenue was where Dorsey *"keeps all her white girls"* (italics in the original). If a successful African American madam was anathema to Guilford, it was unthinkable that white women should work for her.[34]

Gilford's obsession with Dorsey began in 1914, when he reported that she, along with several other madams, was still operating a clandestine brothel, despite the raids in November 1913. Guilford complained that no action had been taken under the abatement act, hinting the elected officials were remiss.[35] Guilford followed Dorsey as she moved her operation around the downtown area, always suggesting that she had official protection. At one point he contrasted her to another madam, May Shultz, whose clientele was drawn from the working class. He reported that Dorsey was running a brothel out of the Churchill Hotel at 626 Hennepin Avenue and claimed to have a list of some of her patrons, complaining that her places were not raided because she had powerful protectors.[36]

Guilford placed a stakeout at 22½ Western Avenue (present-day Glenwood Avenue), another of Dorsey's temporary locations. A block of storefronts with flats above, this building was just the sort of anonymous place to conduct a clandestine brothel.[37] Guilford's report noted that many men entered and left the building from late in the evening to early in the morning. A subsequent raid revealed that Dorsey used the Western Avenue building as a screening area, where customers would be scrutinized to determine whether they were undercover agents. If they passed this test, they would be driven to Dorsey's Marquette Avenue bordello, where her niece, at that time using the name Alvah Lyons, was in charge. Guilford apparently informed the police of Dorsey's operation and they set up a sting. The undercover officers were driven to the Marquette Avenue bordello, where, after they were "'beered' and entertained in regal style," the "cream-colored hostess [Alvah]" was told that she and "the charming damsels assisting" were under arrest. While other newspapers barely mentioned this arrest, Guilford devoted an entire front page to the story and gleefully recounted how his efforts had resulted in Alvah being sentenced to ninety days in jail.[38]

After the raid, Guilford kept up his attacks, questioning why Ida Dorsey herself was not arrested and doing his best to inject xenophobia into the story. Was it because Ida was well connected, or "is it because a slant-eyed Christian Chinaman owns the lease [at Western Avenue]"?[39] When Alvah did not show up to serve her sentence and forfeited the seven-hundred-dollar bail, Guilford again put this story on the front page of his paper, devoting many inches to his rants against Ida Dorsey.[40]

Ida Dorsey's Western Avenue place was another example of how the sex trade had moved throughout the city, far beyond the boundaries of the old red-light districts, as well as illustrating how successful madams changed with the times. The old-style brothels typically had several parlors where individual customers or groups of customers could meet prostitutes yet remain unknown to other customers. Telephones allowed call girls to be sent anywhere, lessening the need for brick-and-mortar bordellos. If a customer did not have a private place to interact with a prostitute, he would still need some sort of brothel or assignation house. The Western Avenue place allowed Dorsey to assess potential customers for signs that they were undercover cops or other potential troublemakers, before allowing them access to her actual bordello.

Dorsey only rented space at the Western Avenue location and apparently had no sex workers on-site. In the unlikely event that she was arrested for prostitution there, it would be the landlord who would be subject to the abatement law. If the Western Avenue place started to attract attention from the authorities or crusaders like Guilford, Dorsey could easily move to another location, all the while shielding her Marquette property.

A year later, Guilford was still writing about Dorsey even though he was aware that she was very sick. After Alvah left town, Ida Dorsey apparently moved into her Marquette Avenue building, where she lived quietly along "with at times a colored maid—at others, a few white girls—'roomers.'" Guilford bragged that "the old hessian, however, was laying low—not through any fear of the law, but through fear of the *Twin City Reporter.* Publicity is an article the black-bats of murky ways cannot stand, and we gave Ida such a publicity bath as she has never had before."[41]

But in reality it was disease, not Guilford's attacks, that halted Dorsey's business. She was dying of cancer, a disease that had carried off many in her family. By February 1918 Alvah had returned to Minneapolis, and while visiting Dorsey in Eitel Hospital she was spotted by a policeman and arrested. Municipal Judge C. L. Smith, who had originally sentenced her, allowed her to serve one day in the workhouse. Smith then considerably shortened Alvah's sentence and let her serve it in the city jail. Smith said he did this "because humanity required that she be where she could conveniently visit her mother occasionally." Predictably, Guilford was outraged at the judge, calling the decision a "serious judicial blunder" and promising the judge that "the ghost of this act will arise to haunt your political life as long as it lasts, and it will last until the voters get another whack at you at the ballot box."[42]

Ida Dorsey died in the summer of 1918. Despite her decades-long notoriety in Minneapolis, Dorsey's passing was little noticed in most newspapers. An African American paper reported it, however, and referred to her as "Mrs. Ida Dorsey," implying she was a widow, as was reported on her death certificate.[43] After a funeral service conducted by Rev. Stovall, she was laid to rest in Lakewood in the family plot.

Dorsey had done her best to provide for her surviving family.

Earlier she had sold the Marquette Avenue property, receiving cash as well as a mortgage for the unpaid balance on the property. Shortly before she died, she transferred the mortgage to her niece, ensuring that Alvah received as much of her property as possible. Alvah in turn sold the mortgage a few months after Dorsey died, thus realizing a substantial amount of cash and bypassing the probate process.[44]

Dorsey left a formal will, naming Alvah Hunton as her chief heir. She left her brother James Burkes one hundred dollars and urged Hunton to "take such care of my servant Cora Taylor as her circumstances will permit."[45] The inventory lists Dorsey's real estate holdings: her residence at 2720 Second Avenue South, her brothel at 212 Eleventh Avenue South, and a property in Anoka that had been left to Dorsey by her brother Moses Burkes. Her jewelry collection was impressive and included several rings each with three-carat diamonds, pearls and emerald pieces, and a platinum brooch with two three-carat diamonds surrounded by thirty smaller diamonds. Unfortunately for Hunton, all these items were pledged as security for loans. The rest of the estate, valued at more than thirteen thousand dollars, was divided among Dorsey's numerous creditors, who had to accept less than their claims were worth.[46]

Alvah left Minneapolis soon after the estate was settled and Dorsey was forgotten, like the other madams who had thrived on the Minneapolis riverfront for several decades. Her Eleventh Avenue bordello, however, survived and, during a twenty-year period, added another chapter to local African American history.

By 1918 the barbering business of Thompson and Carver, previously operated by Bert F. Thompson and Fred S. Carver at 1100 Washington Avenue South, relocated to Dorsey's former building. Thompson, a native of Omaha, was already living in the former bordello next door at 208 Eleventh Avenue South. By 1920 Thompson moved into 212 Eleventh Avenue and took out a permit for alterations to the building; he soon opened a rooming house that catered mainly to African American porters. Like Thompson, all the residents were black men who were transplants, mainly from places like Missouri, Virginia, Georgia, and Tennessee. By 1922 Thompson was listed as the manager of the Colored Railroad Men's Club at 204 Eleventh Avenue South. By the mid-1920s, Thompson apparently offered furnished rooms at 204 and 208 Eleventh Avenue South, as well.[47]

In 1931 Thompson added a café to 212 Eleventh Avenue South. Likely this was for the convenience of his lodgers who might work odd hours and whose access to many restaurants was limited by the segregationist policies of the time. An insurance map from the 1930s characterized it as the "Colored Men's Club." During the late 1920s, Thompson had operated a restaurant at 901 Cedar Avenue South, and perhaps his combination of experience and expertise as a host gave the restaurant wider appeal because by 1937 it was known as the "South Side Nite Club," which offered both food and drink. Judging by a photograph taken during a raid conducted early in 1938, at least some of its patrons were white. Sixty-four-year-old Bert "Dutch" Thompson was identified as the owner and described as a "negro" who was "the boss of the South Side district." No patrons were arrested, but Thompson and two employees (both African American) were taken to jail and later fined for keeping and being found in a disorderly house. After this incident, Thompson apparently lost control of the nightclub operation, but he continued to operate his restaurant there for a few more years. By 1939 the South Side Nite Club was renamed the "Swing Club" and was run by Michael Kraft. The building at 212 Eleventh Avenue South had again become a place of entertainment and that use continued until the early 1940s. After that, the building was converted to an upholstering firm and later still to a shelter for the homeless, its original function long forgotten. The surrounding buildings that formerly housed brothels were razed over time until Dorsey's building was the last one of its kind left standing.[48]

The story of the Minneapolis madams was further obscured when the Sisterhood of Bethany revised its story. Still in operation in 1916, the Sisterhood released its fortieth annual report in which it recapped the organization's history by rewriting it. In this version, the Sisterhood came together because its founders were "disturbed by" the injustice of a "court in sending four [unnamed] women to the state penitentiary for immoral lives, without making any effort to bring their male associates to judgment for the same offenses." By contrast, the 1877 story makes no mention of challenging male privilege, focusing instead on offering a second chance to women who had run afoul of the double standard. The two women for whom the Sisterhood had obtained pardons in 1876 were conflated with the four madams who had been indicted in 1880. Three of them, not four, were sent to Stillwater, and the Sisterhood made no attempt to free Nettie Conley, Sallie Campbell, or Kate Johnson. It was the mayor and other leading citizens who signed the petition, in hopes that the madams would come back and regain control of the local sex industry. By recasting this account, the writer of the fortieth annual report not only obscured the Sisterhood's history, she also helped to erase from city history a group of entrepreneurial females who challenged the traditional notions of a woman's place.[49]

Subsequent accounts of the city such as Marion Shutter's *History of Minneapolis: Gateway to the Northwest* (1923) made no mention of the madams or the period of openly operated sex districts, although Shutter did give an account of Harriet Walker's life, including her work with the Sisterhood of Bethany. Calvin F. Schmid's *Social Saga of Two Cities: An Ecological and Statistical Study of Social Trends in Minneapolis and St. Paul* (1937) acknowledged the existence of former red-light areas but was silent on who might have operated those businesses or lived there.

Over the decades, as the former bordellos were repurposed, razed, and replaced by other structures, most physical traces of the madams' existence disappeared. People who might have recalled the city's unacknowledged history also passed away with time and thus the madams were forgotten. Today, standing in front of Ida Dorsey's former bordello, it is hard to imagine that this was once a neighborhood owned and controlled almost exclusively by women, who, although scorned by respectable society, were running businesses that catered to the forbidden desires of members from that society. These madams influenced municipal government. They helped shape the riverfront through the placement of their bordellos near train stations, theaters, and mills, and contributed to the creation of entertainment districts that even today offer restaurants, bars, and arts venues.

We deserve a complex civic history that gives voice to a class of women who engaged in a morally problematic lifestyle and an account that does not hide the stark economic choices faced by women in the nineteenth century. We need a story that acknowledges that some in city government saw the madams as a means to control the commercial sex trade, while reformers, on the other hand, viewed them as the source of the problem. We should recognize not only the stories of women such as Charlotte Van Cleve and Harriet Walker but also those of Nettie Conley, Jennie Jones, and Ida Dorsey: all these women left their mark on the history of Minneapolis.

NOTES

PREFACE

1. Minneapolis Department of Inspections, building permit index card for 212–214 Eleventh Avenue South. Both "sporting house" and "house of ill fame" were common nineteenth-century euphemisms for brothels.

INTRODUCTION

1. "The 'Social Evil,'" *Minneapolis Chronicle,* April 30, 1867.

2. Ibid.

3. "City Ordinances," *St. Anthony Express,* May 26, 1855; "The Cyprians Routed," *St. Anthony Evening News,* October 2, 1857; "City and State," *Minnesota Republican* (St. Anthony), July 9, 1858; and "Three Men Shot!—Attempt to Take Prisoners out of Jail!" *Minnesota Republican* (St. Anthony), July 23, 1858.

4. For examples of the term "public women" in local newspapers, see "Her Column," *Minneapolis Tribune,* November 12, 1873, and "Painted Women," *Minneapolis Tribune,* December 9, 1878. When Kate Hutton, a St. Paul prostitute, died, her coffin was "followed to Oakland [Cemetery] by most of the public women of her class in the city," according to one newspaper ("St. Paul," *Minneapolis Tribune,* August 28, 1881).

5. For a more complete account of the founding of St. Anthony and Minneapolis, see Lucile M. Kane, *The Falls of St. Anthony: The Waterfall That Built Minneapolis* (1966; repr., St. Paul: Minnesota Historical Society Press, 1987); and William W. Folwell, *A History of Minnesota,* 4 vols. (1921–30; repr., St. Paul: Minnesota Historical Society Press, 1956), 1:431–32.

6. Agnes M. Larson, *The White Pine Industry in Minnesota: A History* (1949; repr., Minneapolis: University of Minnesota Press, 2007), 243, 246.

7. Kane, *Falls of St. Anthony,* 28.

8. "Wholesale Trade: How It Has Grown Up in Minneapolis from Small Beginnings," *Minneapolis Journal,* November 26, 1903.

9. *Saint Anthony Falls Rediscovered* (Minneapolis: Minneapolis Riverfront Development Coordination Board, 1980), 15, 29; Norman Francis Thomas, *Minneapolis–Moline: A History of Its Formation* (New York: Arno Press, 1976), 47–48; Horace B. Hudson, *A Half Century of Minneapolis* (Minneapolis: Hudson Publishing Company, 1908), 432; John M. Wickre, "Farm Implements and Tractors," in *A Guide to the Industrial Archeology of the Twin Cities,* ed. Nicholas Westbrook (St. Paul: Minnesota Historical Society, 1983), 90.

10. Minneapolis City Charter reprinted in the *Minneapolis Chronicle,* January 15, 1867, chapter IV, section 31. The first Minneapolis city ordinance that refers to prostitution that I have been able to find is dated February 20, 1868. The Minneapolis Municipal Library has a box of old ordinances, although most of the original documents, such as the 1868 prostitution ordinance, are missing. Fortunately, each missing ordinance has a "Missing" card that gives the date of the ordinance and a brief description. Another such card refers to an ordinance dated July 15, 1869, to amend section 2 of an ordinance relating to disorderly houses, houses of ill fame, and common prostitutes. The earliest Minneapolis ordinance in written form is dated April 12, 1873. This ordinance prohibited brothels and prostitution in general, and set fines for violators: brothel keepers faced fines of $25–$100; visitors (usually the male customers), $5–$10; landlords who leased to known prostitutes, $50–$100; and ordinary prostitutes, $10–$50. "A Fallen Angel," *Minneapolis Tribune,* March 4, 1868. See also "Police Court," *Minneapolis Tribune,* May 13, May 16, and July 21, 1868.

11. "Police Court," *St. Paul Pioneer Press,* May 14, 1872.

12. Hennepin County Criminal Index, November 25, 1869; "District Court," *Minneapolis Tribune,* June 21, 1870, and June 22, 1870. Stillwater convict records describe Sullivan as a Minnesota native, five feet tall, with brown hair, blue eyes, and a fair complexion that was slightly pockmarked. She began serving her sentence on June 23, 1870.

13. "Police Courts," *Minneapolis Tribune,* May 22, 1872.

14. "Governor Pillsbury," *Hennepin County Mirror,* February 26, 1881.

15. The Pillsburys were natives of New Hampshire, while the Washburns and Prays hailed from Maine. To name only two examples of prominent nineteenth-century Minneapolis families: the Pillsburys traced their first American ancestor to William Pillsbury, who settled in the Massachusetts Bay Colony in 1640; the Washburns' first American ancestor was John Washburn, secretary of the Plymouth Colony in England, who immigrated to Massachusetts and married into a Mayflower family. See Isaac Atwater, *History of the City of Minneapolis, Minnesota* (New York: Munsell, 1893), 591, 545.

16. Merlin Stonehouse, *John Wesley North and the Reform Frontier* (Minneapolis: University of Minnesota Press, 1965), 39. This quote is from a letter to the editor of the *Washington, D.C., National Era,* January 24, 1850.

17. Stonehouse, *John Wesley North,* 36.

18. "Minnesota Affairs," *Minnesota Pioneer* (St. Paul), August 14, 1851. The *St. Anthony Express* was the first newspaper to be published in St. Anthony or Minneapolis. Its first editor was Isaac Atwater, who later published an extensive history of Minneapolis.

19. "The New England Festival," *St. Anthony Evening News,* December 29, 1857. This story takes up almost three pages of the four-page issue. Another four-page newspaper, the *Minnesota Republican,* December 25, 1857, devoted more than one page to the coverage of this story.

20. Joel Best, *Controlling Vice: Regulating Brothel Prostitution in St. Paul, 1865–1883* (Columbus: Ohio State University Press, 1998), 24–25; Josie Washburn, *The Underworld Sewer: A Prostitute Reflects on Life in the Trade, 1871–1909* (1909; repr., Lincoln: University of Nebraska Press, 1997), 27–28; Mara L. Keire, *For Business and Pleasure: Red-Light Districts and the Regulation of Vice in the United States, 1890–1933* (Baltimore: The Johns Hopkins University Press, 2010), 7–9; Al Rose, *Storyville, New Orleans: Being an Authentic, Illustrated Account of the Notorious Red-Light District* (Tuscaloosa: University of Alabama Press, 1974), 8–9.

21. Keire, *For Business and Pleasure,* 89, 107.

22. Clifford's death notice appeared in "Nina Clifford, Long St. Paul Demi-Monde Queen, Is Dead," *St. Paul Daily News,* July 17, 1929. See also Oliver Towne's column in the *St. Paul Dispatch,* August 11, 1958, July 4, 1963; *St. Paul Pioneer Press Dispatch,* October 25, 1987; *Minneapolis Star Tribune,* April 2, 1997; and Paul Maccabee, *John Dillinger Slept Here: A Crook's Tour of Crime and Corruption in St. Paul, 1920–1936* (St. Paul: Minnesota Historical Society Press, 1995), 13–17.

1. WOMEN'S WORK OF ALL KINDS

1. "One More Unfortunate," *Minneapolis Tribune,* November 7, 1874.

2. Joseph F. Kett, *Rites of Passage: Adolescence in America, 1790 to the Present* (New York: Basic Books, 1977), 95–96.

3. Faye E. Dudden, *Serving Women: Household Service in Nineteenth-Century America* (Middletown, Conn.: Wesleyan University Press, 1983), 48.

4. *First Biennial Report of the Bureau of Labor Statistics of the State of Minnesota for the Two Years Ending December 31, 1887–1888* ([Minneapolis]: Thomas A. Clark & Co., 1888), 140. The investigators for the bureau reported conditions and wages for all laborers in Minnesota, but had no power to compel business owners to make their workplaces safer or offer higher wages. The study

did not include women who worked as teachers, possibly because these were salaried positions, as opposed jobs with hourly wages.

5. Ibid., 188.

6. Ibid., 196.

7. *Third Biennial Report of the Bureau of Labor Statistics of the State of Minnesota* (Minneapolis: Harrison and Smith, State Printers, 1893), 75.

8. Ibid. Hennepin County cases are on 109–11; those from Ramsey County are on 111–14.

9. Eva Gay, "Workers in Wool," *St. Paul Daily Globe,* May 20, 1888.

10. Eva Gay, "Eva Gay's Travels," *St. Paul Daily Globe,* May 6, 1888.

11. Eva Gay, "How Girls Clerk," *St. Paul Daily Globe,* June 17, 1888.

12. Eva Gay, "The Girls Rejoice," *St. Paul Daily Globe,* July 1, 1888.

13. Eva Gay, "Song of the Shirt," *St. Paul Daily Globe,* April 8, 1888.

14. Eva Gay, "Sewing Girls," *St. Paul Daily Globe,* June 10, 1888.

15. Eva Gay, "Search for Homes," *St. Paul Daily Globe,* August 5, 1888.

16. Eva Gay, "Eva Gay's Travels," *St. Paul Daily Globe,* April 22, 1888.

17. Timothy J. Gilfoyle, *City of Eros: New York City, Prostitution, and the Commercialization of Sex, 1790–1920* (New York: W. W. Norton, 1992), 60–61; Christine Stansell, *City of Women: Sex and Class in New York, 1789–1860* (Urbana: University of Illinois Press, 1987), 167.

18. Eva Gay, "The White Cross," *St. Paul Daily Globe,* July 8, 1888.

19. *First Biennial Report of the Bureau of Labor Statistics of the State of Minnesota,* 149–50.

20. Gay, "The White Cross."

21. "The Servant Girl Problem," *Minneapolis Tribune,* October 14, 1879.

22. "Met Two Dusky Damsels," *Minneapolis Tribune,* October 22, 1900.

23. "Naked in the Night," *Minneapolis Journal,* June 8, 1889. Leppala was also known as Eleanor Westphal.

24. "Crime's Catalogue," *Minneapolis Tribune,* November 18, 1879.

25. Gilfoyle, *City of Eros,* 60, 69; "The Scarlet Sin," *Minneapolis Journal,* June 16, 1886.

26. "Her Lover Got Angry," *Minneapolis Tribune,* December 23, 1888.

27. "Gracie Davis," *Minneapolis Tribune,* December 6, 1878; "It Was Pitiful," *St. Paul Pioneer Press,* December 6, 1878; "The Suicide," *St. Paul Daily Globe,* December 7, 1878.

28. William W. Sanger, *The History of Prostitution: Its Extent, Causes, and Effects Throughout the World* (1858; repr., New York: Eugenics Publishing Company, 1939), 452–54, 460–61, 539–40, 570–72.

29. "Died Repentant," *Minneapolis Tribune,* November 11, 1889; "A Big Haul," *Minneapolis Tribune,* December 14, 1875.

30. "Lured to a Den of Vice," *Minneapolis Tribune,* July 17, 1888.

31. "A Dramatic Scene," *St. Paul Daily Globe,* December 27, 1886.

32. "Spurned by Her Lover, Mrs. Stewart Seeks Refuge in a Low Resort," *Minneapolis Tribune,* February 2, 1907.

33. Ramsey County District Court document no. 14190, April 5, 1881, Minnesota Historical Society manuscript collections. Lola France was listed as Ida E. France in the 1870 federal census for St. Paul. Mary France states her age as forty-four in this document, meaning she was born in 1837 or 1838. Her death certificate gives her birth date as June 20, 1839.

34. Joel Best, *Controlling Vice,* 142. It is possible that Maria Denley was a pseudonym for Mary France. Denley first appears in the St. Paul directory in 1866, the same year that Mary France became the sole support of herself and her two daughters. Both Denley and France are listed at 63½ Robert, until 1870. The following year Denley disappears from the directory, but France remains at the same address.

35. "The Social Evil," *St. Paul Pioneer Press,* January 21, 1878. The younger daughter, Ida (or Lola in some sources), probably died in 1909 and was buried in the family plot at Lakewood Cemetery in Minneapolis under the name Ida Bouse.

36. Charlotte's death certificate (no. 30531, July 17, 1929) states she was born September 13, 1864, in Red Wing, Minnesota. However, in her signed affidavit provided for her mother's divorce she stated her age as twenty-four, indicating she was born in 1856 or 1857. In this affidavit Charlotte stated that her father left when she was about nine years old, which also supports 1855 or 1856 as her year of birth. Her age is given as fifteen in the 1870 federal census.

37. Rose, *Storyville, New Orleans,* 149–50.

38. "The Scarlet Sorceress," *St. Paul Daily Globe,* February 8, 1889.

39. Ibid.

40. "His Togs on Hertogs," *St. Paul Daily Globe,* June 14, 1889.

41. "More About Mme. Hertogs," *Minneapolis Journal,* June 13, 1889; "His Togs on Hertogs."

42. "This Tells the Tale," *St. Paul Daily Globe,* June 15, 1889. Hertogs was unable to refute the allegations against her and lost her libel suit. "Looks Bad for Hertogs," *Minneapolis Journal,* June 16, 1889; and *Minneapolis Journal,* June 17, 1889. The newspaper noted that Judge Young's instructions to the jury were tilted in favor of the *Globe,* as the newspaper had a duty to expose vice.

43. "The Scarlet Sorceress," *St. Paul Daily Globe,* February 8, 1889.

44. "Will Sidle's Death" and "William H. Sidle," *Minneapolis Tribune,* February 17, 1877.

45. "Emotional Insanity," *Minneapolis Tribune,* June 2, 1877; "Kate Noonan's

Case," *Minneapolis Tribune,* June 4, 1877; and "Fighting for Life," *Minneapolis Tribune,* June 5, 1877.

46. "Not Guilty," *Minneapolis Tribune,* December 24, 1877.

47. Horatio P. Van Cleve, *The Van Cleve Family Pioneers in Minnesota* (New York: Self-published, 1959), 45–49; "The Defense," *Minneapolis Tribune,* December 13, 1877.

48. "Servant-Gal-ism," *St. Paul Pioneer Press,* June 10, 1877.

49. "Ethel Wanted to Die," *Minneapolis Tribune,* November 6, 1894. Ethel attempted suicide with a morphine overdose.

50. Washburn, *The Underworld Sewer,* 176–77.

51. "A Brutal Landlady—A First Street Cyprian on the Warpath—A Serious Case," *St. Paul Daily Globe,* March 13, 1887.

52. Washburn, *Underworld Sewer,* 180–82; Washburn supposedly lived in Minneapolis from 1920 to 1925, long after she left the commercial sex trade (xi). However, she does not appear in any Minneapolis city directories or the 1920 federal census for Minnesota under that name.

53. Madeleine Blair, *Madeleine: An Autobiography,* ed. Marcia Carlisle (1919; repr., New York: Persea Books, 1986), 251. Madeleine visited Minneapolis in about 1897 and described her abortive trip to visit a prostitute she had known in Chicago who lived at a brothel at 25 Main Street. The text does not specify whether it was Main Street Northeast or Main Street Southeast. Both addresses, about two blocks apart, were bordellos at that date, but judging by the policeman's description of the place as "the most notorious bawdy-house in Minneapolis," she was probably looking for Jennie Jones's house at 25 Main Street Northeast.

54. Ibid., 133–34.

55. Ibid., 72–73.

56. Ibid., 72–73, 112.

57. "Professor of Music Is Innocent Cause of War," *Minneapolis Tribune,* February 2, 1904.

58. Blair, *Madeleine,* 140–41.

59. Washburn, *Underworld Sewer,* 183–86.

60. Blair, *Madeleine,* 272–73.

61. Gilfoyle, *City of Eros,* 83.

62. "A Lively Tussle," *Minneapolis Tribune,* August 29, 1893; "Ida Dorsey's Sparks," *Minneapolis Journal,* March 26, 1894.

63. Hennepin County Recorder's Office, Miscellaneous Records Book 4, p. 140. Sarah Medberry was probably involved in the sex trade as well, but efforts to identify her have been unsuccessful. The street on which Ellsworth's brothel was located is now part of the Ninth District Federal Reserve Bank campus.

64. "Minneapolis—The Northfield Robbers," *St. Paul Pioneer Press*, September 20, 1876. The centennial refers to the celebration of the United States' first one hundred years as a nation. The celebration was held in Philadelphia, and presumably this where Jesse James intended to take Mollie Ellsworth.

65. "Mollie Ellsworth," *Minneapolis Tribune*, October 28, 1876.

66. Hennepin County Probate Record no. 000791. Hennepin County Miscellaneous Records Book 6, p. 530. Albert Ovitt, the administrator for Kate Travers/Ellsworth's estate, assigned the lease for 16 Second Avenue North to Kate Campbell in exchange "for [unspecified] valuable consideration." Ellsworth's estate went to Frank Travers of Allegheny, New York, who apparently was her father.

67. "Raid Last Night," *Minneapolis Tribune,* April 14, 1873.

68. Peggy Pascoe, *Relations of Rescue: The Search for Female Moral Authority in the America West, 1874–1939* (New York: Oxford University Press, 1991), 4–6.

69. Atwater, *History of Minneapolis,* 250–52, 977–79.

70. Harriet G. Walker, "History," *Third Annual Report of the Sisterhood of Bethany* (Minneapolis: Wilcox, Young & Co., Printers, 1878), 3.

71. "Two Women Sent to the Penitentiary," *Minneapolis Tribune,* March 22, 1876.

72. Charity, letter to the editor, "That Sentence," *Minneapolis Tribune,* March 26, 1876. Another article placed the number of prostitutes in the city at 300–400 ("The Pardoning Power," *Minneapolis Tribune,* June 6, 1876).

73. Charity, letter to the editor, "That Sentence"; Gilfoyle, *City of Eros,* 58. The population of St. Anthony and Minneapolis had quadrupled in the decade that started in 1865, going from 8,106 to 32,721. U.S. census figures for New York City show a population of 813,669 in 1860 and 942,292 in 1870.

74. "Another Reference to a Sad Case," *Minneapolis Tribune,* March 26, 1876; Austin H. Young to John S. Pillsbury, May 19, 1876, Governor John Pillsbury Records, 111.F.5.9 (B), box 18, file no. 368; Stillwater State Prison convict record 112.D.3.3B-1, pp. 426–27, Minnesota Historical Society manuscript collection; Walker, "History," 4.

75. "Unpleasant Reports," *St. Paul Pioneer Press,* July 23, 1876. "Bagnio" was another term for brothel.

76. "Those Unpleasant Rumors," *St. Paul Pioneer Press,* July 25, 1876; "The Suicide," *St. Paul Pioneer Press,* December 6, 1878.

77. "Yesterdays, Todays, and Tomorrows," *Minneapolis Tribune,* May 15, 1910.

78. "Bethany Home," *Minneapolis Tribune,* January 9, 1878; Charlotte O. C. Van Cleve, "Address of the President," *Third Annual Report of the Sisterhood of Bethany,* 10.

79. "Women's Work—Mrs. Van Cleve's Address," *Minneapolis Tribune,* May 1, 1876.

80. "City Council," *Minneapolis Tribune,* January 29, 1878.

81. Pascoe, *Relations of Rescue,* 4.

82. "Municipal Morality," *Minneapolis Tribune,* March 31, 1879. Governor John Pillsbury called the meeting to order. Many of the town's elite, such as judges, clergy, and aldermen, attended this meeting. Even businessman J. A. Wolverton was on the list of attendees. Many years later, Wolverton's only son would become the male companion of one of Minneapolis's leading madams.

83. "Public Morals," *St. Paul Daily Globe,* March 31, 1879.

84. An 1876 Minnesota law allowed women to vote in school and library board elections, but they could not vote in other city, state, or national elections.

85. "Bethany Home," *Minneapolis Tribune,* December 12, 1879.

86. Harriet G. Walker, "Secretary's Report," *Fourth Annual Report of the Sisterhood of Bethany* (Minneapolis: Johnson, Smith & Harrison, 1879), 13.

2. THE WAR ON THE MADAMS

1. Another account of this brawl stated that Conley operated a "disreputable house," not a bowling alley ("Police Courts," *Minneapolis Tribune,* December 25, 1872).

2. Hennepin County Property Records Miscellaneous Book 197, p. 471. A 1920 affidavit by her nephew, William H. Mack, states that her name was Nettie Conley and variations such as Nellie, Connelly, and Connolly were inadvertent misspellings. The description of Conley was taken from Stillwater Prison convict records.

3. "District Court—Criminal Matters," *Minneapolis Tribune,* May 24, 1873; "Raid Last Night," *Minneapolis Tribune,* April 4, 1873; "District Court—Criminal," *Minneapolis Tribune,* May 27, 1873; "District Court—Keeping House of Ill Fame," *Minneapolis Tribune,* June 3, 1873; "The Nettie Connolly Case," *Minneapolis Tribune,* June 4, 1873; "District Court," *Minneapolis Tribune,* June 5, 1873, and June 10, 1873. Throughout this particular trial, the court documents apparently referred to Conley both as "Nettie Connolly" and "Carrie Blume."

4. Hennepin County probate record no. 021963.

5. Hennepin County death certificates, vol. 102, p. 2297, lists Conley's birth date as December 16, 1849, and her birthplace as New York.

6. Conley's great-grandfather, Peter Angle, was born in New Jersey about 1775. According to RootsWeb.com, Family Trees, Peter's father was William Angle (1747/48–1791), and he lived in New Jersey. William, in turn, was the son of Nicholas Angle (1723–81). Nicholas was the son of William Angle (Engle), who immigrated to America from Holland. A "Willm" [William] Angle shows

up in the town of Saratoga, Albany County, New York, in the 1790 federal census. His household includes four white free males under the age of sixteen, one of whom may have been Peter, who would have been about fifteen.

7. "East Side Amusements," *St. Paul Pioneer Press,* December 24, 1872.

8. Hennepin County criminal index, no. 416, May 22, 1873.

9. "Change of Venue," *Minneapolis Tribune,* May 9, 1873; "District Court—Criminal Matters," *Minneapolis Tribune,* May 24, 1873; "Raid Last Night," *Minneapolis Tribune,* April 4, 1873; "District Court—Criminal," *Minneapolis Tribune,* May 27, 1873; "District Court—Keeping House of Ill Fame," *Minneapolis Tribune,* June 3, 1873; "The Nettie Connolly Case," *Minneapolis Tribune,* June 4, 1873; "District Court," *Minneapolis Tribune,* June 5, 1873; and "District Court," *Minneapolis Tribune,* June 10, 1873. Conley's first establishment seemed to be located at 27 Main Street Southeast.

10. "Around the Town," *Minneapolis Tribune,* June 15, 1873; "Don't Agree," *Minneapolis Tribune,* September 2, 1873; "Brief Mention," *Minneapolis Tribune,* September 3, 1873; "Dissatisfied Wives," *Minneapolis Tribune,* September 27, 1874.

11. "An Objectionable Hat, Experience of an Insurance Agent at an East Side Bagnio," *St. Paul Pioneer Press,* May 27, 1876.

12. "Minneapolis," *St. Paul Pioneer Press,* May 30, 1876. Meanwhile the same newspaper noted other disturbances on the Minneapolis riverfront: "a row of very liberal proportions on the East" had the police looking for the wounded and missing, while a brothel on First Avenue North and Second Street was attacked by vigilantes. Once the inmates fled in their nightclothes, the mob went looking for other targets near the Hennepin Avenue Bridge.

13. "Have We in This City a Licensed System of Prostitution?," *St. Paul Pioneer Press,* January 11, 1878. McKibbin was pastor of Central Presbyterian Church in St. Paul.

14. For a more complete account of the St. Paul campaign, see Best, *Controlling Vice,* 90–93. The 1878–80 campaign led by McKibbin fizzled out after he left to head another congregation in Pittsburgh.

15. "Municipal Morality," *Minneapolis Tribune,* March 31, 1879; "Temperance Rally," *Minneapolis Tribune,* April 1, 1879.

16. "Crime's Catalogue," *Minneapolis Tribune,* November 18, 1879.

17. "Bethany Home," *Hennepin County Mirror,* December 13, 1879.

18. "The Courts," *Minneapolis Tribune,* March 1, 1880.

19. "The City," *Minneapolis Tribune,* October 16, 1880; "Municipal Court," *Minneapolis Tribune,* May 19, 1876.

20. *Minneapolis City Directory for 1877–1878* (Minneapolis: W. M. Campbell, [1877]) and *Minneapolis City Directory for 1878–1879* (Minneapolis: John, Smith,

and Harrison, 1878). Kate Johnson does not appear at the First Avenue address in the 1880 federal census, but another woman, Christine Erickson, who like Johnson was born in Norway, approximately thirty years old, and the head of a brothel, is listed as living at 116 First Avenue South. Johnson and Erickson may have been the same person (1880 federal census, Hennepin County, Minneapolis, Enumeration District 242, p. 265).

21. Hennepin County Miscellaneous Records Book 34, p. 227; Deeds Book 88, pp. 573, 574, 608; and Deeds Book 274, p. 587. Carnahan purchased the three lots for $12,500. She held the property at 213–229 First Street until 1889, when she sold it for $95,000.

22. "The Courts, Two of the Fallen Women Found Guilty at the D'strict Bar," *Minneapolis Tribune,* March 19, 1880, and "The Courts," *Minneapolis Tribune,* March 20, 1880. The latter article noted that Anna Carnahan's trial would be put off until the next court term owing to her illness.

23. "The Courts," *Minneapolis Tribune,* March 22, 1880.

24. "The Scarlet Women," *Minneapolis Journal,* October 29, 1880; and "On to Stillwater, Three Notorious Women Taken Away This Afternoon," *Minneapolis Journal,* October 30, 1880. The article noted, "If the judgment of the district court is good and confirmed by the supreme court, then the ordinance is not a bar to repeating fines and punishments for the same offenses."

25. "The Social Evil Cases," *St. Paul Dispatch,* October 30, 1880. See also *State v. Oleseon* (filed June 9, 1880), *Northwestern Reporter,* 1880, 959–70.

26. "Gone Over the Road," *St. Paul Pioneer Press,* October 31, 1880. The article noted that when Sarah Carnahan's case was taken up in the next term, she would be "undoubtedly convicted."

27. "The Scarlet Women," *Minneapolis Journal,* November 8, 1880. The reporter could not resist a dig at St. Paul, noting that madams there had invited the Minneapolis sex workers to move across the river, "by which it seems that in our sinful sister city there is none to make the bad girls afraid."

28. "The Social Evil, the Spread Throughout the City," *Minneapolis Journal,* November 9, 1880.

29. "The Courts, Municipal," *Minneapolis Journal,* October 29, 1880.

30. "The Courts," *Minneapolis Journal,* December 8, 1880.

31. "The Courts," *Minneapolis Tribune,* January 9, 1881. Judge Young presided over Carnahan's second trial as well. Carnahan/Dunn was still operating her bordello in 1885 when the census taker listed her and thirteen other women living at her First Street property.

32. Governor Pillsbury Records, box 26, file no. 436, Minnesota Historical Society collections; editorial (no title), *Minneapolis Tribune,* February 8, 1881; "The Pioneer Press," *Minneapolis Journal,* April 21, 1881. The petition also

listed the total amount of monthly municipal fines paid by each madam for the period January 26, 1878, to June 30, 1880: Campbell, $856; Conley, $750; and Johnson, $937.

33. *Proceedings of the City Council of the City of Minneapolis from April 13th, 1880 to April 12th, 1881* (Minneapolis: Tribune Job Printing Company, 1886), 184. At that time, all city charter amendments had to be passed by the legislature. Copies of city council proceeds may be obtained at Minneapolis City Hall, 250 Fourth Street South, Minneapolis, the Minnesota Historical Society, or the Hennepin County Central Library, Minneapolis.

34. "The New Charter of Minneapolis," *St. Paul Pioneer Press*, February 11, 1881. The bill's official name was Senate File No. 213/House File No. 256 (SF 213/HF 256). The text of the house version is as follows with the senate amendments underlined:

"Be it enacted by the Legislature of the State of Minnesota That Section 9 of chapter 100 relating to offences against chastity, morality and decency be amended to read as follows: Section 9. Whoever keeps a house of ill fame resorted to for the purpose of prostitution or lewdness shall be punished by imprisonment in the state prison not more than one year *nor less than six months* or by fine not exceeding *five hundred dollars nor less than* one hundred dollars. Provided that any person convicted of the foregoing offence under an ordinance of any municipal corporation shall not be liable to conviction and punishment under this section for the same offense. This act shall take effect and be in force from and after its passage."

35. "The Remarks of the Chaplain Satterlee on the Social Evil," *Minneapolis Tribune*, February 14, 1881; T. A. N., "Chaplain Satterlee's Error," *Minneapolis Tribune*, February 14, 1881; W. W. Satterlee, "Chaplain Satterlee's Error," *Minneapolis Tribune*, February 17, 1881.

36. "The Devil's Own," *Minneapolis Journal*, February 16, 1881.

37. Ibid.

38. "Gov. Pillsbury," *Minneapolis Journal*, February 23, 1881.

39. "Who Shall Cast the First Stone?," *St. Paul Pioneer Press*, April 21, 1881.

40. "The Old and the New—The Social Evil," *Minneapolis Tribune*, April 13, 1881. In his speech, Rand differentiated the reformers like Judge Young from the Sisterhood of Bethany, calling the managers of Bethany Home "a band of heroic women."

Many years after the campaign against the madams, a historian of the police department recalled the failed reform effort: Mayor Rand "took occasion to read a lesson to those citizens of good intent who were meddling with the social evil. It would appear that these good people had been interfering with the functions of the police department by securing indictments against keepers of houses of ill fame. The mayor was a strong advocate of the policy of strict police surveillance of those evils, which afflict society—houses of ill fame, gambling houses, and the liquor saloons." Rand "endeavored to show how such intermeddling only increased and intensified the evils it strove to cure by breaking up well governed disorderly houses and scattered the inmates in private rooms all over the city"; *History of the Police and Fire Departments of the Twin Cities* (Minneapolis: American Land and Title Register Association Publishers, 1899), 47.

41. "Mayor Rand's Attitude," *Hennepin County Mirror*, April 16, 1881.

42. Atwater, *History of Minneapolis*, 326.

43. *Minneapolis City Directory for 1886–1887* (Minneapolis: C. Wright Davison, 1886).

44. "Sackett and Wiggins' Dime Museum" (advertisement), *Minneapolis Tribune*, September 27, 1885. By 1889 the Dime Museum was under new management and had moved to 40–44 Marquette Avenue.

45. "Academy of Music—Oscar Wilde" (advertisement), *Minneapolis Tribune*, March 15, 1882; "Oscar Wilde," *Minneapolis Tribune*, March 16, 1882; "Melange," *Minneapolis Tribune*, December 6, 1879; "Gossip About Town," *Minneapolis Tribune*, December 17, 1879.

46. "The City's Shame: The Theatre Comique and How It Disgraces Minneapolis," *Minneapolis Tribune*, February 10, 1881; "The Road to the Devil" (letter to the editor), *Minneapolis Tribune*, February 9, 1881; "On Sunday Night," *Minneapolis Tribune*, February 4, 1889.

47. "Under the Gaslight," *Minneapolis Tribune*, July 20, 1880; "Brief Mention," *Minneapolis Tribune*, May 13, 1881; "An All-Night Restaurant," *Minneapolis Tribune*, October 3, 1886.

48. "Pulled," *Minneapolis Tribune*, November 2, 1873; "The Gambling Den," *Minneapolis Tribune*, April 10, 1881; "The Gamblers," *Minneapolis Tribune*, September 14, 1881; "Bucking the Tiger," *Minneapolis Tribune*, September 24, 1882. John Flannigan, along with partners Michael Shelly and Col. William A. Tanner, ran what was called a "gambling syndicate" for the next twenty years ("City News" and "A Profitable Business," *Minneapolis Journal*, October 23, 1902).

49. "Chalybeate Springs," *St. Paul Pioneer Press*, August 26, 1876; "Gossip About Town," *Minneapolis Tribune*, October 30, 1876. Pettingill operated the boat rides from 1875 until a portion of the tunnel collapsed on December 23, 1880.

50. *Minneapolis City Directory for 1885–1886* (Minneapolis: C. Wright Davison, 1885); *Minneapolis City Directory for 1886–1887*.

51. "Forefather's Day," *Minneapolis Journal*, December 22, 1881; *First Anniversary of the New England Society of Minneapolis* (Minneapolis: Dimond and Ross Printers, 1881). The publication lists many of the guests, such as Charles

Pillsbury, his brother Frederick, and their father, George Pillsbury; the Reverend Charles Seccombe, one of the founders of the First Congregational Church; James Tuttle, pastor of the First Universalist Church of Minneapolis; mill owners such as Woodbury Fisk, Caleb Dorr, and O. A. Pray; and decorator John Bradstreet.

52. The 1880 figure is quoted from http://www.census.gov/population. Rena Michaels Atchison, *Un-American Immigration: Its Present Effects and Future Perils; A Case Study from the Census of 1890* (Chicago: Charles H. Kerr, 1894), 170, 50, 156, 157.

53. "Instructions to Peter Garrioch" from Franklin Steele, dated January 12, 1841: "In regard to the drinking of wine or other liquors in the store, I shall leave it to your judgment to dictate when, however I wish it dispensed with upon all occasions where it would be likely to promote dissipation" (Henry H. Sibley Papers, Minnesota Historical Society). Lumberman Daniel Stanchfield recalled an incident in 1847 when Steele took a large party to St. Anthony Falls. At that event, "There were good wines in abundance, which made the crowd merry, and two hours were spent in feasting and drinking"; Daniel Stanchfield, "History of Pioneer Lumbering on the Upper Mississippi and Its Tributaries, with Biographic Sketches," *Minnesota Historical Society Collections* 9 (1901), 327.

54. "The Danger," *Minneapolis Journal*, March 30, 1882.

55. Lincoln Steffens, *The Shame of the Cities* (New York: Hill and Wang, 1957), 44.

56. "Democratic," *Minneapolis Journal*, March 30 and 31, 1882.

57. "City Election," *Minneapolis Journal*, April 5, 1882. Loring polled slightly less than 36 percent of the vote; Satterlee received 10 percent.

58. "The City Liquor License," *Minneapolis Journal*, April 4, 1884.

59. "A People's Victory," *Minneapolis Tribune*, April 2, 1884; "The Official Count," *Minneapolis Tribune*, April 3, 1884. Pillsbury received 12,244 votes; Ames, 5,876; and Holt, the third-party candidate, 862.

60. "Pillsbury's Policy—The New Mayor's Message," *Minneapolis Journal*, April 8, 1884.

61. *Proceedings of the City Council of the City of Minneapolis from April 8th, 1884, to April 1st, 1885* (Minneapolis: Tribune Job Printing Company, 1887), 58–60; "The High License Ordinance," *St. Paul Pioneer Press*, April 30, 1884; "The Active Patrol Districts," *St. Paul Pioneer Press*, May 1, 1884.

62. The 1884 Liquor Patrol Limits also included a seven-block area bounded by Twenty-Third Avenue South, Twenty-Fifth Street South, Twenty-Seventh Avenue South, and railroad tracks in South Minneapolis as well as a section of Nicollet Island where the Hennepin Avenue Bridge crossed over it, and a wedge-shaped area just below the Washington Avenue Bridge on the west bank.

63. A representative from the license inspection bureau explained that the patrol limits grew out of a desire to confine lumberjacks to one area The city had nice wooden sidewalks, "but the lumberjacks with their big heavy shoes, most of them with nails, ripped the sidewalks to pieces almost as fast as they were put in. So the city fathers tried to figure out a way to keep the lumberjacks below Sixth Street." The article concluded that the police department was constrained by these outdated limits and often wished that the lumberjacks had not worn hobnailed boots or that the city had put in concrete sidewalks earlier (Jay Edgerton, "Patrol Limits—A Lumberjack 'Hangover,'" *Minneapolis Star,* September 26, 1956).

64. "Turned into the Streets," *Minneapolis Journal,* May 12, 1885; "Additional Local News—In General," *Minneapolis Tribune,* May 13, 1885.

65. "The Courts—Municipal," *Minneapolis Tribune,* November 22, 1881; "The City—In General," *Minneapolis Tribune,* December 19, 1886; "The City's Shame," *Minneapolis Journal,* June 17, 1886, and "Cyprians in Court," *St. Paul Daily Globe,* December 12, 1886. Madams Nettie Conley, Mary France, Sarah Dunn, Carrie Moore, Hattie Brush, and Hattie McBride were indicted for renting out their property as brothels. Although Kate Johnson was born in Norway, the newspapers often used the term "Swede" to denote any Scandinavian.

66. Hennepin County Deeds Book 109, p. 375, recorded July 18, 1882. Some accounts give the address as 203 First Street South.

67. "Police Courts," *Minneapolis Daily Evening News,* July 8, 1872; "Minneapolis—Police Court," *St. Paul Pioneer Press,* May 14, 1872; and "Police Courts," *Minneapolis Tribune,* May 22, 1872.

68. Hennepin County Deeds Book 128, p. 614, dated December 5, 1882, but recorded May 5, 1883. The legal description of Conley's purchase is Lot 11 and a portion of Lot 12 in Block 1 of the Resurvey of Subdivision of the Ground Lots between Pine, Bay, Main and Second Streets. Conley paid $950 in cash, and the Chutes held a mortgage for the balance of the purchase price, which was $3,825.

69. "Minneapolis Globelets," *St. Paul Daily Globe,* May 10, 1883.

70. Hennepin County Liens Book E, p. 487, recorded July 7, 1884, and p. 231, recorded February 12, 1884. Conley, Baker, and Wright signed an agreement dated July 12, 1883, for bricks and labor that was mentioned in Hennepin County Liens Book E, p. 487. Conley had paid for part of this work, but for some unstated reason there was still an outstanding balance on both accounts. There may have been a dispute over quality and workmanship, or perhaps Conley was overextended and suffering from a shortage of cash. Whatever the reason, the two contractors filed liens against the Main Street property that were not fully paid until 1886.

71. "Growth of a Year," *Minneapolis Tribune,* December 31, 1883.

72. *Sanborn Insurance Map, 1885–1889* (New York: Sanborn Map Publishing Company, 1885), vol. 2, p. 59A; St. Anthony Water Power Company photograph dated April 30, 1899, Hennepin History Museum. Minneapolis did not start issuing building permits until 1884.

73. "Fatal," *Minneapolis Tribune,* May 27, 1895; "Lived Only Seven Hours," *Minneapolis Tribune,* May 28, 1895; "Official Inquiries Made," *Minneapolis Tribune,* May 29, 1895.

74. Minnesota state census, 1885, Hennepin County, Minneapolis. Nettie Conley appears as "Nellie Canley"; Seelye is listed as "H. S. Seeley."

75. "City Section," *Minneapolis Tribune,* July 2, 1875, July 3, 1875, August 7, 1875, September 1, 1875, September 5, 1875, October 16, 1875, and October 23, 1875.

76. "The Scarlet Women's Scare," *St. Paul Pioneer Press,* September 25, 1885. "Resort" was another term for brothel.

77. Hennepin County Mortgages Book 115, p. 358, recorded June 25, 1884.

78. Michael Conforti, ed., *Art and Life on the Upper Mississippi, 1890–1915* (Newark: University of Delaware Press, 1994), 67; Hennepin County Mortgages Book 204, p. 236.

79. "Melange," *Minneapolis Tribune,* February 2, 1878. The Island Club performed at the home of John Watson on Nicollet Island. "Melange," *Minneapolis Tribune,* April 20, 1878; "Society," *Minneapolis Tribune,* April 27, 1878; and "The Orphans and Widows," *Minneapolis Tribune,* May 4, 1878. Bradstreet's association with the theater was ongoing. In 1885, his firm supplied "the artistic furniture, curtains, and mirrors for the Sackett and Wiggins' Dime Museum at 214–216 Hennepin Avenue" (advertisement for Sackett and Wiggins' Dime Museum, *Minneapolis Tribune,* September 27, 1885). Bradstreet also redecorated the Grand Opera House in the late 1880s.

80. *Minneapolis City Directory for 1886–1887.*

81. William C. Edgar and Loring Staples, *The Minneapolis Club: A Review of Its History, 1883–1920 and 1920–1974* (Minneapolis: Minneapolis Club, 1974), 7. John Bradstreet was also a member of the Minneapolis Club. For many years, this organization was the most exclusive businessmen's club in town. Membership was limited to white men who could afford the steep dues, but money alone would not guarantee admission to the circle of membership. The Minneapolis Club is now located at 729 Second Avenue South.

82. "John S. Bradstreet Dies," *Minneapolis Tribune,* August 11, 1914. Bradstreet's connection to Bradford was mentioned frequently in accounts of his social activities and professional life.

83. Hennepin County Deeds Book 109, p. 375; Deeds Book 123, pp. 146, 147, 148; Deeds Book 128, p. 614; Deeds Book 127, p. 631; Deeds Book 196, p. 443; Deeds Book 212, p. 480.

84. Hennepin County Deeds Book 126, p. 427; and Hennepin County Mortgages Book 153, p. 175. Hennepin County Miscellaneous Book 197, p. 472. An affidavit by William H. Mack, Conley's nephew, identifies the correct spelling of the name as Henry U. Seelye, although his names appears with several different spellings in various documents, including Henry M. Seely and Seeley.

85. Minnesota state census, Schedule 23, p. 8. The census manuscript gives Seelye's age as twenty-four (about ten years younger than Conley) and states that he was born in Canada. His death certificate, however, lists his birth date as July 11, 1852, suggesting that he was only two years younger than Conley.

86. "Minneapolis News—Minneapolis Globelets," *St. Paul Daily Globe,* May 10, 1881.

87. "Spray of the Falls," *St. Paul Pioneer Press,* February 23, 1884.

88. Hennepin County Deeds Book 426, p. 123.

89. Hennepin County Mortgages Book 95, p. 148; and Mortgages Book 195, p. 279.

90. Hennepin County Mortgages Book 105, p. 84; Mortgages Book 321, p. 318; Mortgages Book 153, pp. 175, 178; Mortgages Book 181, p. 487; Hennepin County Miscellaneous Book 52, p. 299.

91. Best, *Controlling Vice,* 45, 142.

92. Hennepin County Deeds Book 130, p. 590; "Spray of the Falls," *St. Paul Pioneer Press,* August 10, 1883. The reporter got the address wrong: the building was on the corner of Second Avenue and First Street. Mayor O'Brien's campaign against regulated prostitution did little to permanently suppress the sex trade, and the policy was dropped by his successor, Democrat Edmund Rice (Best, *Controlling Vice,* 94–97).

93. Mary France's name or another one of her aliases, "Mrs. Eggelston," appears on Minneapolis building permits A620, A857, A890, A924, A1012, and A1439, issued in 1887 and 1888.

94. "Her Picture," *Minneapolis Tribune,* August 8, 1900.

95. Information from the 1870 federal census, Ancestry.com.

96. LaPorte Genealogical Society website,"Early Marriage," La Porte County, Indiana, Book E, http://www.lpslicer.com/mctartan_5b.htm.

97. The 1860 federal census, Indiana, La Porte County, 271, 289; 1870 federal census, Indiana, La Porte County, 21; Elizabeth died July 8, 1879, and is buried at Rolling Prairie Cemetery in Kankakee. The 1880 federal census, La Porte County, Michigan City, shows Dale living with the Amos C. Hall family.

98. Herbert Asbury, *Gem of the Prairie: An Informal History of the Chicago Underworld* (DeKalb: Northern Illinois University Press, 1986), 95.

99. "The Court Records—Municipal," *Minneapolis Tribune*, August 31, 1883; "The Courts, Minneapolis—Municipal," *St. Paul Pioneer Press*, September 27 and October 30, 1883.

100. "The Courts, Minneapolis—Municipal," *St. Paul Pioneer Press*, November 21, 1884.

101. Hennepin County Deeds Book 131, p. 580. Berry joined the force in 1867 and by 1877 had risen to the rank of captain; see George E. Warner and Charles M. Foote, *History of Hennepin County and the City of Minneapolis* (1881; repr., Marceline, Mo.: Walsworth Company, 1976), 510.

102. Hennepin County Lien Book E, pp. 41, 125, 182. The complaint specifically identifies the property as 228 First Street. The mechanic's lien provides only a partial inventory of all the materials that went into the building, as White had already paid for some items.

103. "The Scarlet Women's Scare," *St. Paul Pioneer Press*, September 25, 1885.

104. Hennepin County Deeds Book 135, p. 300, dated August 21, 1884. Amos Berry held the property for only another year and then defaulted on his mortgage; it was redeemed by Hiram C. Truesdale (Hennepin County Deeds Book 172, p. 335). Jennie Jones, signing as Louise Robbins, gave Truesdale a quitclaim deed to the property in exchange for one hundred dollars (Hennepin County Deeds Book 173, p. 100). A quitclaim deed released Jones's interest in the property without guaranteeing that she actually had a legitimate claim to the real estate. Truesdale, a native of Illinois, settled in Minneapolis in 1882 after receiving a law degree from the University of Iowa. He was a partner in the firm of Lawrence, Truesdale, and Corriston. Two years before his death, Truesdale was appointed the chief justice of the Arizona Territorial Supreme Court by President William McKinley ("H. C. Truesdale Dead," *Minneapolis Journal*, October 29, 1897). The deed from Truesdale to Gage is recorded in Hennepin County Deeds Book 165, p. 574. Although the deed is dated January 12, 1886, it was not recorded until 1889, suggesting that L. J. Gage served as a shield for respectable property owners along First Street. Alfred Condit deeded property in Block 15 to Gage in 1885 (Hennepin County Deeds Book 165, pp. 36 and 41).

105. Minnesota 1885 state census, Schedule 71, p. 4. The women's given ages range from seventeen to thirty-two. Both Jones and Hamilton sliced seven years from their actual ages. Jones was thirty-two, but she was listed as twenty-five; Hamilton was twenty-four, but she is shown as seventeen.

106. Minneapolis building permits A1585, August 21, 1889; A3646, July 22, 1893.

107. "A Fortunate Unfortunate, Death Brings Sweet Release from a Life of Shame," *St. Paul Daily Globe,* March 14, 1887.

108. Lakewood Cemetery, lot 36, section 11. Lake Calhoun is part of the Minneapolis "Chain of Lakes" that includes Lake Harriet, Cedar Lake, and Lake of the Isles. As the city expanded away from the riverfront, the neighborhoods surrounding the "Chain of Lakes" became home to the city's elite.

109. Hennepin County Death Records, vol. 1, p. 275, no. 8.

110. "$35 for a Woman's Yell," *Minneapolis Journal,* June 2, 1885.

111. "Police Courts," *Minneapolis Daily Evening News,* July 8, 1872.

112. Minnesota Death Certificate no. 24601 (June 18, 1918), Minnesota Historical Society. Other sources suggest Ida was born in 1864. Most Woodford County birth records date from 1911 to the present; very few exist from before that year.

113. Only Marie's father is named on her death certificate; Minnesota Death Certificate no. 56-1239 (August 5, 1907), Minnesota Historical Society.

114. Minnesota Death Certificate no. 24601 (June 18, 1918).

115. John Kellogg, "The Formation of the Black Residential Areas in Lexington, Kentucky, 1865–1887," *Journal of Southern History* 48 (February 1982): 36–37; and Marion B. Lucas, *A History of Blacks in Kentucky: From Slavery to Segregation, 1760–1891* (Frankfort: Kentucky Historical Society, 2003), 274.

116. Federal census 1880, Kentucky, Fayette County, vol. 8, ED 68, sheet 59. Most of the ages listed on the census form are different from the birth dates shown on their respective death certificates. Marie would have been thirty-eight, not forty, in 1880; Ida fourteen, not nineteen; Roberta about twelve, not seventeen; and Moses, who was born March 25, 1877, would have been three years old, not fourteen. Only the ages of the two youngest boys—George, age six, and James, five months—are correct. The couple had more children after 1880: Henry was born in 1881 and Nebraska in 1884. Marie, George, and their sons were described as black, while Ida and Roberta were called "mulatto."

117. The 1870 federal census for Woodford County shows William Turner as a sixty-year-old black farmhand possessing three hundred dollars' worth of personal property and one thousand dollars of real estate. He lived with his wife, Ann, fifty-four, and two children.

118. Lucas, *A History of Blacks in Kentucky,* 179.

119. "Ida Dorsey in Trouble," *Minneapolis Tribune,* September 9, 1894.

120. Minnesota state census, Ramsey County, Schedule 6, May 2, 1885. Dorsey may have operated a bordello in St. Paul as May Johnson; "otherwise

Ida Dorsey" paid a monthly fine for occupying a house of ill fame ("Globules," *St. Paul Daily Globe,* March 23, 1886).

121. "Crimes and Criminals," *St. Paul Pioneer Press,* March 22, 1886.

122. "Almost a Babylon," *Minneapolis Journal,* June 15, 1886.

123. Lawrence James Hill, "History of Variety–Vaudeville in Minneapolis, Minnesota" (Ph.D. diss, University of Minnesota, 1979), 93. An 1875 newspaper article cited an ordinance dated May 16, 1873, that prohibited indecent representations and apparently was the basis for the city's ban on the dance.

124. Gilfoyle, *City of Eros,* 161–62.

125. Rose, *Storyville, New Orleans,* 149.

126. "Almost a Babylon."

127. "Scarlet Sorceress," *St. Paul Globe,* February 8, 1889. In another incident Dorsey explained to a judge that she felt compelled to dance, despite a swollen ankle, "because we are colored," playing on another racial stereotype ("Too Accommodating," *St. Paul Daily Globe,* August 27, 1887).

128. "Want Ida Squelched," *Minneapolis Tribune,* June 13, 1888.

129. Ibid.

130. "Couldn't Hold Him," *Minneapolis Tribune,* June 23, 1888; see also "The Municipal Court," *St. Paul Pioneer Press,* June 23, 1888. Both charges against Morris were dismissed.

131. "Closing Them Up," *Minneapolis Journal,* June 25, 1886, and "Charged with Crimes," *St. Paul Daily Globe,* June 26, 1886. The name "Mary Coon" was a racial slur, not an alternative identity that Dorsey created.

132. "Ninety Days at Stillwater," *St. Paul Daily Globe,* July 9, 1886; "The City—Ida Dorsey Sentenced," *Minneapolis Tribune,* July 9, 1886.

133. Hennepin County Criminal Records no. 1661; Stillwater Prison Convict Records, vol. D, p. 636, Minnesota Historical Society collections. The prison records make no mention of the liquor-selling charges, only that she was convicted of keeping a house of ill fame. She was released on September 25, 1886. There is no evidence that Dorsey was ever legally married, but she told at least one census taker that she had given birth to five children.

134. "All Sorts," *St. Paul Daily Globe,* June 26, 1886.

135. "Election Prophets," *Minneapolis Journal,* April 6, 1886.

136. "Like an Avalanche, the Democratic Hosts Pour Down Upon Their Opponents, the Defeat of 1882 Repeated," *Minneapolis Journal,* April 7, 1886; "Yesterday's Revolution," *Minneapolis Tribune,* April 7, 1886.

137. "The Mayor's Order on the Social Evil—It Shall Not Be Recognized and Licensed," *St. Paul Daily Globe,* June 3, 1886.

138. "The Caucuses" and "Dr. Ames (letter to the editor from A. A. Ames),"

Minneapolis Tribune, March 29, 1876; "The Contest for Mayor," *Minneapolis Tribune,* April 2, 1876; "Election Day," *Minneapolis Tribune,* April 4, 1876; "The Election," *Minneapolis Tribune,* April 5, 1876. Van Cleve was elected to the school board. Ames's animosity toward Republicans was manifested in other ways during his third term as mayor. In 1886, Ames was the Democratic nominee for governor. Just before the election, the Republicans held a rally; a group characterized as "Democratic toughs" attacked the rally, throwing stones and wielding clubs. Many prominent Republicans were assaulted, including ex-governor John Pillsbury. The newspapers named several Democrats who led the attack, and although Ames was not present, he was believed to have been the instigator of the attack ("Stoned by a Mob," *Minneapolis Journal,* November 2, 1886). Another account accused Ames and the police force, which he controlled, of aiding and abetting the mob ("Great Parade," *Minneapolis Tribune,* November 2, 1886). Ames lost to Republican Andrew McGill but refused to concede. More than a month after the election, even the *New York Times* carried a story on Ames's contention that he was the victim of election fraud ("Defeated, But Pugnacious," *New York Times,* December 19, 1886). In January Ames, along with two associates "and his magnificent nerve, his constant companion," traveled to St. Paul to be sworn in as governor ("Good as His Word," *Minneapolis Journal,* January 3, 1887, and "Mayor Ames Calls," *Minneapolis Journal,* January 4, 1887).

139. "The Ex-Mayor and Bethany Home," *Minneapolis Journal,* January 8, 1889.

140. Harold Zink, *City Bosses in the United States: A Study of Twenty Municipal Bosses* (Durham, N.C.: Duke University Press, 1930), 338.

141. "The Ex-Mayor and Bethany Home."

142. "Two Cases of Assault," *Minneapolis Tribune,* October 29, 1885; "In General," *Minneapolis Tribune,* June 25, 1886.

143. "Wicked Dames," *Minneapolis Tribune,* December 21, 1886; "More Grand Jury Work," *Minneapolis Tribune,* December 16, 1886; "Just vs. Heinrich," *Minneapolis Tribune,* January 1, 1887.

144. "Minneapolis Event—Judge Young Expresses Some Forcible Views to the Flour City Grand Jury," *St. Paul Daily Globe,* December 8, 1886.

145. "Flour City Sketches—Keepers of Houses of Ill-Fame Brought into Court in Large Numbers," *St. Paul Daily Globe,* December 12, 1886.

146. "A Whole Broadside," *Minneapolis Tribune,* September 12, 1888; "In the Courts," *Minneapolis Tribune,* January 6, 1891.

147. "Court Doings," *Minneapolis Tribune,* October 27, 1885.

148. "Women of Ethiopia," *Minneapolis Tribune,* July 15, 1888; "The Second Offense," *Minneapolis Tribune,* June 22, 1888; "Bits of Police Justice," *Min-*

neapolis Tribune, July 13, 1888; "Colored Fairies in Court," *Minneapolis Tribune,* July 17, 1888; "Fining the Madames," *St. Paul Daily Globe,* July 17, 1889.

3. RED LIGHTS ALONG THE RIVERFRONT

1. Sarah A. Campbell operated a brothel at 127 Second Street North, next door to Ida Dorsey's place at 125 North Second, during the 1880s. In the spring of 1885, she was indicted in Hennepin County District Court under the name of Sarah Weeks for keeping a house of prostitution. The June 24, 1885, *Minneapolis Tribune* reported that she was found guilty. Stillwater Prison records indicate she was sentenced to ten months in the penitentiary.

2. "On the East Side," *Minneapolis Tribune,* January 24, 1891.

3. According to a 1911 vice commission report there were several active bordellos on and near First Street South. See *Report of the Vice Commission of Minneapolis to His Honor James C. Haynes, Mayor* (Minneapolis: Press of H. M. Hall, 1911), 74.

4. Keith Lovald, "Hobohemia to Skid Row: The Changing Community of the Homeless Man" (Ph.D. thesis, University of Minnesota, 1960), 107.

5. "Old Bridge Square Ain't What It Used to Be—Pretty Dead Since the Real Lumberjacks Left," *Minneapolis Tribune,* April 18, 1915.

6. The Athenaeum, originally known as the Minneapolis Library Association, was founded in 1859 as a subscription library. By 1866, its members had raised enough money for a permanent building, and they chose the Bridge Square area for their two-story brick building. Although it was a private organization devoted to encouraging scholarly pursuits, by 1877 its rules had been loosened when the public reading room hours were extended from 5:00 to 9:00 p.m.; the Athenaeum also was open on Sunday afternoons to provide an alternative to saloons and other evil pursuits. The two bookstores were John Guth at 110 Washington Avenue South and Cushman & Plummer at 24 Washington Avenue South. Booksellers Cushman & Moore (later Cushman and Plummer) had been on Washington Avenue between Nicollet and Minnetonka since the 1860s.

7. The 1879–80 *Minneapolis City Directory* lists "intelligence [employment] offices" at 20 Seventh Street North, 709 Third Street South, 20 Fourth Street South, 254 Sixth Avenue South, and 411 Third Street South.

8. When Mary France died in 1909, Charlotte inherited her estate (Hennepin County probate record no. 011793). By that time, France was known as Mary J. Eggelston.

9. Minneapolis electrical permit F1796, March 17, 1896; building permit B42485, March 10, 1899; electrical permit 3267, March 13, 1899; building permit A6204, March 22, 1899; building permit A8660, July 5, 1904; building permit A9751, May 4, 1907; and electrical permit F41897, June 17, 1911.

10. Minneapolis moving permit E6671, dated June 5, 1906. The brothel at 107 First Street South was built prior to 1884, the year the city began issuing building permits.

11. "The Raids," *Twin City Reporter,* April 23, 1915; "Sheriff Makes Raids at Grand Jury's Word; 74 Prisoners Taken," *Minneapolis Tribune,* April 18, 1915.

12. Minneapolis wrecking permit I672, December 28, 1915, for 200, 218, 220–222, 230, and 236 First Street South. The permit conflicts with the *1892 Rascher Insurance Map,* updated to 1906, which shows the buildings at 230–236 First Street South as already razed by 1906.

13. Hennepin County Miscellaneous Book 67, p. 219. The lease is dated August 20, 1890, but it was not recorded until July 25, 1895. The legal description of this property is Lots 6 and 7, Block 45, Town of St. Anthony. Welles, a native of Connecticut, settled in St. Anthony in 1853. Equipped with considerable capital, Welles at first entered the lumber business. In 1855, he was elected the first mayor of St. Anthony. After leaving the lumber business, he concentrated on real estate, railroads, and banking. Welles owned and developed large portions of present-day downtown Minneapolis, was the first president of the Minneapolis and St. Louis Railroad, and served as the president of Northwestern Bank.

14. Hennepin County Miscellaneous Book 67, pp. 227–28, recorded July 31, 1895, but executed February 21, 1891. The lease and subsequent sale of land to Jennie Jones was hardly the first time Welles did business with the madams. He owned the entire block (Block 35, Town of Minneapolis) where Mathilda Waller's bordello was located during the 1870s. He also owned large sections of First Street and, through leases and a series of same-day sales transactions, transferred these properties to those involved in the sex trade or saloons.

15. "To Transfer Resort," *Minneapolis Journal,* December 15, 1905.

16. Minneapolis building permit A2356, April 28, 1891. The original permit gives the building's cost as $15,000, with additional permits for plumbing and electrical bringing the total to $16,035. According to the Inflation Calculator, $16,035 in 1891 is the equivalent of $384,058 in 2010 dollars (http://www.westegg.com/inflation/infl.cgi). To make another comparison, a large house suitable for a middle-class family could be erected in 1891 in Minneapolis for well under $2,500.

17. St. Paul building permit 18543, April 8, 1889; *Improvement Bulletin,* November 30, 1894; and *St. Paul City Directory 1885–1886* (St. Paul: R. L. Polk and Company, 1885), 58. Terhune's brothel was one of several located along Washington and Eagle Streets, all of which were razed in 1931.

18. "To Transfer Resort."

19. Hennepin County probate record no. 6428; Joanna Richardson, *Gustave Doré: A Biography* (London: Cassell, 1980), 65–66; Virginia Rounding, *Grandes Horizontales: The Lives and Legends of Four Nineteenth-Century Cour-*

tesans (New York: Bloomsbury, 2003). After Cora Pearl's death in 1886, a set of books illustrated by Doré was found among her possessions. For his part, Doré owned a photograph of Cora Pearl, inscribed, "Remember. C. P."; Katie Hickman, *Courtesans: Money, Sex and Fame in the Nineteenth Century* (New York: HarperPerennial, 2004), 331–32. Doré also had romantic friendships with other well-known women, such as opera singer Adelina Patti and actress Sarah Bernhardt; Dan Malan, *Gustave Doré: A Biography* (St. Louis: MCE Publishing, 1996), 91–113.

20. Minnesota state census 1895, Ward 1, Precinct 8. It lists thirteen women, ranging in age from eighteen to twenty-five, who lived at 25 Main Street Northeast, plus a thirty-one-year-old housekeeper and her twelve-year-old son, and a thirty-year-old male janitor.

21. "One Dive to Go," *Minneapolis Journal,* September 14, 1893.

22. Minneapolis building permit A2805, February 16, 1892; plumbing permit D6916, March 3, 1892; electrical permit F411, March 5, 1892; building permit A3597, June 23, 1893; building permit A5845, May 8, 1896.

23. Hennepin County Deeds Book 427, p. 593, recorded August 6, 1895.

24. *The First Fifty Years: Young-Quinlan Company* (Minneapolis: Young-Quinlan Company, 1944).

25. "The City-Town Talk," *Minneapolis Journal,* September 19, 1899; and "Death of Jennie Jones," *Minneapolis Tribune,* September 19, 1899. Jones's death certificate was issued under the name of Louise Robbins and lists the primary cause of death as fibroid and cystic disease of the uterus and the immediate cause as acute renal congestion. Deaths in the State of Minnesota, Death Register, 1899, H. L. Staples, attending physician, p. 1052.

26. "Another Robbin's Heir," *Minneapolis Journal,* May 14, 1900.

27. "Jennie Jones' Son," *Minneapolis Journal,* December 13, 1899; "Minneapolis Fortune Awaits a St. Louis Teamster," *Minneapolis Tribune,* December 14, 1899; "Was a Rover," *Minneapolis Tribune,* August 4, 1900.

28. Hennepin County Court guardianship file no. G04806.

29. "Many Claim Jennie Jones Estate," *Minneapolis Tribune,* March 14, 1900; "Was He a Son?" *Minneapolis Tribune,* August 3, 1900.

30. "Jennie Jones' Son," *Minneapolis Journal,* December 13, 1899.

31. "Could Not Rattle Her. Edna Hamilton on the Witness Stand in Probate Court," *Minneapolis Times,* June 19, 1900.

32. "Wm. Colvin's Bomb," *Minneapolis Journal,* June 13, 1900; "Jennie Jones' Estate," *Minneapolis Journal,* June 18, 1900; and "Showed a Bill of Sale," *Minneapolis Journal,* June 19, 1900. Hamilton described the valuables that Jones gave her as "a pair of diamond ear drops, a gold watch, a necklace, a sealskin cape, and a butterfly pin set with diamonds."

33. "Complicated," *Minneapolis Tribune,* August 9, 1900; "Colvin Not A

Son," *Minneapolis Journal,* August 11, 1900; "Contest Ended," *Minneapolis Tribune,* December 8, 1900; "Irish Heirs Get the Money," *Minneapolis Tribune,* December 8, 1900.

34. Hennepin County Deeds Book 531, p. 274, recorded December 6, 1900, executed November 8, 1900; and Book 537, p. 43, recorded December 6, 1900, executed November 19, 1900.

35. Minneapolis building permit A171, March 24, 1886. The architect is listed as Gilbert LeVeille.

36. "A Sliding Scale," *St. Paul Daily Globe,* July 16, 1889.

37. Minneapolis building permits A2089, September 5, 1890; A2541, August 1, 1891; Hennepin County Miscellaneous Book 53, p. 155, recorded January 9, 1892. Apparently, the first building, which was to be a four-story hotel, was never built, as there are no subsequent electrical or plumbing permits. However, a three-story apartment was completed on the site late in 1891. Frederick A. Clarke was the architect. The address for the building is something of a puzzle. Building permits show it as 13 Main Street Southeast, while city directories and census documents list it as 21 Main Street Southeast; Hennepin County Miscellaneous Book 53, p. 155, recorded January 9, 1892; Hennepin County Lien Book 6, pp. 553–54, recorded June 6, 1892. A mechanic's lien filed by contractor James W. Cashen indicated the building had parquet floors.

38. Minneapolis building permit A2929, April 14, 1892; "Lost Lover and Pup," *Minneapolis Tribune,* July 7, 1894.

39. Minneapolis state census, 1895; Minneapolis building permit A1098, October 2, 1888. The original structure was described as a twenty- by twenty-foot shed (building permit A254, August 12, 1886). The 1888 building permit lists madam Anna Hoist as the owner, but she was the tenant of owners Richard and Samuel Chute.

40. "Easily Equal to It," *Minneapolis Tribune,* May 10, 1891.

41. "Local Monte Carlo," *St. Paul Daily Globe,* March 18, 1892.

42. The Minnesota Historical Society owns a photograph of this building, dating from 1948 (MH5.9MP3.1R p7).

43. Hennepin County Deeds Book 55, p. 8, and Minneapolis building permit A730, March 13, 1888. By 1875 Thomas Lowry was the owner of the building and was responsible for the additions.

44. Hennepin County Miscellaneous Book 58, p. 25, recorded November 3, 1892, but executed February 15, 1892. The text reads: "In case however of said work being stopped by city authorities said penalty is not to be paid while the work is so stopped." Nels Peterson, a building contractor, may have simply served as a "straw man" owner to put some distance between the respectable seller and the buyer from the demimonde. His last name was sufficiently com-

mon to be confused with any number of other people, and his profession would allow him to maintain that he was only hired to perform construction work. Often the names of contractors or architects were listed as the owners on building permits of brothel property to divert attention from the actual deed holder. Edwin Stebbins served as the Minneapolis School Board architect for many years; among his notable buildings are Gethsemane Episcopal Church (1883), Holy Rosary Catholic Church (1887), and Sidney Pratt School (1898).

45. "Outside the Hall," *New York Times,* June 8, 1892. An earlier article reported sleeping car berths were offered for one dollar a night on the west side of the river ("Convention Notes," *New York Times,* June 4, 1892).

46. "Everyone Likes Us," *Minneapolis Journal,* June 9, 1892; "Two Expert Opinions," *Minneapolis Journal,* June 11, 1892; and "It's Time to Blush," *Minneapolis Journal,* June 15, 1892.

47. Gilfoyle, *City of Eros,* 232–34.

48. "Lots of Red Paint," *Minneapolis Tribune,* January 21, 1891. There is no listing for the Minneapolis Theatrical Union in Minneapolis city directories, suggesting this name was an alias to shield the true identities of the party's sponsors.

49. "'Behind the Mask," *Minneapolis Tribune,* February 14, 1896; "Masks and Faces, *Minneapolis Tribune,* February 12, 1897; "Free Rein to Vice," *Minneapolis Journal,* November 22, 1901.

50. *Minnesota City Directory for 1889–1890* (Minneapolis: Minneaplis Directory Company, 1889).

51. "They Do Protest," *St. Paul Globe,* February 8, 1891; Hennepin County Miscellaneous Book 48, pp. 290, 293, recorded February 7, 1891. William and John Sexton were the sellers of these two parcels. The total price for both parcels was $136,000. Cole was to pay each seller $150 a month until 1901, when a $100,000 balloon payment would be due. A building permit (A2258) for "inside alterations on a three-story brick building" at 1013 Second Street South is dated February 14, 1891. A building permit dated November 2, 1891 (A2699), for minor alterations to the property at 1017 Second Street South lists Hattie Cole as the owner.

52. "They Do Protest."

53. "The Sixth Ward Kick," *Minneapolis Journal,* February 9, 1891.

54. "Removing the Madams," *Minneapolis Tribune,* February 8, 1891.

55. "A Loud Protest," *Minneapolis Tribune,* February 10, 1891. A similar protest meeting scheduled for Dania Hall on Cedar Avenue did not materialize ("Very Large Red 'No,'" *St. Paul Globe,* February 10, 1891).

56. "A New Plague Spot," *Minneapolis Journal,* February 7, 1891.

57. "Naked in the Night," *Minneapolis Journal,* June 8, 1889; "Eminent

People Arrested—In a High-Toned Assignation House in Minneapolis," *St. Paul Daily Globe,* June 8, 1889.

58. "A New Plague Spot."

59. "Very Large Red 'No.'" Lars Rand claimed that since Sixth Warders were not of the class that patronized bordellos, such establishments should not be inflicted upon the neighborhood. Swan Turnblad, publisher of the *Svenska Amerikana Posten* newspaper, proposed that if the brothels were allowed on Eleventh Avenue, then all the fallen women should be driven out of the city by force. He volunteered to join such a posse.

60. Hennepin County Deeds Book 331, p. 99, recorded March 14, 1891, but executed February 5, 1891; Minneapolis building permit A2480, June 30, 1891; "An Elopement," *Minneapolis Tribune,* April 8, 1892. The property, purchased for $30,000, is described as Lot 7, Block 113, Town of Minneapolis, and the building cost more than $14,000 to complete.

61. Minneapolis building permits A2278, March 9, 1891; A2269, February 25, 1891.

62. Using her maiden name, Mary E. Kerns, Mabel married Robert H. Bleakie on April 6, 1887, in St. Croix County, Wisconsin (Wisconsin Historical Society, Wisconsin Genealogy Index Home Page; www.wisconsinhistory.org/vital records/index.asp?id=2217008). Mary Kerns and her sister Frances are listed in the 1870 federal census as living with their parents, Patrick and Mary, and several siblings in Detroit, Michigan (Heritage Quests Online).

63. "An Elopement."

64. Hennepin County Deeds Book 261, p. 148, recorded July 12, 1888. The property was located at 2822 Fifteenth Avenue South and purchased under the name of Mary E. Bleakie.

65. "He Turned the Tables," *Minneapolis Tribune,* September 4, 1891; "Mabel's Friends Get Out Too," *Minneapolis Tribune,* September 15, 1891.

66. "An Elopement"; "Oh, Miss Mabel!," *Minneapolis Times,* April 8, 1892.

67. "A Duel with Knives," *Minneapolis Tribune,* July 18, 1894; and "Slashed with a Knife," *St. Paul Daily Globe,* July 18, 1894.

68. "Took Bad Aim," *Minneapolis Tribune,* March 22, 1897. Bleakie apparently survived the suicide attempt. It is not clear that Mabel/Mary actually married William S. Allen, but she did assume his last name and identified herself as his widow after his death in 1915.

69. Minneapolis building permits A6815, July 6, 1900, and A6818, July 7, 1900, describe the dimensions of each building as forty by sixty feet. The cost of each building was $13,000; with the plumbing and electrical work the total cost for each was close to $15,000. Among Bertrand and Chamberlin's notable designs are Asbury Hospital (1898); Dean and Company Warehouse (1902); the

Minneapolis Athletic Club (1912; now the Grand Hotel); the Chamber of Commerce Annex (1919); and Shriner's Hospital (1921).

70. Minneapolis building permit A9101, June 20, 1905. Mary Allen's former brothels at 200–208 Eleventh Avenue South were razed in March 2006 to make way for a condominium development.

71. Minneapolis building permits A2526, July 22, 1891; A2917, April 7, 1892; and plumbing permit D7177, April 30, 1892. Frances Stewart was also buying this property via an agreement for deed, according to Hennepin County Miscellaneous Book 51, p. 122, July 17, 1891.

72. Biographical information on Andrew Haugan can be found in *Illustrated Minneapolis: A Souvenir by the Minneapolis Journal* (Minneapolis: Minneapolis Journal, 1891), 98; "Death Takes Haugan; Queer Career Ends," *Minneapolis Times,* November 26, 1902; and "A Shock to His Friends," *Minneapolis Journal,* November 26, 1902.

73. Hennepin County Deeds Book 325, p. 134, recorded November 25, 1890. The Haugans sold the rear fifty feet of lots 6 and 7 in Block 113, Town of Minneapolis on November 25, 1890. Carolina's name appears as Caroline Anderson in some sources.

74. Minneapolis building permit A2214, December 16, 1890. The building permit simply lists "Hunt" as the architect. This could be one of three architects practicing in the Twin Cities around that time. I am grateful to Barbara Bezat of the Northwest Architectural Archives for identifying three possible candidates: William A. Hunt of Minneapolis, who left for Duluth in 1889; Peter Hunt, who was listed in the *Minneapolis City Directory* for 1886–1887 and for 1887–1888; and William S. Hunt, who seems to be the most likely one. William S. Hunt, a graduate of Beloit College, studied architecture in Chicago before relocating to Minneapolis in the 1880s. In 1888, he began a solo practice that continued until his death in 1919. He specialized in residences, apartment buildings, and small-scale commercial buildings. Some of his extant works include a block of apartments (1891) at 1818–1826 Fifth Street South and an apartment building at 1802 Eleventh Avenue South. An 1892 quitclaim deed (Hennepin County Deeds Book 377, p. 14) states Carolina was married to Zacharias Anderson. Although the building permit index card indicates that "L. Anderson" served as the building contractor for 212 Eleventh Avenue South, the handwritten initial on the permit actually reads "Z. Anderson," meaning Zacharais Anderson was the contractor for Dorsey's brothel. Early in 1891, a plumbing permit for $1,000 was taken out, meaning the bordello cost at least $13,000 to complete. The minimum cost of building Dorsey's bordello, including land, was $21,000. According to the Inflation Calculator, $21,000 in 1890 is the equivalent of $495,055 in 2009 dollars. This does not include the cost of its furnishings.

75. Hennepin County Lien Book 5, p. 575, recorded October 10, 1891. The lien notes that Simonson Bros. supplied lumber to the bordello from April 16 to July 7, 1891.

76. Haugan, Stoft, and the Simonsons had another connection, namely, as officers of the South Minneapolis Building and Loan Association. In August 1890 Stoft became its president, Haugan the treasurer, and Hans Simonson a director ("Personal and General," *Minneapolis Tribune,* June 19, 1886).

77. "Stole Her Diamonds," *Minneapolis Tribune,* March 25, 1894.

78. "The Raids," *Twin City Reporter,* April 23, 1915.

79. "The Fire Element," *Evening Bulletin* (Maysville, Ky.), September 25, 1891.

80. "Women and Wine Rooms," *Minneapolis Tribune,* June 22, 1891.

81. "Slumming Again," *Minneapolis Tribune,* August 25, 1891.

82. Dorsey and her sister Roberta apparently continued a connection to their place at 116 Second Avenue South for some time after the Eleventh Avenue bordello was completed. It was there on January 27, 1891, that Dorsey gave birth to a stillborn daughter, and on October 15 of that same year that Alvah was born to Roberta ("Birdie Berkes") (Lakewood Cemetery records and Hennepin County birth records, Minnesota Historical Society).

83. "The Pearl Loses a Fight," *St. Paul Daily Globe,* July 31, 1891; "The Original Black Pearl," *St. Paul Daily Globe,* March 1, 1903.

84. "The Boldest Yet," *Minneapolis Times,* March 25, 1894; "Stole Her Diamonds"; "The Dorsey Robbery," *Minneapolis Tribune,* March 26, 1894; Pat Crowe, *Spreading Evil: Pat Crowe's Autobiography* (New York: Branwell Company, 1927), 133–36. Crowe came to Minneapolis while on the run from other crimes. He targeted Dorsey, whom he described as "the beautiful Creole" with many valuable jewels and "a great favorite of an elderly man then living in Minneapolis." Crowe was a notorious bank and train robber who was perhaps best known for the 1900 kidnapping of Edward Cudahy Jr. in Omaha.

85. The 1895 Minnesota state census lists Maria Burkes, several of her sons, and three-year-old Alvah, Dorsey's niece, at 1119 Washington Avenue South. The house Dorsey purchased was located at 2720 Second Avenue South. Dorsey's stepfather, George, died in 1892 and is buried at Lakewood.

86. Hennepin County Death Records, vol. 9, p. 222, July 23, 1898. Roberta was listed as a widow on this record, although no husband's name is given.

87. Hennepin County probate record 020733.

88. Hennepin County Deeds Book 604, p. 447, recorded June 7, 1906. The purchase price in this document was listed as $12,000. By 1906 ownership of 212 Eleventh Avenue had passed to Henry E. and Aimee Wunder of St. Louis County, Minnesota, and these two deeded the property to Dorsey.

89. Minneapolis building permits B5728, B5729, and 5769, all dating from January 1886, indicate this was a two-story wooden building with storefronts on the first level and ten apartments above. The property also had a barn and a "wooden factory" building. Apparently another dwelling was added a year later. During the 1880s the Liljengren Furniture Company occupied the site.

90. Hennepin County Deed Book 630, p. 236, recorded April 16, 1907; Hennepin County Deed Book 627, p. 29, recorded April 16, 1907; Hennepin County Deed Book 705, p. 88, recorded January 17, 1911.

91. Roland J. Mulford, *History of the Lawrenceville School, 1810–1935* (Princeton, N.J.: Princeton University Press, 1935), 134; "At the Hotels," *New York Times,* April 2, 1899, March 22, 1900, and November 27, 1903; "In Social Circles," *Minneapolis Journal,* February 2, 1901; His Majesty's High Court of Justice, Principal Probate Registry, will of Carleton Cook Pillsbury, June 8, 1923; *Minneapolis City Directory* for 1903 and 1904; "Minneapolis Socially," *Minneapolis Tribune,* December 31, 1903; "Got the Reward," *Minneapolis Journal,* April 24, 1905. Pillsbury broke the Minneapolis–Northfield automobile record, making the 108-mile round-trip run in a twelve-horsepower Franklin in three hours and fifty-five minutes. He had set the record the previous year, when he completed the same race in slightly less than five hours.

92. "Roosevelt Club's Show," *Minneapolis Tribune,* November 5, 1904; "Extremely Gorgeous Is the Roosevelters' Play," *Minneapolis Tribune,* January 24, 1905; "'Cinderella and the Prince' Revealed Tomorrow Night," *Minneapolis Tribune,* January 22, 1905.

93. "Notice," *Minneapolis Tribune,* March 7, 1905; Minnesota Secretary of State File No. 7457-AA, March 4, 1905; "Floating Along" as seen on www .hulapages.com and "De Cleanin' Man" as seen on the Library of Congress website. Gardner Greenleaf and William La Grange Dana were the other two incorporators of Pillsbury's music company.

94. Howard A. Guilford, "Unlucky Thirteenth," *Twin City Reporter,* August 18, 1916.

95. "The Negro's Greatest Enemy" (editorial), *Twin City Star,* January 18, 1913.

96. State of Minnesota death certificate no. 19,011, dated August 25, 1910; Hennepin County probate record no. 12974. M. Callahand filed her claim on April 1, 1911, and it was subsequently dismissed. Any vouchers supporting claims against Pillsbury's estate were destroyed in 1950, making it impossible to determine the nature of Dorsey's claim. Carleton Pillsbury's estate was valued at more than $260,000. His will (no. 12974) is dated August 16, 1910.

97. State of Minnesota death certificate no. 20744, October 1, 1916.

98. Hennepin County Miscellaneous Book 105, p. 325, dated November 26,

1897, twenty-year lease of Lots 6 and 7, Block 112, Town of Minneapolis, to Mattie and John Nichol; Johnson was apparently leasing Lot 8 to another madam, Mamie Lacy. See also Hennepin County Deeds Book 609, p. 318, recorded November 20, 1905 (Dickerson to Mamie Lacy); Deeds Book 609, p. 316, recorded November 20, 1905 (Dickerson to Ida Malling); Deeds Book 598, p. 287, recorded January 25, 1906 (Dickerson to John M. and Josie D. Price).

99. Hennepin County Deeds Book 536, p. 147, recorded April 10, 1901. Frank Cottom sold these parcels to Nettie Conley for $10,000 (Hennepin County Deeds Book 535, p. 302, recorded April 9, 1901).

100. Minneapolis building permit B49138, dated July 5, 1901. The building was twenty-five feet across the front and sixty feet in depth. The initial cost was $8,000, with electrical and plumbing adding several hundred dollars more to the cost. The permit shows the address as 1111 Second Street South, but the legal address is listed as Lot 1 of Baker's Rearrangement of Block 112, the land that Conley purchased in 1901. The Rascher Insurance map clearly shows a three-story brick building called a "female boarding house" at 1109 Second Street South that fronted on Lot 1 of this subdivision. The building at 1111 Second Street South was razed in 1934 (Minneapolis wrecking permit I4084). The firm of Bertrand and Chamberlin designed this building, like all the others that Conley built in the Eleventh Avenue district.

101. Minneapolis building permit B58333 describes the 1904 building at 1101 Second Street South as a store, but the subsequent electrical permits call it a saloon. An 1892 Rascher Insurance map, updated to 1906, labels the building a saloon as well. The building permit index card acknowledges the dual nature of the building by listing 207–211 Eleventh Avenue as the alternative address. The 1910 federal census lists it as 205 Eleventh Avenue South.

102. Federal census for 1910.

103. Minnesota state census for 1905.

104. Minneapolis building permit B63233, dated May 31, 1905. Bertrand and Chamberlin were the architects. The building permit listed the cost as $8,000; the various electrical and plumbing permits taken out in 1905 for this structure total $705. The electrical and plumbing permits were taken out from July through November 1905, indicating the building was ready for occupancy in the autumn of 1905.

105. Federal census for 1910, Hennepin County, Minneapolis.

4. REFORMING THE CITY

1. "Police in Sudden Raid on Resorts," *Minneapolis Journal,* April 14, 1910.

2. "After the 'Roomers,'" *Minneapolis Journal,* September 8, 1891.

3. "Ten Long Months," *Minneapolis Tribune,* November 7, 1891; "Madam

Lloyd Pleads Guilty," *Minneapolis Tribune,* November 6, 1891. Stillwater records describe Lloyd, a native of Wales, as five feet four inches tall, 160 pounds, with gray hair, a fair complexion, blue eyes, and a scar on her wrist. The widowed Lloyd neither smoked nor drank. She was literate and a Methodist. Stillwater Prison Convict Record, vol. D, p. 368, Minnesota Historical Society collections.

4. "In the Courts," *Minneapolis Tribune,* August 28, 1889.

5. "Barred Them Out," *Minneapolis Tribune,* November 18, 1891; "So Very 'Practical,'" *Minneapolis Journal,* November 18, 1891; "Drawing the Line," *Minneapolis Times,* November 18, 1891.

6. "Waifs Barred from the Schools," *Minneapolis Tribune,* November 19, 1891; "Libel on the Eighth Ward," *Minneapolis Tribune,* November 20, 1891; "But Four Signed," *Minneapolis Tribune,* November 20, 1891.

7. "The Case Argued," *Minneapolis Tribune,* November 25, 1891; "It Won't Give In," *Minneapolis Tribune,* November 28, 1891; "Didn't Back Water," *Minneapolis Times,* November 28, 1891; "A Suicidal Move," *Minneapolis Tribune,* November 29, 1891; "Law for the City School Board," *Minneapolis Tribune,* November 29, 1891; "Shaw Talks Back," *Minneapolis Tribune,* December 1, 1891.

8. "A Suicidal Move."

9. "A Clash of Authority," *Minneapolis Tribune,* February 18, 1897; "In 1897 the fine was raised to $100 (the maximum that could be imposed by the court) for the proprietor; and fining of the inmates, except when prosecuted for special cause, was discontinued"; *Report of the Vice Commission of Minneapolis to His Honor James C. Haynes, Mayor,* 23.

10. Carl H. Chrislock, *The Progressive Era in Minnesota, 1899–1918* (St. Paul: Minnesota Historical Society, 1971), 25–26.

11. "A Political Possibility," *Minneapolis Journal,* July 24, 1900; editorial cartoons, *Minneapolis Tribune,* July 31 and August 1, 1900; "An Inevitable Effect," *Minneapolis Journal,* September 10, 1900; "The Mayoralty," *Minneapolis Journal,* September 17, 1900; "John A. Schlener for Mayor," *Minneapolis Tribune,* September 17, 1900; "Certain," *Minneapolis Tribune,* September 20, 1900; "Total Votes Received by Nominee," *Minneapolis Tribune,* September 21, 1900; "Tribute to Ames," *Minneapolis Tribune,* November 5, 1900; "It's Ames," *Minneapolis Journal,* November 7, 1900; "Local Results," *Minneapolis Tribune,* November 8, 1900. In the Republican primary election, Ames garnered 11,638 votes; John Schlener, 10,007; and James Elwin, 1,700.

12. "Ames Held a Levee," *Minneapolis Journal,* January 5, 1901; "'A Republican Machine,'" *Minneapolis Journal,* February 13, 1901.

13. Lincoln Steffens, "The Shame of Minneapolis," *McClure's Magazine,* January 1903, 234.

14. "By Mayor's Order," *Minneapolis Journal,* May 11, 1901.

15. "Mayor Ames' Ideal," *Minneapolis Journal*, May 13, 1901.

16. "Will Probe Deeper" and "Resort Proprietors Flee," *Minneapolis Journal*, May 13, 1901.

17. "On the Street," *Minneapolis Journal*, May 16, 1901.

18. Transcript included in Ames's appeal to the Minnesota Supreme Court, 91 Minn. 365, January 29, 1904.

19. "Big Storm Is Brewing," *Minneapolis Journal*, March 19, 1902.

20. "Two Indictments Coming Tomorrow," *Minneapolis Tribune*, May 15, 1902; "Indictment against Mayor Ames to Have Been Returned," *Minneapolis Tribune*, June 17, 1902; "Grand Jury Finds Four Indictments," *Minneapolis Tribune*, July 30, 1902.

21. "To Leave the Staff," *Minneapolis Journal*, July 1, 1902.

22. "Mayor Jones Does Not Favor Narrow Administration," *Minneapolis Tribune*, August 10, 1902.

23. "Get Near the River," *Minneapolis Tribune*, September 10, 1902; "Low Resort Limits," *Minneapolis Journal*, September 10, 1902.

24. "Low Resort Limits." In 1905 Jones continued his campaign against what he saw as public vice when he closed all saloons on Sunday (*Minneapolis Journal*, October 31, 1905).

25. "The Tax Rate Fixed," *Minneapolis Journal*, October 4, 1902; "Tax Levy Is Pared Down," *Minneapolis Tribune*, October 4, 1902.

26. "A Tax Levy Is Agreed Upon," *Minneapolis Journal*, October 5, 1902; "The Tax Rate Fixed." Eustis served as mayor of Minneapolis from 1892 to 1894.

27. "A Step Forward," *Minneapolis Journal*, October 9, 1902.

28. "A Tax Levy Is Agreed Upon."

29. "The Tax Rate Fixed."

30. Lincoln Steffens, *The Autobiography of Lincoln Steffens* (1931; repr., Berkeley, Calif.: Heyday Books, 2005), 374–75.

31. Zink, *City Bosses in the United States*, 341–42, 344.

32. "Guilty Verdict in Ames Case—Ex-Mayor Crushed by Awful Blow," *Minneapolis Tribune*, May 8, 1903; "A. A. Ames Given 6-year Sentence," *Minneapolis Tribune*, May 18, 1903.

33. "Acquittal for Minneapolis," *Minneapolis Tribune*, May 8, 1903.

34. "Clean Out Main Street," *Minneapolis Journal*, August 4, 1903.

35. "'Red Light' Blight," *Minneapolis Journal*, August 5, 1903.

36. "Appeal to Mayor," *Minneapolis Journal*, August 11, 1903; "Park for East Side," *Minneapolis Tribune*, August 2, 1903; "Say Main Street Dives Must Go," *Minneapolis Tribune*, August 20, 1903.

37. "The Mayor Is Cautious," *Minneapolis Tribune*, September 5, 1903; "Will Keep His Land," *Minneapolis Tribune*, September 10, 1903; "The Dives Are

Doomed," *Minneapolis Tribune,* September 10, 1903. After much wrangling, the East Side did get another park, Richard Chute Square, although it was not located directly on the riverfront ("Richard Chute Square a Beautiful Addition," *Minneapolis Tribune,* December 15, 1904).

38. "Resorts Will Close," *Minneapolis Tribune,* January 21, 1904.

39. "Hennepin Ave. Is Stirred Up," *Minneapolis Journal,* February 5, 1904.

40. "Resorts Will Close"; "To Clean up Main Street," *Minneapolis Tribune,* April 2, 1904; "Main Street Is Dark," *Minneapolis Tribune,* April 17, 1904.

41. "A Sweeping Order," *Minneapolis Journal,* September 11, 1903.

42. "Say Main St. Dives Must Go," *Minneapolis Tribune,* August 20, 1903.

43. Minnesota state census, 1905; "Edna Hamilton Raided," *Minneapolis Tribune,* March 28, 1905.

44. Minneapolis building permit B63233, dated May 31, 1905. The building permit listed the cost as $8,000, while the various electrical and plumbing permits taken out in 1905 for this structure total $705. The electrical and plumbing permits were taken out from July through November, indicating the building was ready for occupancy late in 1905.

45. "Edna Hamilton's Main Street House Will Be New Hospital," *Minneapolis Journal,* December 15, 1905.

46. "Recruits at the Jumbo," *Minneapolis Journal,* March 4, 1890.

47. Ibid.

48. Gilfoyle, *City of Eros,* 274.

49. "Mr. Philbin Arraigns the District Leaders," *New York Times,* October 25, 1901.

50. "Citizens Chosen as Anti-vice Leaders," *New York Times,* December 1, 1900; Gilfoyle, *City of Eros,* 198.

51. "Hideous Crime of a Procurer," *Minneapolis Journal,* September 29, 1904; "Lure Girls to Ruin," *Minneapolis Tribune,* October 1, 1904.

52. "Hideous Crime of a Procurer."

53. Ibid.

54. "Saved from Prison," *Minneapolis Tribune,* November 2, 1904; "Convicted Man Is Finally Free," *Minneapolis Tribune,* December 4, 1904.

55. "Chinese Debauch Many Innocent Girls," *Minneapolis Tribune,* October 8, 1904; "Shocking Crime Charged to Them," *Minneapolis Journal,* October 7, 1904; "The Race Question in the Raw" (editorial), *Minneapolis Tribune,* October 10, 1904; "The Local Chinese Scandal" (editorial), *Minneapolis Tribune,* October 11, 1904; "Alleged National Syndicate Which Supplies Chinaman with White Slaves," *Minneapolis Tribune,* October 13, 1904.

56. "Chinaman Who Has a White Wife," *Minneapolis Tribune,* October 21, 1904; "John Leon Case Has New Aspect," *Minneapolis Tribune,* October 22,

1904; "Chinaman Goes Free; Stepdaughter Sentenced," *Minneapolis Tribune,* October 30, 1904.

57. "Chinese New Year," *Minneapolis Journal,* January 30, 1900; "Counted the Chinks," *Minneapolis Journal,* May 21, 1905; "Official," *Minneapolis Tribune,* July 22, 1905; *Davison's Minneapolis City Directory, 1903* (Minneapolis: Minneapolis Directory Company, 1903); *Davison's Minneapolis City Directory, 1905* (Minneapolis: Minneapolis Directory Company, 1905); "Twin City Chinese Guests of Restaurateur," *Minneapolis Tribune,* February 22, 1904. The 1905 state census counted 261,974 people in Minneapolis.

58. "For Protection of Young Girls," *Minneapolis Journal,* October 11, 1904.

59. "Women Are Wrought Up," *Minneapolis Journal,* October 15, 1904.

60. "Protection for Girls," *Minneapolis Journal,* October 17, 1904.

61. "Chinese Debauch Many Innocent Girls."

62. "R. Sing First Chinaman to Be Placed on Trial," *Minneapolis Tribune,* November 16, 1904; "Chinamen Prepare for Next Trial," *Minneapolis Tribune,* November 19, 1904; "County Jail Prisoners Will Have Chinese Cook," *Minneapolis Tribune,* December 16, 1904.

63. "Jim Moe [Moy] Faces Jury," *Minneapolis Tribune,* November 29, 1904; "Moy Jim Goes Free by Verdict of Jury," *Minneapolis Tribune,* December 3, 1904; "Gee Lee and Jim Lee Given Their Liberty," *Minneapolis Tribune,* December 14, 1904.

64. "Ames Case Reversed," *Minneapolis Tribune,* January 30, 1904; "No Verdict in Ames Case," *Minneapolis Tribune,* May 15, 1904; "Jury in Ames Trial Evenly Divided," *Minneapolis Tribune,* October 22, 1904; "Eleven Jurors Are Stubborn," *Minneapolis Tribune,* November 1, 1904; "Ames Jury Is Not Talkative," *Minneapolis Tribune,* December 14, 1904; "Few Attending Dr. Ames' Trial," *Minneapolis Tribune,* December 9, 1904.

65. "Much-Tried Ames Goes Scot Free" and "No More Ames Trials" (editorial), *Minneapolis Journal,* December 14, 1904; "Public Approval of Municipal Graft" (editorial), *Minneapolis Tribune,* December 14, 1904.

66. Zink, *City Bosses in the United States,* 343.

67. "Red Lights Ordered from Second Street," *Minneapolis Journal,* November 11, 1904.

68. "The Dives Must Clear Out," *Minneapolis Journal,* January 14, 1905.

69. "The Raids," *Twin City Reporter,* April 23, 1915.

70. Minneapolis building permit A9116, July 8, 1905. The initial permit lists the cost of the building as $3,500 and additional permits for electrical and plumbing total $180. William Hunt was probably the architect who designed Ida Dorsey's bordello that still stands at 212 Eleventh Avenue South.

71. Minneapolis building permits A9221, October 3, 1905; and A9263,

November 10, 1905; electrical permits F14884, November 1, 1905 ($25); F19067, November 16, 1906 ($5); and F42199, July 1, 1911 ($35). No plumbing permits are listed for the structure, which was razed in 1913. The building had two mirror-image units divided by a central party wall. Minneapolis building permits describe it as a one-story dwelling made of concrete blocks. The address for this building is given as 212–214 First Street South on the Rascher Insurance map of 1892, updated to 1906.

72. "Civic Organizations Are Interested in Properly Beautifying Bridge Square," *Minneapolis Tribune,* March 7, 1908.

73. "Striking and Comprehensive Plan for Laying Out Minneapolis on New Lines of Use and Beauty," *Minneapolis Journal,* December 2, 1906.

74. "Interesting History of Post Office Sites," *Minneapolis Tribune,* December 9, 1906. Block 40, Town of Minneapolis is bounded by Washington Avenue South, Third Avenue South, Second Street South, and Second Avenue South, and was finally chosen as the site of the 1913 post office.

75. "Citizens Object to New Invaders," *Minneapolis Tribune,* March 26, 1908.

76. "Cleaning Up Bridge Square," *Minneapolis Journal,* March 28, 1908.

77. *Western Architect* 12, no. 6 (December 1908), 63–65. Lowell A. Lamoreaux, Edwin H. Hewitt, and Jacob Stone Jr. were the architects who submitted sketches for remaking the Bridge Square area.

78. "Prayers Heard in Homes of Infamy," *Minneapolis Journal,* February 27, 1907.

79. Ibid.

80. Ibid.

81. "Wanted—New Location: South Side People Eager for Suggestion on Red Light Problem," *Minneapolis Journal,* April 1, 1908.

82. Ibid.

83. "Organize New Body," *Minneapolis Tribune,* November 8, 1907.

84. "'Police Force Is Blind to Evils,'" *Minneapolis Tribune,* January 4, 1909.

85. "Women Organize to Aid in Vice Crusade," *Minneapolis Tribune,* January 8, 1909; "Drugs and Cigaretes Held as Big Evils," *Minneapolis Tribune,* February 27, 1909; "Burlesque Houses Branded Immoral," *Minneapolis Tribune,* March 16, 1909; "My! My! Even Choir Boys Smoke Naughty Cigarete," *Minneapolis Tribune,* June 12, 1909; "Purity Squad's Work Nets City Thousands," *Minneapolis Tribune,* December 12, 1909.

86. "Bills for Social Purity," *Minneapolis Journal,* April 17, 1909.

87. "National White Slave War," *Minneapolis Tribune,* September 29, 1909; "Some Hope for Evil Chicago," *Minneapolis Tribune,* October 1, 1909; "W.C.T.U. Hears of Slavery," *Minneapolis Tribune,* October 26, 1909; "Congress Knew of

White Slave Trade," *New York Times,* October 27, 1909; "White Slave Story False, Says Guide," *New York Times,* October 28, 1909; "Mulry Says Turner Slandered the City," *New York Times,* October 29, 1909; "Prof. Jenks Upholds White Slavery Charge," *New York Times,* October 30, 1909; "To Curb White Slavery," *New York Times,* November 25, 1909; George Kibbe Turner, "The Daughters of the Poor," *McClure's Magazine,* November 1909; "White Slave Story True, Says M'Clure," *New York Times,* November 28, 1909.

88. "To Curb White Slavery."

89. "Pastor Fails to Find Organized Girl Traffic," *Minneapolis Tribune,* February 7, 1910; "Wants Girls Protected," *Minneapolis Journal,* February 7, 1910.

90. "Pamphlet Warns of City Dangers," *Minneapolis Journal,* January 27, 1910.

91. "No White Slave Evidence Found," *Minneapolis Journal,* January 22, 1910.

92. "White Slave Bill Passed," *New York Times,* February 12, 1910; "Agree on White Slave Bill," *New York Times,* March 17, 1910; "Taft Got Much Legislation," *New York Times,* June 25, 1910.

93. "South Siders to Begin Campaign," *Minneapolis Journal,* February 15, 1910.

94. "Police in Sudden Raid on Resorts."

95. "'Exclusion from Ward Crusaders' Sole Aim," *Minneapolis Tribune,* April 15, 1910.

96. "Problems Follow in Wake of Raid," *Minneapolis Journal,* April 15, 1910.

97. Ibid.

98. "All Bound Over to Grand Jury," *Minneapolis Journal,* April 22, 1910.

99. "Ask Authorities to Drop Action," *Minneapolis Tribune,* April 28, 1910; "Jury Gets Resort Petition," *Minneapolis Tribune,* April 29, 1910.

5. VICE REPORT

1. "Seek to Root Out Evil," *Minneapolis Journal,* July 8, 1910; "Vice Commission Asked," *Minneapolis Tribune,* July 9, 1910.

2. *Report of the Vice Commission of Minneapolis to His Honor, James C. Haynes, Mayor,* 77.

3. Ibid., 14.

4. Ibid., 33.

5. Ibid., 99-100.

6. Ibid., 71.

7. Ibid., 75, 102.

8. Ibid., 103.

9. Ibid.

10. "Citizens Protest Against Reopening," *Minneapolis Journal,* July 1, 1911.

11. "Vice Board's Report Advises Suppression," *Minneapolis Tribune,* July 14, 1911; "The Vice Commission's Report" (editorial), *Minneapolis Journal,* July 15, 1911; "Will the Mayor Act?" (editorial), *Minneapolis Journal,* July 18, 1911; "The Mayor Again" (editorial), *Minneapolis Journal,* September 18, 1911.

12. "What Other People Think—The Journal and the Vice Commission."

13. "Good Citizenship" (editorial), *Minneapolis Tribune,* July 15, 1911.

14. "The Vice Problem" (letter to editor), *Minneapolis Journal,* July 31, 1911; *Report of the Vice Commission of Minneapolis,* 64.

15. *Minneapolis City Directory, 1926* (Minneapolis: Minneapolis Directory Company, 1926).

16. The Minneapolis city directories for the years 1912–15 show a Josephine Dale living at 4500 or 4509 Bloomington Avenue South. At that time, the Minneapolis city limits stopped at Fifty-Fourth Street, and this area was sparsely populated; the nearest streetcar line was several blocks away. The 1914 *Minneapolis Atlas* shows no buildings at either address. Josephine may have even left Minneapolis for a few years. The 1920 federal census, vol. 21, ED 19, lists Josephine Dale as the head of household plus five male boarders ranging in age from thirty to fifty-seven, with occupations of lathers and cooks.

17. The January 31, 1890, *Minneapolis Tribune* noted that the marriage of Barrows and Wolverton took place in her parents' home. In this account, Wolverton was described as doing government work in McAlister, Indian Territory, which probably refers to McAlister, Oklahoma.

18. Hennepin County Civil Case no. 80319. Lydia claimed William, though able-bodied, stopped supporting her in 1893, just about the time their first child was born. Up to the date of their final break on March 20, 1897, Lydia said William regularly came home drunk and abused her.

19. Based on numbers from the Inflation Calculator (www.westegg.com), $5,000 in 1932 would be the equivalent of $79,037 in 2010 dollars.

20. Hennepin County death record no. 4444 states Walter Dale died November 19, 1933, and lived in Minneapolis for thirty-five years. Online records at Ancestry.com give the details of the fifty-five-old-year Alfred Dale's death as April 29, 1897, at Michigan City, Indiana. The same source indicates that Dale lived at 132 East Michigan Street and worked as a drayman during the 1890s. It is unclear what happened to Jenny Wilcox, his second wife and mother of Walter.

21. Minnesota death certificate no. 19,429, March 8, 1937. The informant is simply listed as Lucia Camp. Lucia W. (Wolverton) Camp was William's sister; her daughter, Lucia H. Camp, was William's niece.

22. "1,000 Big Dollars," *Minneapolis Tribune,* April 25, 1901. Samuel Hines

was charged with abduction; Dolly Taylor was sent to the state training school for reform after appearing in court with her mother, who claimed she had tried, without success, to keep Dolly at home, away from bad influences. A newspaper described Dolly as "calm and unmoved. It did not concern her how her mother suffered. On one side was duty, honor and poverty. On the other side dishonor, ultimate remorse, but fine clothes" ("Chose a Life of Dishonor," *Minneapolis Tribune,* April 4, 1901).

23. Conley's probate documents show that she held mortgages for Lot 27, Auditor's Subd. 33; Motor Line Addition, Block 4; and Remington's Third Addition Block 40, Lot 2, all of which are located in South Minneapolis. She also held the mortgage for 616 Fillmore Street Northeast (Ramsey and Lockwood Addition, Block 8, Lot 21), which was owned by her brother William.

24. Julia A. (Angle) Buckley died June 8, 1922, and was buried in West Plaine, Missouri. Her death certificate lists her parents as Charles Angle and Harriet Connors [Converse]. Minnesota state death certificate no. 18758.

25. Minnesota state death certificate no. 27,757, dated December 28, 1918, lists Ella's father as Charles Angle, her mother as Harriet Converse, and her birthplace as New York. Conley's half brother George Angle, born in 1872, was institutionalized in a Wisconsin state hospital for the insane for many years.

26. Minnesota state death certificate no. 19,957. Conley died in Swedish Hospital on June 9, 1919, and was buried at Hillside Cemetery in Minneapolis.

27. Hennepin County probate record no. 21963. The appraiser placed a value of $50,614.70 on Conley's estate; the Inflation Calculator website converts this to $632,235 in 2010 dollars.

28. Minneapolis wrecking permit I21446, dated March 3, 1987 (1107 Second Street South). It is not clear when 1101 Second Street South (a.k.a. 205 Eleventh Avenue South) was razed, but it was probably in 1987, when the other building went down.

29. "Halt Graft Trial to Probe Charges Against Juror," *St. Paul Daily News,* February 11, 1914. Nina Clifford operated a brothel at 145–147 South Washington Street. The thousand dollars probably represented only a down payment on the property. See also "Declares She Gave Diamond to Turner," *St. Paul Pioneer Press,* February 13, 1914. In this account, Clifford stated that she had known Ida for twenty-seven years.

30. "Resort Keepers Ready to Depart," *St. Paul Pioneer Press,* May 25, 1913; "Resort Inmates to Begin Hegira Today," *St. Paul Pioneer Press,* May 26, 1913. The reporter took a jab at Minneapolis when he speculated that most of the inmates who populated the sixty-two known brothels in St. Paul would relocate to Minneapolis, where enforcement was lax.

31. "Halt Graft Trial to Probe Charges Against Juror, *St. Paul Daily News,* February 11, 1914.

32. "Despite Flanagan's Injunction Woman Says She Paid Tribute to Graft Ring," *St. Paul Pioneer Press,* January 31, 1914; Minnesota state death certificate no. 23050, March 16, 1918. Henry may have been the child of Roberta, Dorsey's sister. The death certificate lists his parents as Roberta Bailey and Henry Burkes, but more likely their last names were switched and should have read Roberta Burkes and Henry Bailey.

33. "Wench Puts Blame on Daughter," *Twin City Reporter,* April 17, 1917.

34. "Our 'Smoked Friend' Ida Dorsey Refuses to Quit—At It Again, Eh?" *Twin City Reporter,* April 20, 1917.

35. "Minneapolis Resorts Raided by Detectives Several Months Ago, Said to Be Running; No Abatement Actions Begun, Why?" *Twin City Reporter,* August 7, 1914.

36. "The Raids," *Twin City Reporter,* April 23, 1915. "Ida has never been molested. Why not raid her? Some pretty big guns would be grabbed there and the papers would have some great stories."

37. Dorsey was not the first to use 22½ Western Avenue in connection with the sex trade. In 1913, another woman, Carrie Durgin, was arrested for running a house of prostitution at the same address ("Sleuths Hired by Grand Jury Bring About Big Raids," *Minneapolis Journal,* November 20, 1913).

38. "Disorderly House Keeper Sentenced," *Minneapolis Tribune,* April 21, 1917; "Big and Little Fish," *Twin City Reporter,* April 6, 1917; "Wench Puts Blame on Daughter." Alvah seemed to use a number of pseudonyms, including Alvah Dorsey and Alvah Hunton.

39. "The Why and the Why-Not," *Twin City Reporter,* April 20, 1917.

40. "Woman Resort Keeper Forfeits $700 Bail," *Minneapolis Tribune,* April 26, 1917; "What's Rotten and Where," *Twin City Reporter,* May 4, 1917.

41. "Dorsey Brat Is Now a Free Woman," *Twin City Reporter,* March 29, 1918.

42. "Vice Fugitive, Home to Dying Mother, Jailed," *Minneapolis Journal,* February 12, 1918; "Ida Dorsey Dying; Her Daughter Sent to Jail," *Minneapolis Tribune,* February 13, 1918; "Judge Suspends 90 Day Sentence of Resort Keeper," *Minneapolis Journal,* March 20, 1918; "Dorsey Brat Is Now a Free Woman."

43. Minnesota state death certificate no. 24601, June 18, 1918. "Death of Ida Dorsey," *Twin City Star,* June 22, 1918. Dorsey died of liver cancer that had begun as breast cancer. The *Minneapolis Journal* carried a paid obituary for Dorsey.

44. Hennepin County Warranty Deed Book 867, p. 136 (signed February 1, 1918), recorded February 7, 1918; Hennepin County Mortgage Books 1024, p. 55, recorded February 7, 1918; Mortgage Book 939, p. 306; and Mortgage Book 1022, p. 461 (signed February 1, 1918), recorded September 19, 1918.

45. Hennepin County probate record no. 20733, February 14, 1918.

46. The Inflation Calculator website indicates $13,000 in 1918 dollars is the equivalent of $186,580.35 in 2010 dollars.

47. *Davison's Minneapolis City Directory* for 1918, 1922, 1923, and 1924 (Minneapolis: Minneapolis Directory Company, 1918, 1922, 1923, 1924); *Minneapolis City Directory* for 1925, 1926, 1927, and 1928 (Minneapolis: Minneapolis Directory Company, 1925, 1926, 1927, 1928); *Minneapolis Directory Company's Minneapolis, Minnesota City Directory* for 1929 and 1930 (Minneapolis: Minneapolis Directory Company, 1929, 1930). Minneapolis building permit A14865, February 21, 1920; fourteenth census of the United States, 1920, Hennepin County, Minneapolis, ED 109, sheet 14.

48. *Minneapolis City Directory for 1928; Minneapolis Directory Company's Minneapolis, Minnesota City Directory for 1929;* Minneapolis city directories for 1937–42. Minneapolis electrical permit F245938, February 24, 1931; Minneapolis building permit A209957, September 17, 1932; Sanborn Insurance Map, 1912–30, Hennepin County History Museum; *Minneapolis Tribune* photographs, Minneapolis Special Collections, Hennepin County Central Library; "Grand Jurors and Police Raid Night Spots, Arrest 7," *Minneapolis Journal,* January 6, 1938; "Closing of Raided Night Clubs to Be Asked in Council," *Minneapolis Tribune,* January 7, 1938; "Jury Raids Tipped Off, Leach Says," *Minneapolis Journal,* January 7, 1938.

49. *Annual Report of the Fortieth Year of the Bethany Home Association October 1, 1915 to 1916* [Minneapolis: Sisterhood of Bethany, 1916], 6; *Second Annual Report of the House of Bethany of Minneapolis, Minnesota* (Minneapolis: Johnson, Smith and Harrison, 1877), 3.

INDEX

African Americans, 83, 85–89, 92,
104, 116, 117–18, 145, 169, 170–72,
192n, 193n, 195n, 203n
Aldrich, Cyrus, 10
Allen, Lizzie, 37
Allen, Mary E. (also known as Mabel
Baker, Mary E. Bleakie, and
Mary E. Kerns), x, 110, 112, 113,
119, 120, 200n, 201n
Allen, T. F., 115
Allen, William (Montana Jack), 112
Ames, Albert (Doc Ames), 10, 71–72,
89–92, 128–32, 133, 134–35,
144–45
Ames, Fred, 129–30, 132
Ames, William, 76
Anderson, Carolina, 114, 201n
Anderson, Johanna S., 80
Anderson, John L., 114
Anderson, John W., 80
Anderson, May, 29
Anderson, Zacharias, 114, 201n
Angle, Charles Henry, 55, 212n
Angle, George, 166, 212n
Angle, Harriet (Converse), 55, 212n
Angle, Naomi (Nettie). See Conley,
Nettie

Angle, Nicholas, 182n
Angle, Peter, 182n
Angle, William, 166, 182n, 212n
Angle, William (Engle), 182n
Ankey, A. T., 128
Anti-Saloon League, 124
Asbury, Herbert, 81, 191n
Atwater, Isaac, 3, 44, 66, 176n, 177n,
181n, 186n

Babb, E. C., 91
Badger, W. C., 137
Bailey, Henry (also known as Henry
Burkes), 168, 213n
Baker, Mabel. See Allen, Mary E.
Baker, Norma Jean, 54
Barrows, Lydia F., 163, 211n
Bell, Pauline, 60
Benedict, Beatrice, 98
Berry, Amos C., 82, 191n
Berry, Jennie, 82
Bertrand and Chamberlin, 112, 139,
200n, 204n
Berts, Birdie. See Burkes, Roberta
Best, Joel, 30, 177n, 179n, 183n, 190n
Bethany Home, 28, 45, 46, 47–48, 49,
51, 58, 59, 60, 63, 65, 74, 90–91,

PENNY A. PETERSEN is a researcher for a historical consulting company in Minneapolis. She is the author of *Hiding in Plain Sight: Minneapolis' First Neighborhood*, a history of the Marcy–Holmes neighborhood. She has worked as a historic site interpreter and site technician for the Minnesota Historical Society at St. Anthony Falls.